Community Sport and Social Inclusion

This book examines sport as an inclusive and developmental environment, exploring the conditions by which community sport initiatives can promote personal development, health and social cohesion, particularly for at-risk youth.

At the empirical core of the book is a multiple disciplinary study of community sport programmes in Flanders, Belgium, involving researchers from social sport sciences, social work, pedagogy and health care sciences. Drawing on this cutting-edge, realist research, the book considers the implications for sport development policy and practice around the world. The book considers community sport as a vehicle for promoting social inclusion and the ways it allows people of all backgrounds and abilities to participate and access social and health benefits whilst touching on key issues including monitoring and evaluation; exercise and health; youth welfare; and volunteering.

This book is fascinating reading for any student, researcher or practitioner working in sport for development, sport management, sport coaching, social work, education, sociology or urban studies.

Marc Theeboom is Professor at the Faculty of Physical Education and Physiotherapy and at the Faculty of Psychology and Educational Sciences of the Vrije Universiteit Brussel, Belgium.

Hebe Schaillée is Assistant Professor and postdoctoral researcher in the Department of Movement and Sport Sciences at the Vrije Universiteit Brussel, Belgium.

Rudi Roose is Professor of Social Work at the Department of Social Work and Social Pedagogy at Ghent University, Belgium.

Sara Willems is Professor of Equity in Health Care and the head of the Department of Public Health and Primary Care in the Faculty of Medicine and Health Sciences at Ghent University, Belgium.

Lieve Bradt is Professor of Social Pedagogy at the Department of Social Work and Social Pedagogy at Ghent University, Belgium.

Emelien Lauwerier is Professor of Health Psychology and postdoctoral researcher at the Department of Experimental-Clinical and Health Psychology in the Faculty of Psychology and Educational Sciences and the Department of Public Health and Primary Care in the Faculty of Medicine and Health Sciences at Ghent University, Belgium.

Routledge Research in Sport, Culture and Society

Social Activism in Women's Tennis
Generations of Politics and Cultural Change
Kristi Tredway

Sport, Welfare and Social Policy in the European Union
Nicola R. Porro, Stefano Martelli and Alberto Testa

Disability, the Media and the Paralympic Games
Carolyn Jackson-Brown

Sport, Film and National Culture
Edited by Seán Crosson

Female Fans, Gender Relations and Football Fandom
Challenging the Brotherhood Culture
Honorata Jakubowska, Dominik Antonowicz and Radosław Kossakowski

Gym Bodies
Exploring Fitness Cultures
James Brighton, Ian Wellard and Amy Clark

Sport and Secessionism
Edited by Mariann Vaczi and Alan Bairner

Discrimination in Football
Christos Kassimeris

Doping in Non-Olympic Sports
Challenging the Legitimacy of WADA?
Lovely Dasgupta

Social Capital and Sport Organisations
Richard Tacon

Community Sport and Social Inclusion
Enhancing Strategies for Promoting Personal Development, Health and Social Cohesion
Edited by Marc Theeboom, Hebe Schaillée, Rudi Roose, Sara Willems, Lieve Bradt and Emelien Lauwerier

Cricket and Contemporary Society in Britain
Crisis and Continuity
Russell Holden

For more information about this series, please visit: www.routledge.com/sport/series/RRSCS

Community Sport and Social Inclusion

Enhancing Strategies for Promoting Personal Development, Health and Social Cohesion

Edited by Marc Theeboom, Hebe Schaillée, Rudi Roose, Sara Willems, Emelien Lauwerier and Lieve Bradt

LONDON AND NEW YORK

First published 2022
by Routledge
2 Park Square, Milton Park, Abingdon, Oxon OX14 4RN

and by Routledge
605 Third Avenue, New York, NY 10158

Routledge is an imprint of the Taylor & Francis Group, an informa business

© 2022 selection and editorial matter, Vrije Universiteit Brussel and Universiteit Gent; individual chapters, the contributors

The right of Vrije Universiteit Brussel and Universiteit Gent to be identified as the author of the editorial material, and of the authors for their individual chapters, has been asserted in accordance with sections 77 and 78 of the Copyright, Designs and Patents Act 1988.

All rights reserved. No part of this book may be reprinted or reproduced or utilised in any form or by any electronic, mechanical, or other means, now known or hereafter invented, including photocopying and recording, or in any information storage or retrieval system, without permission in writing from the publishers.

Trademark notice: Product or corporate names may be trademarks or registered trademarks, and are used only for identification and explanation without intent to infringe.

British Library Cataloguing-in-Publication Data
A catalogue record for this book is available from the British Library

Library of Congress Cataloging-in-Publication Data
A catalog record for this book has been requested

ISBN: 978-0-367-35614-9 (hbk)
ISBN: 978-1-032-12528-2 (pbk)
ISBN: 978-0-429-34063-5 (ebk)

DOI: 10.4324/9780429340635

Typeset in Times New Roman
by Apex CoVantage, LLC

Contents

Contributors   vii

PART 1
Introduction and general findings   1

1. **Introduction**   3
   MARC THEEBOOM, HEBE SCHAILLÉE, DORIEN BROSENS, SARA WILLEMS, EMELIEN LAUWERIER, RUDI ROOSE AND LIEVE BRADT

2. **Community sport and social inclusion: necessary and sufficient conditions**   23
   HEBE SCHAILLÉE, MARC THEEBOOM, SHANA SABBE, KAREN VAN DER VEKEN, PIETER DEBOGNIES AND DORIEN BROSENS

PART 2
Thematic insights into community sport and social inclusion   43

3. **Reflective practices in a volunteer community sport coach training programme**   45
   DORIEN BROSENS, HEBE SCHAILLÉE, MARC THEEBOOM AND PIETER DEBOGNIES

4. **Health promotion in the context of community sport: illustration of a theory-informed approach to programme development and evaluation**   64
   EMELIEN LAUWERIER, KAREN VAN DER VEKEN, KAATJE VAN ROY AND SARA WILLEMS

5 **Facilitating conditions for establishing social cohesion through structural approaches in community sport** 83
SHANA SABBE, LIEVE BRADT AND RUDI ROOSE

PART 3
Broader perspectives on community sport and social inclusion 101

6 **The evolution of evaluation: from the black box to programme theory** 103
FRED COALTER

7 **Realist inquiry and action research** 127
GUY KEGELS AND BRUNO MARCHAL

8 **Problematising the concept of social inclusion through sport: opportunities and challenges through the lens of aspirations and capabilities** 145
EMRAN RIFFI ACHARKI AND RAMÓN SPAAIJ

PART 4
General reflections 157

9 **General reflections** 159
MARC THEEBOOM, HEBE SCHAILLÉE, SARA WILLEMS, EMELIEN LAUWERIER, RUDI ROOSE AND LIEVE BRADT

Index 180

Contributors

Emran Riffi Acharki, Amsterdam University of Applied Sciences and University of Amsterdam, the Netherlands

Lieve Bradt, Ghent University, Belgium

Dorien Brosens, Vrije Universiteit Brussel, Belgium

Fred Coalter, Vrije Universiteit Brussel, Belgium, and Leeds Beckett University, UK

Pieter Debognies, Vlaams Instituut Gezond Leven, Belgium

Guy Kegels, Institute of Tropical Medicine, Belgium

Emelien Lauwerier, Ghent University, Belgium

Bruno Marchal, Institute of Tropical Medicine, Belgium

Rudi Roose, Ghent University, Belgium

Kaatje Van Roy, Ghent University, Belgium

Shana Sabbe, Ghent University, Belgium

Hebe Schaillée, Vrije Universiteit Brussel, Belgium

Ramón Spaaij, Victoria University and University of Amsterdam, the Netherlands

Marc Theeboom, Vrije Universiteit Brussel, Belgium

Karen Van der Veken, Ghent University, Belgium

Sara Willems, Ghent University, Belgium

Part 1
Introduction and general findings

1 Introduction

Marc Theeboom, Hebe Schaillée, Dorien Brosens, Sara Willems, Emelien Lauwerier, Rudi Roose and Lieve Bradt

Setting the scene

The central theme of this book relates to the asserted potential of community sport for realizing social inclusion of young people in socially vulnerable situations. This chapter provides the rationale for this theme, which starts from the observation that there are a substantial number of young people in the EU who live at risk of social exclusion. For example, in 2019 more than 5 million 15- to 24-year-olds in the EU-28 were considered as NEETs (i.e. neither in education, employment nor in training) (Eurostat 2020a, 2020b). With long-term youth unemployment at record highs, there is a high risk that these NEETs will become socially and economically marginalised. Data in 2018 also revealed that 26.3 per cent of young people aged 16–29 years living in the EU are at risk of poverty, experience severe material deprivation and/or live in households with very low work intensity (Eurostat 2019). This corresponds to about 20.6 million young people in total. With only minor fluctuations over the past decade, the fact that a substantial number of young people are living in a socially vulnerable situation is regarded by many as an important societal challenge. In reference to young people, Vettenburg et al. (1984) have defined societal vulnerability as an interactional process between adolescents and societal institutions. The key assumption of their societal vulnerability theory is that an accumulation of negative experiences and contacts with official societal institutions may lead to an unfavourable societal perspective of this group. In a more general sense, several factors have been described that characterise social (societal) vulnerability (e.g. level of poverty, lack or limited access to resources such as information, knowledge and technology or to political power and representation, lack or limited social capital including social networks and connections, and vulnerable residential settings) (Cutter et al. 2003). While over the years, social inclusion policies have tried to provide better opportunities and equal rights for as many young people as possible, challenges remain to reach out to the most vulnerable youth. Noteworthy is that over the past decades, a growing number of policymakers at different levels have stated that community sport is a (cost-effective) means for achieving social policy objectives by reaching out and empowering marginalised and deprived groups in general and young people in particular (Bloyce and Smith 2010; Coalter 2007; Harris and Houlihan 2016; Platts 2018). However, given the dominant focus within such policy debates on the asserted outcomes of sport programmes, researchers have pointed to the need for more critical research and theory that identifies the processes through which (community) sport can (or cannot) be linked to outcomes at individual level (e.g. personal development and health) and impacts at societal level (e.g. social inclusion and civic engagement) (see e.g. Agergaard 2018; Coalter 2013; Kennett 2014; Tacon 2007).

This book looks critically at the potential of community sport for social inclusion of young people in a socially vulnerable situation. It looks at the extent to which community sport is expected to have a positive impact on the lives of these young people and how it is used in an attempt to help to overcome some of the difficulties that this youth is facing and, as such, trying to bring them into a less socially vulnerable situation. The book draws upon the findings from a comprehensive study conducted in the region of Flanders (Belgium) on community sport and social inclusion. The project was entitled: *Community sport for AT-risk youth: Innovative strategies for promoting personal development, health and social CoHesion* (with the acronym CATCH). The CATCH project started in January 2016 and ended in December 2019 and was commissioned by the *Flanders Innovation and Entrepreneurship Agency* of the Flemish Government (VLAIO). Its aim was to get an in-depth understanding of why, how and in what circumstances community sport programmes can have an effect on *social inclusion* for young people in socially vulnerable situations. As will be discussed later on in this chapter, social inclusion was operationalised by means of the following three objectives: *personal development, health* and *social cohesion*. These objectives were selected on the basis of a benchmark study among community sport providers in Flanders (Van Poppel 2015).

A unique consortium was set up for the CATCH project consisting of a multi-disciplinary research team and several non-academic partners (the latter referred to as *social users*). The research team, with 15 Flemish and four international researchers, comprised three university teams: *Sport and Society* (Vrije Universiteit Brussel) as the coordinating group, *Social Inequality in Health Care* (Ghent University) and the *Department of Social Work and Social Pedagogy* (Ghent University). The non-academic partners came from 18 community sport programmes and 22 umbrella organisations who represented stakeholders in, among others, youth work, organised sport, local health services and welfare organisations. In addition, the *Flemish Institute of Sport Management and Recreation Policy* (Vlaams Instituut voor Sportbeheer en Recreatiebeleid – with ISB as its Flemish Acronym), a recognised expertise centre on community sport in Flanders, ensured knowledge translation between researchers, practitioners and policymakers.

Apart from the rationale of the project, this chapter describes the project's general set-up. Given the often-overgeneralised notions that are used with regard to social inclusion and community sport in general and in relation to young people in particular, we will first clarify how these concepts have been interpreted within our project.

Social inclusion/exclusion and young people in socially vulnerable situations

Notwithstanding the term's popularity in policy statements, different interpretations of *social inclusion* exist in the academic debate. While some scholars have characterised it by a series of inter-connected dimensions (i.e. spatial, relational, functional and power) (Bailey 2008), others have labelled it as 'not a simple, unambiguous concept' (Lindsey 2003: 3). Consequently, it has been indicated that the concept is often ill-defined and interpreted differently (Glazzard 2011; Levitas 2005; Silver 2010). Hodkinson (2012) argued that, as a concept, social inclusion has frequently been used to focus on notions of assimilation rather than representing a struggle for equality and social justice. Moreover, according to Hickey and du Toit (2007), its discourse is often based on an underlying moral meta-narrative which assumes that social inclusion is inherently good and desirable, although this statement is debatable from a critical stance. It is noteworthy that social inclusion is often considered as the opposite of *social exclusion*, which in turn also has a wide range of definitions. Levitas, Pantazis, Fahmy, Gordon, Lloyd and Patsios (2007: 21) indicated that the definitions they identified in the literature are in general pitched at two different levels: 'They refer to structures, processes and characteristics of the society as a whole, as well as to the experience of individuals situated within these'. Omtzigt (2009: 7) argued that 'Definitions are caught between trying to provide an exhaustive list of everything the socially excluded is excluded from and listing the processes underlying the poverty and social exclusion'. In their own definition, Levitas and her colleagues (2007: 9) take a broad view of social exclusion as they see it as:

> a complex and multidimensional process. It involves the lack or denial of resources, rights, goods and services, and the inability to participate in the normal relationships and activities, available to the majority of people in a society, whether in economic, social, cultural or political arenas. It affects both the quality of life of individuals and the equity and cohesion of society as a whole.

These authors have developed an operational measurement framework identifying 3 domains and 10 sub-domains of potential social exclusion which relate to a lack of resources (economic, social and access to services) and an inability to participate (economic, social, cultural, civic and political participation), resulting in low quality of life (health and well-being, living environment, crime, harm and criminalisation). The multidimensional perspective of social exclusion is also emphasised in the often quoted definition of the European Commission from 1993 (Omtzigt 2009: 4):

> social exclusion refers to the multiple and changing factors resulting in people being excluded from the normal exchanges, practices and rights of modern society. Poverty is one of the most obvious factors, but social exclusion

also refers to inadequate rights in housing, education, health and access to services. It affects individuals and groups, particularly in urban and rural areas, who are in some way subject to discrimination or segregation; and it emphasizes the weaknesses in the social infrastructure and the risk of allowing a two-tier society to become established by default.

In terms of combating social exclusion, different perspectives on responsibilities within social inclusion policies have been described. Noteworthy here is Veit-Wilson's (1998: 45) distinction between two different policy discourses on social exclusion, namely a weak and a strong version:

> In the 'weak' version of this discourse, the solutions lie in altering these excluded peoples' handicapping characteristics and enhancing their integration into dominant society. 'Stronger' forms of this discourse also emphasise the role of those who are doing the excluding and therefore aim for solutions which reduce the powers of exclusion.

Other authors, such as Smyth (2017), have referred to a similar distinction between two interpretations regarding the causation of exclusion affecting the nature of social inclusion policies. One strategy relates to mending the bonds that bind people to society, and the other focuses on the way in which power is deployed in producing exclusionary social structures. Regarding the latter, Smyth (2017: 1) argued that 'Envisaging how structural impediments operate, as well as doing something about it, has been much more problematic than in the former case'.

Within current European social policies targeting young people, there seems to be a dominance of weak discourses regarding the causation of social exclusion. For example, the *EU Youth Strategy 2019–2027* emphasises three areas of action among the Member States: (1) to engage young people's participation in civic and democratic life; (2) to connect young people across the EU to promote volunteering, opportunities to learn abroad, solidarity and intercultural understanding and (3) to empower young people through boosting innovation, as well as the quality and recognition of youth work (European Commission 2018a). This EU Youth Strategy has a particular interest in outreach and active involvement of young people who are in socially vulnerable situations, which is legitimated as follows: 'Youth struggling with disadvantages are generally less active citizens and have less trust in institutions' (European Commission 2018b: 1). The European Commission (2010) emphasised that its policy to address these challenges focuses on providing better opportunities for employment, training and education for as many young people as possible, as well as promoting social justice and fundamental rights relating to the values of respect for human dignity and solidarity. Yet, the emphasis is on empowering young people through skill, competence and knowledge development, allowing them to become more active citizens. Within this framework, youth work and non-formal education activities are considered to be important providers for this development and, consequently, for social inclusion.

Sport and social inclusion

Over the past decades, policymakers at various levels have increasingly begun to regard sport as a means for achieving social policy objectives, not only in relation to improving people's health but also, among others, to reach out and empower, to build communities, as well as to help shape society at large (Fletcher 2014; McDonald 2005; Spaaij et al. 2014). Coalter (2007) has argued that social inclusion sport policies are mostly shaped by a dual focus on extending social rights and citizenship (i.e. through access to participation) and emphasizing various individual and collective benefits presumed to be associated with sport participation. Social inclusion, as put forward in most public policies of sport, is an ideal that governments, policymakers and community leaders pursue in order to prevent and mitigate the marginalisation of particular social groups. It is clear that over the years, the expectations regarding the potential of sport to realise social inclusion have become higher. For example, in the mid-1970s, European policymakers saw sport primarily as 'an aspect of socio-cultural development' (European Sport for All Charter 1975/76: article III). At present, however, it is believed that sport in Europe will help 'to ensure sustainable development and to adequately tackle the overarching socio-economic and security related challenges facing the EU, including migration, social exclusion, radicalisation that may lead to violent extremism, unemployment, as well as unhealthy lifestyles and obesity' (Council of the European Union 2017: 5). Today, one of the EU sport policy priorities is 'to foster a sense of social inclusion and integration through sport, particularly for marginalised groups' (European Commission – Sport and Society 2018, Website Sport).

This broad social potential of sport has been widely asserted by both policymakers at various levels and representatives of sport organisations and agencies. Over the years, it has been asserted that sport has been positively linked to a variety of social outcomes (e.g. intercultural dialogue, social and moral development, civic engagement, community development and deradicalisation of extremism). But despite the increased interest and beliefs among many policymakers, sport organisations and agencies in the social value of sport, various scholars have referred to the weak evidence base for this (see, e.g. Coalter 2007; Green 2008; Long and Sanderson 2001; Nicholls et al. 2010). For example, it has been argued that sport and social inclusion policy programmes are often only concerned with measuring and delivering quantitative outputs (Kennett 2014). This primarily relates to the number of people (particularly from underrepresented target groups) that are actively participating or refers to the frequency of their participation. These outputs are often short-term and are relatively easy to measure. However, in most cases whether this participation will eventually lead to specific outcomes and has an actual social impact is less certain as this relates to longer-term changes in the lives of individuals, groups, communities and possibly even society at large. A major concern here is how to measure the social impact of sport.

Challenges for evidence-informed policy and practice

Several authors have made critical remarks regarding the methodologies of studies that have attempted to measure the social impact of sport. For example, Tacon (2007) has described a series of factors that impede robust evaluative research of sports-based social inclusion projects (e.g. no clear definitions of measurable outcomes, limited duration of programmes, cross-sectional analyses and anecdotal data from unrepresentative samples). A systematic review of research on the social impact of sport including 232 studies by Taylor, Davies, Wells, Gilbertson and Tayleur (2015) concluded that there are several deficiencies in the reported evidence. Among other things, this related to a very generic perspective on sport with a lack of insight into differential effects of different activities and on different sub-groups of the population; limited testing of causality; no focus on the strength and duration of the effects or on the effects of frequency, intensity and duration of the sport participation. Taylor et al. (2015) also mentioned that the evidence reported in the existing research on the social impact of sport is very different when compared to the literature on sport's physical health benefits where the highest quality evidence was presented. Similar remarks regarding the weaknesses of the reported evidence have been made in relation to empirical studies that have attempted to evaluate sport's social value to youth development (see, e.g. Hermens et al. 2017; Jones et al. 2017). In most cases, there was an absence of information on the logic and rationale of programmes and interventions which were presumed to lead to the expected social outcomes. This lack of attention to the analysis of process illustrates that too often sport's social outcomes are regarded as inevitable and self-evident. This is exemplified by Green (2008: 132), who argued that 'the belief that sport builds character is so ingrained that neither providers nor participants feel it necessary to do anything more than to provide opportunities'.

Taylor et al.'s (2015) review of research on the social impact of sport showed that only 12 per cent of all studies conducted a qualitative evaluation with an intensive descriptive or explanatory analysis of an individual, group or intervention. One of the possible reasons for this is that much of the sport impact research has primarily been undertaken for accountability to management and funders that are often more interested in quantifiable outputs. This means that most studies that have investigated the social impact of sport have focused on measuring intervention effects without much understanding of the actual processes that are assumed to produce them. Conventional (experimental) evaluation research in general often uses designs where interventions are controlled through randomisation and compared with control settings to identify causal links with observed results. These designs have been criticised for disregarding the fact that interventions take place in complex open and dynamic social systems (see, e.g. Henry and Ko 2014). Among other things, this refers to the inability to separate sport programmes from other wider socio-economic or socio-cultural contexts which complicates the set-up of controlled environments. But even if one may assess whether the expected results occurred and whether an intervention played a role, conventional approaches often do not explore the reasons why it did or did not work. Therefore, there is a need to understand the conditions in a programme under which one can expect positive changes to occur. For example, Coalter (2007) has argued for a better understanding of the *necessary* and *sufficient conditions* of sports-based developmental practices. The former refers to the conditions that are needed to get people into sport (e.g. in terms of appeal, accessibility, recruitment and sustained involvement). The latter relates to conditions that are required to produce desirable developmental outcomes (e.g. effective mentoring, active involvement of participants, and provision of learning opportunities and relevant experiences).

Scholars have, therefore, argued to extend and diversify research approaches regarding the necessary and sufficient conditions for the social impact of sport and, at the same time, attribute these results to actual interventions (see, e.g. Kay 2009). An important challenge that has emerged from the literature is to move away from simple 'input-output approaches' when evaluating sports-based social interventions and shift the focus to a better understanding of contexts, processes and outcomes (see, e.g. Chen et al. 2014). This has led a number of scholars to propose the use of a *theory-based evaluation approach* (TBE) when investigating outcomes of sport and social inclusion policies and programmes (see, e.g. Agergaard 2018; Coalter 2013; Henry and Ko 2014; Kennett 2014; Tacon 2007). TBE provides a way to assess the extent to which an intervention has produced or influenced observed results and why this has occurred (see, e.g. Pawson 2006; Weiss 1995). Instead of merely investigating *if* a programme or policy works (what most evaluative research does), TBE intends to understand *why* and *how* it does (or does not) and *in what circumstances*. Central to the TBE approach is the notion that all programmes have an implicit *programme logic* or *programme theory* (Pawson 2001; Weiss 1995). There is a general expectation that *if* specific resources and activities are provided to specific subjects and *if* specific conditions are met, *then* these subjects may choose to adopt them, thus changing the behaviour in a favoured direction (Pawson 2006). A programme theory seeks to explain how an intervention is understood to contribute to a chain of results that can produce outcomes and impacts (at individual, community or even societal level). Chapter 6 reflects on the scope and capacity of different monitoring and evaluation approaches and their relation to the social impact of sport.

Before we introduce the set-up of the CATCH project, we will first describe the rationale for the focus on community sport and will clarify what is meant here by this term as different interpretations exist. We start with a brief description of the specific context and evolution of community sport in Flanders.

Community sport in Flanders

Studies have shown repeatedly that marginalised groups are often less involved in sport compared to a general population. For example, according to the most recent *Eurobarometer on sport and physical activity* (European Commission 2018c), engagement in sport is less prevalent among people with lower levels of education and among those with financial difficulties (i.e. having difficulties paying bills).

Flemish sport participation data have confirmed this (Theeboom et al. 2015). Data from the JOP-schoolmonitor 2, conducted by the *Youth Research Platform* in 2018 with more than 8,000 adolescents (aged 12–18 years) going to secondary schools in Brussels, Antwerp and Ghent and a control group of students going to Flemish schools outside these three cities, showed that 53.3 per cent of young people without a migration background indicated that they were currently member of a sport club, whereas for those with a migration background (second generation) this percentage was only 31.4 per cent. Participation levels also differed according to the educational level of the parents. For young people with parents with higher education, the percentage of active sport participants was 51.1 per cent compared to 28.9 per cent for those with parents with lower or no education.

To promote sport participation among these 'hard-to-reach' groups, local policymakers have started to make use of alternative (more open access) sport organisational formats. One of the most commonly used formats in Flanders for this is community sport. In general, community sport refers to programmes that provide grassroots sports for a wide variety of people in collaboration with, among others, local schools, community centres and voluntary-based sport clubs (Evans et al. 2019; Jeanes et al. 2018). But while this term is commonly used in sport policy literature, more precise definitions are rarely given. Platts (2018: 5) argued that it is problematic to define community sport:

> If defining what we mean by community is fraught with complexity, a similar fate awaits us when trying to determine what is meant by community sport and PA [Physical Activity]. Rather than the definitions of the words being the issue here – although the separate terms of sport and physical activity are often mistaken for each other and used interchangeably – it is the various forms of sport and PA that exists within a community setting that makes defining it problematic.

Policy changes have also made it harder to provide a clear definition for community sport. For example, Harris and Houlihan (2016) have indicated that the evolution of community sport policy over the last 20 years in the UK was characterised by a broad shift from 'sport for sport' to 'sport for good'. While the former relates to traditional sport development outcomes (such as recreation and health enhancement), the latter refers to the use of sport to achieve broader social outcomes (most notably social inclusion). A similar evolution can be noticed with regard to Flemish community sport policy. In Flanders, the concept of community sport (in Dutch *buurtsport*) originally arose from the observation that while sport was considered to offer social inclusion opportunities for inner-city youths, traditional sport providers (i.e. sport clubs, federations and municipal sport services) were unable to attract the most vulnerable groups (often with an ethnic minority background). From the early 1990s onwards, open access sport activities were organised in deprived inner-city areas specifically targeting these hard-to-reach groups (Theeboom and De Maesschalck 2006). The first initiatives were primarily organised within the youth welfare sector and were focused on social inclusion for target groups in socially vulnerable situations (Theeboom and De Knop 1992). Theeboom and De Maesschalck (2006) noted that as municipal sport services in later years became more actively involved in the organisation of community sport, a shift was noted from a social inclusion perspective for disadvantaged groups towards promoting recreational sport in people's own neighbourhood, with an emphasis on those not involved in sport. In addition, they argued that this evolution also led to a wide variety of initiatives turning community sport into a 'container concept'. In 2014, Flemish Institute of Sport Management and Recreation Policy (ISB) launched its *community sport expertise centre*, a knowledge, dissemination and support platform for community sport practices of Flemish municipalities. Through this centre, ISB started to encourage local authorities to reflect more critically on the ambitions and objectives with regard to their own community sport policy in an attempt to position it more clearly compared to their general sport-for-all policy. This reflection has resulted in a revised definition where community sport is now viewed as (Van der Sypt 2019: 31):

> an umbrella term for low-threshold and community-oriented initiatives, based on a vision that seeks to guarantee optimum accessibility of sport for disadvantaged groups. Sport is used with or without an explicit focus on development at the individual and/or community level.

A survey in 2019 among all Flemish local authorities had shown that 23 per cent of the 308 municipalities organised community sport and that a majority of these programmes (85 per cent) specifically targeted groups in socially vulnerable situations (Van der Sypt 2019). The new definition is more in line with the original interpretation where community sport is viewed from a social inclusion perspective targeting disadvantaged groups. The renewed ambition for community sport provision by policymakers was the main reason for setting up the CATCH project.

Social inclusion objectives of community sport in Flanders

As policymakers in Flanders on different levels have repeatedly linked community sport to social inclusion, mostly in relation to young people in socially vulnerable situations, the general goal of the CATCH project was to get an in-depth understanding of *why, how* and *in what circumstances* this type of impact can be expected. The project's central research question was therefore: *What are the working mechanisms and facilitating conditions in community sport initiatives that relate to the promotion of social inclusion for young people in socially vulnerable situations?*

As indicated earlier, the operationalisation of social inclusion was based on insights from a benchmark study among Flemish community sport programmes which identified three social inclusion objectives as the most important ones when working with young people in socially vulnerable situations (Van Poppel 2015). These objectives were *personal development, health* and *social cohesion*. It should be noted that operationalizing social inclusion by means of these three objectives has restricted the perspective on the situation of the young people who were targeted in the project. Considering the multidimensionality of the definition of social exclusion, as we saw earlier, a number of aspects that have been mentioned by Levitas et al. (2007) have not been taken into account, for example, the availability of material and economic resources (e.g. income and debts), opportunities for economic participation (e.g. employment; working adults in household in paid work) and housing and local environment (e.g. housing quality, neighbourhood safety and access to open space). However, the CATCH project has deliberately started from the perspective of the Flemish community sport organisations and how they defined social inclusion. It should be noted that for the remainder of this book when referring to social inclusion in relation to the CATCH project, this perspective is used. Although these three specific social inclusion objectives were commonly mentioned by practitioners and policymakers in relation to community sport in Flanders, their meaning still remains vague, as well as ways of attempting to achieve them. It was therefore necessary to also look at how practitioners operationalised these objectives. The following chapters will discuss this in selected community sport practices in Flanders. As a way of general introduction to each of the three objectives, a brief description is next.

Personal development

Based on preliminary consultations with social users and community sport practitioners, it became clear that this objective primarily referred to the provision of positive learning experiences within a supportive social climate characterised by developmental mentoring based on mutual respect and trust. This could then lead to the acquisition of transferable life skills (e.g. decision-making, conflict resolution and communication skills) and to changed values and attitudes. Coalter (2013) has used the term *sport-plus* to refer to programmes in which sport is the core activity and used to work towards developmental objectives. Another term that has often been used in this perspective is *positive youth development* (PYD) through sport (Hermens et al. 2017; Holt 2008). While many have stated that sport is potentially beneficial for the personal development of young people (Danish et al. 2004; Kay 2009), it has been indicated that research examining *how* to promote youth development through sport remains in its infancy (Holt 2008). However, many agree that the quality of social relationships between coaches (or mentors) and participants is an important contributor to effective sports-based developmental practices for youth at-risk. For example, Coalter (2012) emphasised the importance of creating a social climate in which respect, trust and reciprocity can be developed as a basis for potential attitude and behaviour change among young participants in sports-based developmental programmes. Among other things, this relates to the presence of interested and caring adults and facilitating a sense of belonging and perceived competence at a particular (sport) activity (such as through volunteering). These and other strategies provide a context for *experiential learning* which is often a key concept in youth work practice and emphasises the development of real-life situations and transformative experiences. Apart from specific youth mentoring strategies focusing on relationship building, it has been indicated that a developmental approach also includes reflective practice. Super et al. (2018) have argued that the stimulation of critical self-reflection can be regarded as an essential aspect in the personal development of young people in socially vulnerable positions. Chapter 3 refers to widely recognised theoretical models (i.e. Kolb and Fry's experiential learning theory and Gibbs' reflective cycle) and how they can be used as conceptual frameworks for reflective practice in community sport.

Health

Health, as stated by the World Health Organization (WHO 1946), is 'a state of complete physical, mental, and social well-being and not merely the absence of disease or infirmity'. While important in its own right – by stressing aspects of health beyond physical disease indicators – recent theory and studies add to this definition. One important theoretical perspective is that of positive psychology. It means the study of the contributors to a healthy life for self and others (such as positive emotions, life meaning, engaging work and close relationships) (Seligman and Csikszentmihalyi 2000). From this perspective, studying health requires the investigation of broad indicators of biological, psychological and social well-being. As such, it is clear that the concept of health is closely connected to the objectives of personal development and social cohesion. Traditionally, health approaches tended to focus on disease prevention and, therefore, the study of those factors that were linked to poor health, such as smoking, physical inactivity, a sedentary lifestyle and alcohol abuse. For the past several years, researchers have become aware of the independent and added contribution of 'health assets' to health. Examples of such health assets are self-regulation, life meaning and purpose, civic engagement and good social relationships (Park et al. 2016). In the CATCH project, healthy behaviour was seen to be linked to having a sense of 'life meaning' and 'growth' (personal development) and 'building meaningful connections with others' (social cohesion), leading to intermediate changes of increased self-esteem, perceived self-efficacy and ultimately motivation to change behavioural pattern and behave more healthily. Chapter 4 describes a way of developing and evaluating a health-promoting intervention based on an initial programme theory that was developed and that combined risk factors and health assets, as well as relationships between those factors as they together contribute to better health in the long term. A planned and participatory approach was followed (i.e. Bartholomew et al.'s intervention mapping), and behaviour change theories (i.e. Bandura's social-cognitive learning theory, Ajzen's theory of planned behaviour and Prochaska and DiClemente's transtheoretical model) were used to bring depth into the underlying causal assumptions through which risk or protective factors may lead to the desired outcomes.

Social cohesion

This objective is considered a key ingredient for strong and healthy societies (Kearns and Forrest 2000; Novy et al. 2012). As mentioned earlier, it also appeared to be a pinnacle objective for community sport in Flanders. Notwithstanding the importance of social cohesion as an objective for community sport practices, it is claimed to be a rather contested notion (Bailey 2005; Chan et al. 2006). It is often referred to as a 'concept of convenience', referring to its pragmatic, chameleon-like and often instrumental use (Chan et al. 2006). Especially in the current context of the post-welfare state, social cohesion is liable to be given form from a focus on private obligations, human capital, individual autonomy, choice and responsibility at the expense of attention for collective responsibilities (Kessl 2009; Lorenz 2016). Within sports-based practices, this is believed to debouch in the dominance of instrumental approaches above more structural approaches (Coakley 2011; Darnell et al. 2016; Hartmann and Kwauk 2011; Nols 2018). Within such an instrumentalised approach, community sport practices are mainly concerned with improving young people's individual knowledge, skills and resilience. Such practices might risk to become blind for challenging the structural exclusion mechanisms which young people in vulnerable situations are facing (Crabbe 2009; Ekholm 2016; Kelly 2011). Chapter 5 elaborates on the struggle of community sport practitioners to install a 'socio-pedagogical shift' (Haudenhuyse et al. 2013) and thus in developing a more structural understanding and approach to social cohesion, focused on reducing the powers of exclusion.

Aims of the CATCH project

As mentioned before, the general goal of the CATCH project was to get an in-depth understanding of why, how and in what circumstances community sport involvement can be effectively linked to social inclusion of young people in socially vulnerable situations. The project had two specific aims: (a) to obtain insights into processes of community sport provision in relation to the three selected objectives (i.e. *research aim*) and (b) an exchange of knowledge between researchers, practitioners and policymakers (i.e. *knowledge translation aim*). How both of these specific aims of the project were pursued will be described next.

Understanding process

Regarding the research aim, two consecutive phases were set up. In the first phase, after consultation with the social user group, nine community sport programmes in Flanders were selected, all primarily targeting young people in socially vulnerable situations. Each of the three identified objectives (i.e. personal development, health and social cohesion) was covered within three of the nine selected programmes. The Flemish Community Sport Benchmark (Van Poppel 2015) had shown that a degree of overlap between the three objectives was inevitable, which also became apparent as several programmes indicated to target more than one objective at the same time. During the first phase, a TBE approach was used to get a better understanding of the inner workings of the selected community sport programmes. Although two prominent TBE approaches can be distinguished (i.e. *theory of change* and *realist evaluation*), each with their own merits, a realist evaluation approach was used for the first phase of the CATCH project. While both approaches have often been used interchangeably, important differences have been described (Blamey and Mackenzie 2007). On the one hand, a theory of change approach focuses on developing a theory that can show how a specific intervention is intended to work and the assumptions behind that theory (Weiss 1995). It is primarily concerned with overall programme outcomes and synergies between the various components of an intervention. Although not exclusively, according to Blamey and Mackenzie (2007), it is more associated with a (complex) macro-programme level with large-scale multi-topic interventions aiming for multiple outcomes. On the other hand, a realist evaluation approach regards programme evaluation as a way to identify 'What works for whom in what circumstances and in what respects, and how?', using *Context, Mechanism* and *Outcome* (CMO) configurations (Pawson and Tilley 2004). This approach has mostly been linked to micro-level aspects of programme theories. As most interventions in community sport are primarily situated at micro- and meso-level (often dealing with young participants at individual and smaller group level), the CATCH project was more in line with realist evaluation. Blamey and Mackenzie (2007) also noted that within this approach, it is more common that evaluators use their own knowledge and experience to develop a programme theory, whereas in a theory of change approach this is done by stakeholders based on their own views and then discussed with evaluators. Regarding the second approach, it should be noted that as many organisations lack the experience to do this work on their own, evaluators tend to assist them in this process. The researchers in the CATCH project made use of mixed methods to collect data which included participant observation, individual in-depth interviews with various stakeholders (participants, community sport coaches, youth workers, coordinators and partners) and focus groups with key witnesses and social users. These insights were then used to develop an evidence-informed framework including the contextual assets and practices that shape the necessary and sufficient conditions through which community sport programmes may foster social inclusionary outcomes (see Chapter 2).

In the second phase, three community sport contexts were selected to set up action-oriented research in which interventions were developed and tested in close collaboration with practitioners. The approach was based on the knowledge that was developed in the first phase (such as the evidence-informed framework). As will be explained in the following chapters, each context in this second phase used a different approach and focused on one of the three specific objectives. For personal development, this was done through consulting, advising and redesigning an existing training course emphasizing soft-skill development for young volunteers to become city coaches in local community sport programmes. For health, the intervention consisted of the development and organisation of a training programme for community sport coaches with a focus on motivational coaching.

16 *Marc Theeboom et al*

In relation to social cohesion, the research focused on structural work (i.e. strategies focused on reducing the powers of exclusion) by conducting a single-case study in one good practice in Flanders. Chapters 2 to 5 will discuss in detail the methods and most important findings of the different parts of the research.

Knowledge translation

The second aim of the CATCH project was related to *knowledge translation*. The process of knowledge translation has been defined as the exchange, synthesis and application of knowledge through a dynamic and iterative process of interactions between relevant stakeholders to improve the societal or economic impact of research (Straus et al. 2013; Sudsawad 2007). In general, knowledge translation practices can occur on three different levels: (1) *strategic* (i.e. raising and maintaining the interest and commitment of different actors involved and managing power relations between them), (2) *cognitive* (i.e. identifying and circulating users' knowledge and needs in terms of project design, content and meaning) and (3) *logistic* (i.e. facilitating and supporting strategic and cognitive practices as they enable knowledge translation during the different project phases). The major activities of the knowledge translation strategies that were used during the CATCH project will be described next. We have elsewhere elaborated more on these strategies (Schaillée et al. 2019).

Firstly, there was an active involvement by practitioners in the formulation of the research aims, questions, products and methods which started during the preparatory phase of the project. This enabled researchers to gain insight into the opportunities and benefits that the research outcomes would hold for practitioners and to identify research questions that addressed the needs of community sport practices in relation to the three identified community sport objectives. However, it became evident that most practitioners experienced difficulties in determining the actual impact of their programmes with regard to these objectives. This illustrated their concern of not fully understanding how the provided activities would effectively contribute to such aims and therefore recognised the need for additional understanding of the inner workings of their own programmes. Although both aspects (i.e. understanding how to work effectively and how to determine impact) were regarded as equally important, it was decided by the CATCH team to focus on the practitioners' first concern. There was a consensus with the fact that, without a better understanding of the process, it is very difficult to determine effectiveness and causality. Secondly, through consultation with practitioners (such as during the project's kick-off meeting) and initial data collection (e.g. extended participatory observations in research phase one), researchers gained critical insight into the inner workings of the community sport programmes resulting in the development of an evidence-informed framework related to the three identified objectives (see Chapter 2). In turn, this directly informed the design of the approaches to be used during the subsequent action-oriented research in the three community sport practices of research phase two (see Chapters 3, 4, and 5). Thirdly, on various occasions over the course of the project, several workshops, seminars, learning labs and annual meetings with local policymakers were organised, which provided opportunities for linkage and exchange activities with practitioners, social users and policymakers. Fourthly, knowledge translation practices also related to the production of a series of non-academic research outputs aimed at different audiences. These included a practical handbook for community sport practitioners, 10 publications in media outlets and professional journals geared towards end users, a two-page project flyer, a quick scan (i.e. a topic list to assess the current situation in a community sport practice), a training module for community sport coaches, a mobile online reflection tool for young volunteer community sport city coaches, a TBE-based social impact tool for community sport coordinators (the *community sport impact wizard*) and a symposium bringing together international experts and local practitioners. In addition, during the project 5 *community sport labs* (CSLs) were established to interact with a broader group of users who were not directly involved in the research. They served as a *community of practice*, bringing together a group of relevant stakeholders with an interest in community sport. The CSLs also acted as locally embedded steering groups, where the knowledge translation products were developed, implemented and tested. Fifthly, it is also noteworthy that ISB played a crucial role as a *boundary spanner* operating at the interface between local community sport practices and policymakers. ISB was selected on the basis of its specific expertise, network and capability to safeguard post-project sustainability. This facilitated the research team's access to key stakeholders and end users. ISB was responsible for establishing and managing the CSLs and supporting the activities of the social user group and created platforms where practice-based tools were developed and tested. They also contributed to the effective communication of research-based knowledge to a wide range of end users. Finally, knowledge strategies also comprised efforts to contribute to the uptake of research by policymakers. This included annual briefings with Flemish government cabinet members and senior civil servants in different departments (i.e. youth, welfare and sport). The briefings enhanced policymakers' awareness and recognition of the research and led to various exchanges in which they sought research-based advice and input from the research team.

Chapter overview

This book consists of nine chapters. Through four sections, it provides insights into a number of specific aspects of the CATCH project with contributions, each focusing on one particular topic with relevance to the central aim of the project. Chapters 1 and 2 form the first section (*Introduction and general findings*), with Chapter 2 presenting an evidence-informed framework including the contextual assets and practices that shape the necessary and sufficient conditions through which community sport programmes may foster social inclusionary outcomes. In the second section (*Thematic insights into community sport and social inclusion*), insights are described that are related to the work that was done regarding each of the three selected social inclusion objectives within the CATCH project (i.e. Chapter 3 on conceptual frameworks for reflective practice in community sport in relation to personal development; Chapter 4 on an intervention aimed at promoting health in the context of community sport practice and Chapter 5 on the efforts of community sport practitioners to develop a more structural understanding and approach to social cohesion). In the third section (*Broader perspectives on community sport and social inclusion*), a broader perspective is provided with regard to specific issues relevant for the central topic and/or approaches used in the CATCH project (i.e. Chapter 6 on different approaches to monitoring and evaluation and its relevance for sport for development (SfD); Chapter 7 on a realist inquiry frame-of-mind that can contribute to substantiate, structure and deepen action research and Chapter 8 on critical reflections on the concept of social inclusion and its application and operationalisation in social science research on community sport). In the final section of this book (*General reflections*), consisting of Chapter 9, we reflect on what we have learned through our involvement in the CATCH project, including the value and challenges of its multidisciplinary approach, the specific role and importance of sport in community sport practice for targeting selected social inclusion objectives and the level of expertise of community sport coaches to work towards these objectives.

References

Agergaard, S. (2018) *Rethinking sport and integration: Developing a transnational perspective on migrants and descendants in sports*, London: Routledge.

Bailey, R. (2005) 'Evaluating the relationship between physical education, sport and social inclusion', *Educational Review*, 57(1), 71–90. DOI: 10.1080/0013191042000274196

Bailey, R. (2008) 'Positive youth development through sport', in: N.L. Holt (ed) *Youth sport and social inclusion*, London: Routledge, pp. 85–96.

Blamey, A. and Mackenzie, M. (2007) 'Theories of change and realistic evaluation: Peas in a pod or apples and oranges?', *Evaluation*, 13(4), 439–455. DOI: 10.1177/1356389007082129

Bloyce, D. and Smith, A. (2010) *Sport policy and development – an introduction*, London and New York: Routledge.

Chan, J., To, H.P. and Chan, E. (2006) 'Reconsidering social cohesion: Developing a definition and analytical framework for empirical research', *Social Indicators Research*, 75(2), 273–302. DOI: 10.1007/s11205-005-2118-1

Chen, S., Henry, I. and Ko, L.M. (2014) 'Meta-evaluation, analytic logic models and the impact of sport policies', in: I. Henry and L.M. Ko (eds) *Routledge handbook of sport policy*, London: Routledge, pp. 33–47.

Coakley, J. (2011) 'Youth sports: What counts as "positive development?"', *Journal of Sport and Social Issues*, 35(3), 306–324. DOI: 10.1177/0193723511417311

Coalter, F. (2007) *A wider social role for sport: Who's keeping the score?* London: Routledge.

Coalter, F. (2012) '"There is loads of relationships here": Developing a programme theory for sport-for-change programmes', *International Review for the Sociology of Sport*, 48(5), 594–612. DOI: 10.1177/1012690212446143

Coalter, F. (2013) *Sport for development: What game are we playing?* London: Routledge.

Council of the European Union (2017) *EU work plan for sport 2017–2020*, Resolution of the Council and of the Representatives of the Governments of the Member States, meeting within the Council, on the European Union Work Plan for Sport, Official Journal of the European Union, C 189/5. Available HTTP: https://eur-lex.europa.eu/legal-content/EN/TXT/HTML/?uri=CELEX:42017Y0615(01)&from=EN (accessed 23 April 2020)

Crabbe, T. (2009) 'Getting to know you: Using sport to engage and build relationships with socially marginalised youth', in: R. Levermore and A. Beacom (eds) *Sport and international development*, Houndmills: Palgrave Macmillan, pp. 176–198.

Cutter, S.L., Boruff, B.J. and Shirley, W.L. (2003) 'Social vulnerability to environmental hazards', *Social Science Quarterly*, 84(2), 242–261. DOI: 10.1111/1540-6237.8402002

Danish, S., Forneris, T., Hodge, K. and Heke, I. (2004) 'Enhancing youth development through sport', *World Leisure Journal*, 46(3), 38–49. DOI: 10.1080/04419057.2004.9674365

Darnell, S.C., Chawansky, M., Marchesseault, D., Holmes, M. and Hayhurst, L. (2016) 'The state of play: Critical sociological insights into recent "sport for development and peace" research', *International Review for the Sociology of Sport*, 53(2), 133–151. DOI: 10.1177/1012690216646762

Ekholm, D. (2016) *Sport as a means of responding to social problems: Rationales of government, welfare and social change*, Doctoral dissertation, Linköping University, Linköping.

European Commission (2010) *The European platform against poverty and social exclusion: A European framework for social and territorial cohesion*, Communication from the Commission to the European Parliament, the Council, the European Economic and Social Committee and the Committee of the Regions, Brussels, 16 December, COM (2010) 758 final. Available HTTP: https://eur-lex.europa.eu/LexUriServ/LexUriServ.do?uri=COM%3A2010%3A0758%3AFIN%3AEN%3APDF (accessed 4 May 2020)

European Commission (2018a) *Empowering young people and building their resilience: A new EU youth strategy*, Factsheet, Brussels: European Commission. Available HTTP: https://ec.europa.eu/youth/sites/youth/files/factsheet-youth-may2018-en.pdf (accessed 17 April 2020)

European Commission (2018b) *Engaging, connecting and empowering young people: A new EU youth strategy*, Communication from the Commission to the European Parliament, the European Council, the Council, the European Economic and Social Committee and the Committee of the Regions, Brussels, 22 May, COM (2018) 269 final. Available HTTP: https://ec.europa.eu/youth/sites/youth/files/youth_com_269_1_en_act_part1_v9.pdf (accessed 13 April 2020)

European Commission (2018c) *Special eurobarometer 472: Sport and physical activity*, Brussels: DG Education, Youth, Sport and Culture.

European Commission – Sport and Society (2018) *Website sport*. Available HTTP: https://ec.europa.eu/sport/policy/society_en (accessed 17 April 2020)

European Sport for All Charter (1975/76) *Appendix to resolution (76) 41: Article III: Adopted by the committee of ministers on 24 September 1976 at the 26th meeting of the ministers' deputies*. Available HTTP: www.europa.clio-online.de/quelle/id/q63-28550 (accessed 17 April 2020)

Eurostat (2019) *Young people – social inclusion: Eurostat. Statistics explained*. Available HTTP: https://ec.europa.eu/eurostat/statistics-explained/index.php/Young_people_-_social_inclusion#Young_people_at_risk_of_poverty_or_social_exclusion (accessed 13 April 2020)

Eurostat (2020a) *Population on 1 January by age and sex*. Available HTTP: https://appsso.eurostat.ec.europa.eu/nui/show.do?dataset=demo_pjan&lang=en (accessed 17 April 2020)

Eurostat (2020b) *Young people aged 15–24 neither in employment nor in education and training (NEET), by sex – annual averages*. Available HTTP: https://appsso.eurostat.ec.europa.eu/nui/show.do?dataset=lfsi_neet_a&lang=en (accessed 4 May 2020)

Evans, L., Bolton, N., Jones, C. and Iorwerth, H. (2019) '"Defnyddiwch y Gymraeg": Community sport as a vehicle for encouraging the use of the Welsh language', *Sport in Society*, 22(6), 1115–1129. DOI: 10.1080/17430437.2019.1565399

Fletcher, G. (2014) 'You just wanna be like everyone else: Exploring the experiences of gay, lesbian, bisexual and queer sportspeople through a languaging lens', *Annals of Leisure Research*, 17(4), 460–475. DOI: 10.1080/11745398.2014.956130

Glazzard, J. (2011) 'Perceptions of the barriers to inclusion in one primary school: Voices of teachers and teaching assistants', *Support for learning*, 26(2), 56–63. DOI: 10.1111/j.1467-9604.2011.01478.x

Green, B.C. (2008) 'Sport as an agent for social and personal change', in: V. Girginov (ed) *Management of sport development*, Burlington, MA: Butterworth-Heinemann, pp. 129–145.

Harris, S. and Houlihan, B. (2016) 'Implementing the community sport legacy: The limits of partnerships, contracts and performance management', *European Sport Management Quarterly*, 16(4), 433–458. DOI: 10.1111/1467-9248.00247

Hartmann, D. and Kwauk, C. (2011) 'Sport and development: An overview, critique, and reconstruction', *Journal of Sport and Social Issues*, 35(3), 284–305. DOI: 10.1177/0193723511416986

Haudenhuyse, R., Theeboom, M. and Nols, Z. (2013) 'Sport- based interventions for socially vulnerable youth: Towards well-defined interventions with easy-to-follow outcomes?', *International Review for the Sociology of Sport*, 48(4), 471–484. DOI: 10.1177/1012690212448002

Henry, I. and Ko, L.M. (2014) 'Analysing sport policy in a globalising context', in: I. Henry and L.M. Ko (eds) *Routledge handbook of sport policy*, London: Routledge, pp. 3–10.

Hermens, N., Super, S., Verkooijen, K.T. and Koelen, M. (2017) 'A systematic review of life skill development through sports programs serving socially vulnerable youth', *Research Quarterly for Exercise and Sport*, 88(4), 408–424. DOI: 10.1080/02701367.2017.1355527

Hickey, S. and du Toit, A. (2007) *Adverse incorporation, social exclusion and chronic poverty*, Chronic Poverty Research Centre Working Paper No. 81. Available HTTP: https://ssrn.com/abstract=1752967 (accessed 3 December 2019)

Hodkinson, A. (2012) 'All present and correct? Exclusionary inclusion within the English education system', *Disability and Society*, 27(5), 675–688. DOI: 10.1080/09687599.2012.673078

Holt, N. (2008) *Positive youth development through sport*, London: Routledge.

Jeanes, R., Spaaij, R., Magee, J., Farquharson, K., Gorman, S. and Lusher, D. (2018) '"Yes we are inclusive": Examining provision for young people with disabilities in community sport clubs', *Sport Management Review*, 21(1), 38–50. DOI: 10.1016/j.smr.2017.04.001

Jones, G.J., Edwards, M.B., Bocarro, J.N., Bunds, K.S. and Smith, J.W. (2017) 'An integrative review of sport-based youth development literature', *Sport in Society*, 20(1), 161–179. DOI: 10.1080/17430437.2015

Kay, T. (2009) 'Developing through sport: Evidencing sport impacts on young people', *Sport in Society*, 12(9), 1177–1191. DOI: 10.1080/17430430903137837

Kearns, A. and Forrest, R. (2000) 'Social cohesion and multilevel governance', *Urban Studies*, 37(5–6), 995–1017. DOI: 10.1177/0042098012444890

Kelly, L. (2011) '"Social inclusion" through sports-based interventions?', *Critical Social Policy*, 31(1), 126–150. DOI: 10.1177/0261018310385442

Kennett, C. (2014) 'The evaluation of sport and social inclusion policy programmes', in: I. Henry and L.M. Ko (eds) *Routledge handbook of sport policy*, London: Routledge, pp. 253–263.

Kessl, F. (2009) 'Critical reflexivity, social work, and the emerging European post-welfare states', *European Journal of Social Work*, 12(3), 305–317. DOI: 10.1080/13691450902930746

Levitas, R. (2005) *The inclusive society? Social exclusion and new labour*, 2nd edition, Basingstoke and Hampshire: Palgrave Macmillan.

Levitas, R., Pantazis, C., Fahmy, E., Gordon, D., Lloyd, E. and Patsios, D. (2007) *The multi-dimensional analysis of social exclusion*, London: Department for Communities and Local Government (DCLG).

Lindsey, G. (2003) 'Inclusive education: A critical perspective', *British Journal of Special Education*, 30(1), 3–12.

Long, J. and Sanderson, I. (2001) 'The social benefits of sport: Where's the proof?', in: C. Gratton and I. Henry (eds) *Sport in the city*, London: Routledge, pp. 187–203.

Lorenz, W. (2016) 'Rediscovering the social question', *European Journal of Social Work*, 19(1), 4–17. DOI: 10.1080/13691457.2015.1082984

McDonald, I. (2005) 'Theorizing partnerships: Governance, communicative action and sport policy', *Journal of Sport Policy*, 34(4), 579–600.

Nicholls, S., Giles, A.R. and Sethna, C. (2010) 'Perpetuating the "lack of evidence" discourse in sport for development: Privileged voices, unheard stories and subjugated knowledge', *International Review for the Sociology of Sport*, 46(3), 249–264.

Nols, Z. (2018) *Social change through sport for development initiatives: A critical pedagogical perspective*, Doctoral dissertation, Vrije Universiteit Brussel, Brussel.

Novy, A., Swiatek, D.C. and Moulaert, F. (2012) 'Social cohesion: A conceptual and political elucidation', *Urban Studies*, 49(9), 1873–1889. DOI: 10.1177/0042098012444878

Omtzigt, D.J. (2009) *Survey on social inclusion: Theory and policy*, Working Paper, Oxford: Oxford University, Oxford Institute for Global Economic Development. Available HTTP: https://ec.europa.eu/regional_policy/archive/policy/future/pdf/1_omtzigt_final_formatted.pdf (accessed 21 December 2020)

Park, N., Peterson, C., Szvarca, D., Vander Molen, R.J., Kim, E.S. and Collon, K. (2016) 'Positive psychology and physical health: Research and applications', *American Journal of Lifestyle Medicine*, 10, 200–206. DOI:10.1177/1559827614550277

Pawson, R. (2001) *Evidence based policy, vol. 1, in search of a method*, ESRC UK Centre for Evidence Based Policy and Practice, Working Paper 3, London: Queen Mary University of London.

Pawson, R. (2006) *Evidence-based policy: A realist perspective*, Thousand Oaks, CA: Sage.

Pawson, R. and Tilley, N. (2004) *Realistic evaluation*, London: Sage.

Platts, C. (2018) 'Introducing community sport and physical activity', in: R. Wilson and C. Platts (eds) *Managing and developing community sport*, London: Routledge, pp. 3–14.

Schaillée, H., Spaaij, R., Jeanes, R. and Theeboom, M. (2019) 'Knowledge translation practices, enablers, and constraints: Bridging the research-practice divide in sport management', *Journal of Sport Management*, 33(5), 366–378. DOI: 10.1123/jsm.2018-0175

Seligman, M.E.P. and Csikszentmihalyi, M. (2000) 'Positive psychology: An introduction', *American Psychology*, 55(1), 5–14. DOI: 10.1037/0003-066X.55.1.5

Silver, H. (2010) 'Understanding social inclusion and its meaning for Australia', *Australian Journal of Social Issues*, 45(2), 183–211.

Smyth, J. (2017) 'Social inclusion', *Education and society*, July. DOI: 10.1093/acrefore/9780190264093.013.129

Spaaij, R., Magee, J. and Jeanes, R. (2014) *Sport and social exclusion in global society*, London: Routledge.

Straus, S., Tetroe, J. and Graham, I.D. (2013) *Knowledge translation in health care: Moving from evidence to practice*, London: Wiley.

Sudsawad, P. (2007) *Knowledge translation: Introduction to models, strategies, and measures*, Austin, TX: Southwest Educational Development Laboratory, National Center for the Dissemination of Disability Research.

Super, S., Verkooijen, K. and Koelen, M. (2018) 'The role of community sports coaches in creating optimal social conditions for life skill development and transferability – a salutogenic perspective', *Sport Education and Society*, 23(2), 173–185. DOI: 10.1080/13573322.2016.1145109

Tacon, R. (2007) 'Football and social inclusion: Evaluating social policy', *Managing Leisure*, 12(1), 1–23. DOI: 10.1080/13606710601056422

Taylor, P., Davies, L., Wells, P., Gilbertson, J. and Tayleur, W. (2015) *A review of the social impacts of culture and sport*, The Sport Industry Research Centre and Centre for Regional Economic and Social Research (Sheffield Hallam University) and Business of Culture (BOC), London: Department for Culture, Media, and Sport CASE Program.

Theeboom, M. and De Knop, P. (1992) 'Inventarisatie binnen het jeugdwelzijnswerk in Vlaanderen [Inventarisation in the youth welfare work in Flanders]', in: P. De Knop and L. Walgrave (eds) *Sport als integratie: Kansen voor maatschappelijk kwetsbare jongeren*, Brussel: Koning Boudewijnstichting, pp. 119–130.

Theeboom, M. and De Maesschalck, P. (2006) *Sporten om de hoek: Een brede kijk op buurtsport in Vlaanderen [Sport around the corner: A broad view on neighbourhood sport in Flanders]*, Sint-Niklaas: ISB.

Theeboom, M., Haudenhuyse, R. and Vertonghen, J. (2015) *Sport and sociale innovatie: Inspirerende praktijken en inzichten [Sport and social innovation: Inspiring practices and insights]*, Brussel: Academic Scientific Publishers.

Van der Sypt, P. (2019) 'Buurtsport in Vlaanderen en Brussel anno 2018: De 2-meting buurtsport [Community sport in Flanders and Brussels anno 2018]', *Vlaams Tijdschrift voor Sportbeheer*, 271, 30–35.

Van Poppel, M. (2015) *Benchmark buurtsport: Buurtsport in Vlaanderen anno 2014 [Benchmark community sport: Community sport in Flanders anno 2014]*, Research Report, Sint-Niklaas: ISB.

Veit-Wilson, J. (1998) *Setting adequacy standards*, Bristol: Policy Press.

Vettenburg, N., Walgrave, L. and Van Kerckvoorde, J. (1984) *Jeugdwerkloosheid, delinquentie en maatschappelijke kwetsbaarheid: Een theoretisch en empirisch onderzoek naar de veronderstelde band tussen werkloosheid en delinquentie bij 17–19 jarigen [Youth unemployment, delinquency and societal vulnerability: A theoretical and empirical study of the assumed connection between unemployment and delinquency among 17 to 19 year-olds]*. Antwerp, Belgium: Kluwer.

Weiss, C.H. (1995) ' "Nothing as practical as good theory": Exploring theory-based evaluation for comprehensive community initiatives for children and families', in: J. Connell, A. Kubisch, L. Schorr and C.H. Weiss (eds) *New approaches to evaluating community initiatives: Concepts, methods, and contexts*, New York: The Aspen Institute, pp. 65–92.

World Health Organization (1946) *Preamble to the constitution of the World Health Organization as adopted by the International Health Conference, New York, 19–22 June*, Official Records of the World Health Organization, Geneva, Switzerland: World Health Organization.

2 Community sport and social inclusion

Necessary and sufficient conditions

Hebe Schaillée, Marc Theeboom, Shana Sabbe, Karen Van der Veken, Pieter Debognies and Dorien Brosens

Towards an empirically informed understanding of community sport and social inclusion

As shown in the previous chapter, both in and beyond Flanders the scientific knowledge base of community sport – and specifically regarding using sport as a tool for social inclusion – is emergent. As noted in Chapter 1, community sport is an important alternative sport context in Flanders that attracts young people in socially vulnerable situations and often strives towards increasing young people's personal development, health and social cohesion (Van Poppel 2015). To date, especially in the Flemish context, there is, however, little systematic scientific research on how to use sport as a tool for social inclusion in a community setting. To date, there is no evidence-informed framework on how community sport can contribute to the promotion of social inclusion. The *Community sport for AT-risk youth: Innovative strategies for promoting personal development, health and social CoHesion* (CATCH) project aims at co-creating a scientific breakthrough in this matter supported by stakeholders from the field of practice. The project was designed to advance our scientific understanding of the contribution of community sport provisions on social inclusion. The chapter will specifically focus on how community sport programmes can pursue social inclusionary objectives (i.e. personal development, health and social cohesion).

In Chapter 1, we outlined the broad contours of the CATCH project. Following from it, this chapter describes necessary and sufficient conditions for each social inclusionary outcome. A realist evaluation approach was used to assess the extent to which an intervention – in our case: a community sport programme – may achieve social inclusionary objectives – in relation to personal development, health and social cohesion – and why this can occur in these specific community sport interventions (see, e.g. Pawson 2006; Weiss 1995). Instead of merely investigating if a programme or policy works (what most evaluative research does), a *theory-based evaluation approach* (TBE) intends to understand why and how it does (or does not) and in what circumstances. Central to the TBE approach is the notion that all programmes have an implicit programme logic or programme

DOI: 10.4324/9780429340635-3

theory (Pawson 2001; Weiss 1995). TBE is fundamentally concerned with theory development, refinement and evaluation and is not a specific method or technique but an approach to evaluation. This approach – see also Chapter 6 – aims for an in-depth understanding of the mechanisms, triggered by contextual conditions, within a specific programme or activity. The necessary and sufficient conditions presented in this chapter, derived from data of the CATCH project, attempt to explain how community sport programmes targeting young people in socially vulnerable situations support participants' personal development, health and social cohesion.

Methods

As discussed in Chapter 1, there is uncertainty among scholars not merely about the potential social contribution of sport but also about the capacity of research to reveal this contribution (Kay 2009). Chapter 1 outlines various critical remarks regarding methodologies of existing studies including the lack of analysis of the particular and generalisable necessary and sufficient conditions that underpin implementation and delivery. The first research phase of the CATCH project sought to address these issues via a case study design in Flanders. As argued by Yin (2004), when strategically chosen, cases can strengthen the study results and make the interpretations and explanations more robust. Spaaij (2011) indicated that if each case is sought to be understood individually and as much in-depth as possible, it can illuminate patterns of similarity and difference. The cross-case comparison in CATCH was used to increase our insights into similarities and differences between community sport cases and between the pursuit of different social inclusionary objectives. This analysis served as a basis for the necessary and sufficient conditions outlined in this chapter. The multiple-case design involved nine community sport cases that align with the three social inclusionary objectives (i.e. personal development, health and social cohesion). For each social inclusionary objective, we selected three cases.

Case selection

One explicit research strategy was to embed co-design through the project. Co-design refers to the stimulation and facilitation of practitioners' active involvement alongside the research team (Schaillée et al. 2019). In the CATCH project, co-design started with the pre-project phase in which collaboration with practitioners led to (1) the formulation of the central research questions (see Chapter 1), (2) supported decisions on the research methodology, (3) the selection of knowledge translation practices and deliverables (see Chapters 1 and 9) and (4) a shared vision to focus on personal development, health and social cohesion as the three central social inclusionary objectives within the CATCH project.

All community sport programmes that sought to contribute to one of these objectives were invited to the kick-off event of the CATCH project. Eighteen community sport programmes were willing to participate in our research project and all but one attended the kick-off. The objective of the meeting was not only to present our project to those working in the field but also to attain a well-informed decision about our case selection. During the meeting, the community sport stakeholders were invited to share their thoughts on statements such as: *community sport programmes should primarily be focused on young people in socially vulnerable situations*. Statements were used as a means to position themselves and, combined with group discussions, to gain more insight into different key aspects of each community sport programme (e.g. characteristics of their target group(s) and attitude towards hosting a researcher). As we only wanted to select nine cases (i.e. three per thematic focus), the following two criteria were used for the selection:

- The extent to which the cases believed to focus on a specific approach (i.e. mission, vision, goal setting) and content (i.e. mid and long-term projects) in relation to each of the three topics;
- Ensuring a wide variety across our selection to make our results useful/interesting for a variety of other community sport programmes.

Regarding the second criterium, our goal was to select a diversity of community sport programmes for each social inclusionary outcome as it is believed that diversity across cases is valuable when external conditions are thought to produce much variation in the phenomenon being studied (Yin 1994). The community sport programmes within each thematic category varied on the basis of a number of aspects, including age range of their target group, the number of participants, the number of full-time equivalents, executing agency, the number of years of operation and geographical spread. The diversity among the nine selected programmes is illustrated in Table 2.1.

Table 2.1 Diversity among the selected community sport programmes

Theme	City of CSP[1]	Target groups[2]	Number of inhabitants	Number of FTE[3]	Executing agency
Personal development	Brussels	Young adolescents, adolescents, young adults	>1,000,000	22.6 FTE	Community sport, since 2001
	Mechelen	Children, young adolescents, adolescents, young adults	+/–85,000	1 FTE	Community sport, since 1993
	Ninove	Young adolescents, adolescents, young adults	+/–39,000	1 FTE	Youth work, since 2013
Health	Ghent	Adolescents, young adults	+/–260,000	13.6 FTE	Youth work, since 2009
	Leuven	Young adolescents, adolescents, young adults	+/–100,000	2 FTE	Sport, since 2006

(*Continued*)

Table 2.1 (Continued)

Theme	City of CSP[1]	Target groups[2]	Number of inhabitants	Number of FTE[3]	Executing agency
	Lier	Adolescents, young adults	+/–35,000	0.2 FTE	Welfare and sport, since 2008
Social cohesion	Bruges	Children, young adolescents, adolescents	+/–120,000	6 FTE	Welfare, since 2009
	Kortrijk	Children, young adolescents	+/–76,000	6 FTE	Sport, since 2009
	Ronse	Children, young adolescents, adolescents, young adults	+/–26,000	1 FTE	Community sport, since 2003

Notes.
[1] CSP is the abbreviation for Community Sport Programme.
[2] The target group was divided into children (<11 years), young adolescents (11–13 years), adolescents (14–17 years) and young adults (18–25 years) according to the categorisation of Curtis (2015).
[3] FTE is the abbreviation of full-time equivalents.

Data collection

The research took place between February 2016 and June 2017 (i.e. 17 months) and combined several complementary data collection methods: field visits, individual in-depth interviews and focus groups. Three researchers each immersed themselves in three of the selected community sport programmes to gain trust of the practitioners and participants. Issues of trust were crucial to the process of collecting data, which were negotiated in large part through being physically present, listening carefully and respectfully demonstrating concern for research participants and their interests. The field visits provided the opportunity for direct observation, which enabled the researchers to obtain impressionistic information concerning community sport activities, practitioners' job content, differences and similarities across programmes, as well as participants and staff's actions during the community sport activities. By generating the feeling of what it is like to be in a particular social situation, the researcher is more able to make sense of what people have to say and the ways in which they describe and interpret their social world (Brewer 2000; Madden 2010).

This resulted in 64 field visits, accounting for a total of 179 hours of field visits over a period ranging from three to seven months, across the nine cases. The field visits lasted between 30 and 180 minutes (on average 123). During the field visits, the three researchers attended sport activities (e.g. boxing), side activities (e.g. homework guidance), staff meetings and events (e.g. neighbourhood party) co-organised by practitioners within the local communities of the programmes. The impressions, views and personal reflections of each researcher were kept in a reflective diary.

In order to gain richer insights into practitioners' experiences, opinions and aspirations, individual in-depth interviews with 30 partners (e.g. municipal sport services, sport clubs, social work and youth work services), 25 coordinators and 27 coaches were conducted. The interviewees were recruited across the nine programmes through a purposive sampling method (DiCocco-Bloom and Crabtree 2006) in order to enhance the richness of the data. Most interviewees were practitioners with knowledge on the research topic that were appointed to the researchers by the directors of the programmes before the first series of field visits (between February and July 2016). A snowball technique (Jones et al. 2013) was subsequently used to further increase the range of perspectives. All interviewees in this first stage worked with socially vulnerable (young) people in the context of community sport. This included, for example, coaching sport activities or providing homework guidance. The age of the interviewees ranged between 18 and 60 years (on average 34.3 years). The interview guide focused on (1) how practitioners conceptualise the three social inclusionary objectives (i.e. personal development, health and social cohesion) and on (2) how they see their programmes contributing towards these outcomes. The individual in-depth interviews were guided by four main questions:

1 What do you seek to achieve when taking personal development, health or social cohesion as an objective of community sport?
2 What are the expected effects with regard to personal development, health or social cohesion?
3 How and to what extent does community sport currently contribute to personal development, health or social cohesion?
4 Which mechanisms and contextual resources contribute to participants' personal development, health or social cohesion?

The second stage consisted of another round of field visits at the nine research sites and individual in-depth interviews with participants (n = 59) to complement the initial data set. On request of the community sport practitioners, researchers immersed themselves for the second time into the programmes. This resulted in 20 additional field visits, accounting for a total of 140 hours of participant observations over a period of six months (from August 2016 until January 2017). Similar to the first series of field visits, a wide range of activities were observed. This second phase of field visits was crucial, especially given the fact that community sport has huge fluctuations regarding the in- and outflow of participants. Using a fieldwork approach allowed us to be as flexible as possible and to 'keep the participants on-board' (Van Hove and Claes 2011: 91) between the field visits and the interviews, which followed in a later phase. Fifty-nine participants were recruited to further increase the range of perspectives on how community sport can contribute to one of the objectives. The interviewed participants (44 males and 15 females) attended or participated[1] in one of the community sport programmes. Their age ranged between 10 and 49 years (M = 22.6 years). A substantial number of participants (n = 31) had a foreign background (such as Moroccan, Somali,

Syrian, French, Turkish and Congolese). The majority (81.3 per cent) of the participants who provided information regarding their educational background were enrolled in technical or vocational secondary education (n = 24), primary education (n = 14) or had no qualification (n = 10). The interviews with the participants focused on the meaning that was attributed to community sport in their lives.

In a third stage, focus groups with community sport practitioners were conducted to complement the field notes and the data from the interviews. A focus group enables the researcher to study the interaction within the group and the collective construction of meaning. The latter is particularly true in relation to how people respond to each other's opinions and form their own opinion out of the interaction that takes place within the group (Bryman 2012). The dynamics of a focus group can produce data that would not arise from an interview in which particular questions have been scripted by a researcher (Morgan 1988). A total of eight focus groups (i.e. two for health, three for personal development and three for social cohesion) were held, each comprising between 6 and 12 participants. The objective of the focus groups was to gain insight into the different perspectives on the facilitating conditions in the context of community sport and to search for the reasons why particular views are held by individuals and groups (i.e. similarities and differences).

The final stage of this iterative research process consisted of a *community sport lab* for the social user group of the CATCH project. The social user group comprised 18 community sport programmes and 22 umbrella organisations. The latter are (regional or Flemish) organisations from different policy domains (sport, youth, welfare, poverty and culture) that support (local) primary community sport programmes or are involved in facilitating a community sport offer at a local level. The results from the previous stages were presented during this community sport lab and a more in-depth insight was provided to the attendees in order to increase their understanding into the underlying processes (necessary and sufficient conditions) within community sport. This community sport lab was also used as a platform to reflect on the usefulness of our results for the social users.

Data analysis

The field notes were kept in a research diary, while the interviews and focus groups were audio recorded and anonymised. Interview and focus group data were managed using qualitative data management package NVivo 11 (GSRInternational) and subjected to thematic analysis. This process involved familiarisation with the data (i.e. reading and re-reading) and assigning broad thematic codes. Investigator triangulation was applied. The researchers from the different thematic foci met regularly (on average once every two weeks) to discuss issues around coding and to revise the coding strategy if necessary. The broad higher-order themes deriving from specific codes were data driven. Coded data were charted to allow comparisons across cases and themes. The last stage consisted of interpreting the data. The interpretative stage was performed through

Table 2.2 Assets and practices that shape the necessary and sufficient conditions of community sport programmes

Necessary and sufficient conditions	Assets or practices
1 Building caring relationships with mentors and coaches	• The person-oriented approach • A 'thousand chances' philosophy • The cultural capital • Mutual exchange of knowledge
2 Creating an experiential learning context	• Hands-on learning opportunities • Reflective practices
3 Developing an enlarged and diversified social network	• Anti-stigma interventions • Interorganisational partnerships

discussions within the CATCH research team and the international scientific steering committee.

In this chapter, we aim to contribute to existing knowledge on community sport by identifying a particular set of conditions that enables community sport programmes to foster social inclusionary outcomes, as some of the conditions have been described elsewhere and they will only be cited here. The results presented in this chapter relate to necessary and sufficient conditions that the three researchers encountered independently of their own thematic focus. According to Coalter (2007), necessary conditions need to be fulfilled to reach your target group, whereas sufficient conditions maximise a programme's capacity towards achieving social inclusionary objectives. Findings showed that the community sport programmes deploy a particular set of conditions to contribute to participants' personal development, health and social cohesion (See Table 2.2):

1   Building caring relationships with mentors and coaches
2   Creating an experiential learning context
3   Developing an enlarged and diversified social network.

Building caring relationships with mentors and coaches

Community sport practitioners focused on establishing caring relationships with participants and regarded it as a necessary and sufficient condition to facilitate the achievement of social inclusionary objectives. According to Haudenhuyse (2012), the division between necessary and sufficient conditions needs to be viewed as the poles of a continuum, implying a potential interplay between both types and consequently also a challenge in making a clear-cut distinction necessary (i.e. reach the target group) and sufficient conditions (i.e. work with the target group). In line with the international literature on targeted sport-based youth programmes (see, e.g. Bailey 2008; Coalter 2007; Kelly 2011), the relational aspect is viewed as the cornerstone of working with young people in a community sport context. In caring relationships, participants report high levels of respect and trust towards the coaching staff, which can eventually lead to reciprocity (such as participants not engaging in rule-breaking behaviour) (Coalter 2013). In this study, four contextual assets appeared to contribute to the development of caring relationships: (1) a person-oriented approach, (2) a 'thousand chances' philosophy, (3) the cultural capital of practitioners and (4) a two-way exchange of knowledge.

Firstly, related to the *person-oriented approach*, community sport participants across the different programmes experienced that coaches attach great importance to participants' well-being. By addressing each participant individually, participants noticed that community sport coaches were sensitive and responsive to their personal lives (e.g. family situation, culture, school results, neighbourhood characteristics). Such person-oriented perspective furthermore allows practitioners to get insight into the unique stories and experiences of young people and to establish customised, one-on-one approaches (Sabbe et al. 2019a). This was emphasised by one social worker as follows:

> They are not obliged to come with a question or with a problem. By being yourself (and people feel that), without wanting to come with all solutions, but just by offering a listening ear, by giving people attention and showing interest in who they are and what they're capable of . . . approaching them in this manner, makes that you more rapidly trust a person. Then you can achieve much more with them. And sometimes people are stuck in the same situation for years, but then it is what it is. We are not going to push them. Just trying to remain standing besides them and, yes, showing interest in what they can do and as such putting them into their strength and trying to approach them positively.
>
> (social worker, 37 years, male, health)

Another community sport coordinator reported:

> You cannot work with young people if you don't know them. So, first you should get to know them and their life situation . . . and this has nothing to do with measuring how vulnerable they are or not. No, you should really put some efforts in getting to know them because by doing so needs will show up, which allow you to organise more meaningful activities or better provide help.
>
> (coordinator, male, 37 years, personal development)

Pawson (2006) suggested that befriending relationships are crucial as such relationships create a context in which the mentee (here community sport participant) recognises the legitimacy of other people (such as the coach) and other perspectives. The primary objective of befriending is the creation of bonds of trust and not to prioritise the setting or achievement of objectives (Pawson 2006). Moreau et al.'s (2018) analysis related to the Canadian sport for development (SfD) programme DesÉquilibres showed that social bonds are formed at the micro-level. They reveal that the ongoing presence and the participation of coaches during the activities facilitated relationship building based on mutual respect and trust with participants. One of the community sports coaches in our study mentioned that such social bonds enabled him to move beyond merely community sport participation: 'I'm strongly convinced that if you cannot create that feeling of safety, you will continue to struggle.... It's kind of a necessary condition to take next steps' (coordinator, male, 29 years, health).

A second contextual asset that seems to contribute to the development of caring relationships is a *thousand chances philosophy* (Debognies et al. 2019). Practitioners mentioned that they embraced the idea that people deserve a second chance. In many community sport programmes, it was clearly stated that expectations in terms of behaviour exist (e.g. in relation to showing respect for others, having discipline during the training sessions and not offending other people), but that rule-breaking behaviour would not immediately lead to the exclusion of participants. Rule-breaking behaviour is rather perceived as an opportunity for young people to learn from their mistakes. As one of the practitioners stated:

> We start from a thousand-chances-philosophy, which implies that we keep giving chances and opportunities to young people ... while at sport clubs people are often not welcome anymore, for example, after they stole something. In our programme we then choose to ask young people why they stole something, but afterwards we close the incident and give them a second chance.
>
> (coordinator, male, 30 years, personal development)

The importance of this approach was also reported by this community sport coordinator:

> I think we make the difference at the moment that someone crosses the lines by the way we deal with it. Almost all people we work with have been showing undesirable behaviour in school or feel they are not receiving any chances or are been set aside. I think we have to try to make the difference there by ... precisely deal with [that/them] in a way that they think: 'Ok, here I do receive another chance" or "I have not been put aside as a person here'.
>
> (coordinator, male, 34 years, health)

This approach is also perceived and highly appreciated by the participants, as illustrated in the following quote:

> If you don't respect the others, you don't have to come back. But if you want to do better afterwards, then you might get another chance, you can get new chances here, a lot of new chances.... When you behaved badly or you have been rude to one of the coaches, he will ask you to leave, but the next day you can come back and talk with the coaches, say sorry and thereafter you can participate again.
>
> (participant, male, 14 years, personal development)

During one focus group the importance of this approach was emphasised by one of the practitioners as follows:

> Sanctioning, you might do it with athletes. But, at this level, I think, sanctions will make you lose more people than you win. Of course, sometimes a sanction is necessary, but even then, our door stays open.
>
> (coach, male, 36 years, personal development)

In that sense, practitioners stressed the difference between prevention and repression. As such, community sport prevents behaviour that has the potential to evolve towards deviant actions. However, community sport practitioners strongly believe in doing so from a non-repressive and unconditional approach (Debognies et al. 2019; Sabbe et al. 2019a; Van der Veken et al. 2020b). This was emphasised by one of the practitioners as follows:

> I think disciplining young people is a good thing per definition. However, I do think it is not community sport that has to discipline them. Community sport should be about having fun, relaxing and coming in whenever you feel like it.
>
> (coach, female, 29 years, social cohesion)

However, practitioners mentioned that this thousand chances philosophy is not a boundless frame (Schaillée et al. 2017). For example, (short-term) exclusion will evolve if the behaviour of participants endangers the freedom of other individuals or constrains the practical organisation of activities (e.g. participants' tardiness could affect the participation of the remaining participants). Many participants perceived that the thousand chances philosophy common in community sport programmes stands in contrast to teachers' way of working in formal educational contexts. Practitioners in this study also avoided positioning themselves as authoritarian figures. This is potentially also one of the underlying reasons that explain why the community sport coaches are viewed by young people as being different from other social agents, such as teachers or law enforcers (Sabbe et al. 2019a). This was illustrated by one of the practitioners as follows:

> Community sport in general should not be the buffer against nuisance. We are no police officers; instead, we try to work with these young people, not against them.
>
> (coach, male, 39 years, social inclusion)

Another aspect that is somehow different from the formal educational settings is the *cultural capital of the coaching staff*, which is considered as a third contextual asset that contributes to the development of caring relationships with youngsters. In each programme, there were some members of the coaching staff that shared a good portion of cultural capital with participants. Many practitioners argued that such similarities are a strength, as highlighted in the following quotes:

> I live in the same neighbourhood as most of my participants, I know where they live, I know the context in which they grow up. I also know their parents, their family situation etc. This allows me to engage them in a tailored way to their needs and situation. In contrast, most teachers in schools are living outside of the city and, although they provide young people with opportunities for learning, their position allows them less to give attention to individual students, and in particular those who are underperforming.
>
> (coach, female, 30 years, personal development)

> I come from the neighbourhood and used to be part of the target group. And that is important. When we organise something, I know what to take into account, which obstacles the target group is struggling with. . . . I have also a . . . similar background. It makes it easier for me as I speak the same language, I understand them and, yes, I grew up here, so I know the neighbourhood very well, I know these people very well.
>
> (coordinator, male, 37 years, health)

Crabbe (2007: 35) described such similarities as the 'shared cultural capital' of coaches in relation to participants. This type of capital has been identified as having a significant influence not merely on a programme's ability to attract young people from socially vulnerable situations but also when intending to work with them towards social inclusionary objectives (Coalter 2013; Crabbe 2008; Haudenhuyse et al. 2012; Schaillée 2016). Participants in the community sport programmes confirmed the finding in earlier research (Crabbe 2005; Spaaij 2011) that staff members with a similar cultural background can more easily connect with the target group rather than with those who are not. This finding concurs with studies on the contributions of peer educators and role models in SfD programmes (Coalter 2007; Nicholls 2009; Meier and Saavedra 2009). The community sport programmes investigated here employed several coaches whose cultural backgrounds are broadly similar to those of the target group and give former project participants, whose socio-cultural distance to participants is relatively small, opportunities to take up a role as a coach. A participant expressed the impact of employing such coaching profiles as follows:

> The boys that work here as a coach, they've been through a lot. And if they come to us, for example our teachers at school, those are also good people, they aren't bad, but if they would talk to us, they will understand us less well than our coaches. They [community sport coaches] know what we are experiencing, because they have been in similar situations when they were young, hanging on the streets with their friends. They have more experience and are

> thus wiser than us, they can teach us things. . . . They have another impact on us compared to our teachers from school.
>
> (participant, male, 18 years, personal development)

However, in this study a disparate array of staff with distinct skills and backgrounds was present. It has been argued in previous research that such diversity is not necessarily a constraining condition. For example, Spaaij (2011) argued that a diversity of profiles among coaching staff might lead to the development of different types of social capital. Whereas small socio-cultural differences might lead to more social bonding between coaches and participants; these so-called 'cultural intermediaries' can potentially open:

> access to social worlds and opportunities which are not currently accessible to the young people with whom they work, in order that those young people are in a stronger position to make positive life choices from a wider range of options.
>
> (Crabbe et al. 2006: 15)

A last contextual asset that operates in community sport programmes and contributes to the development of caring relationships relates to the approach of community sport practitioners to the equal treatment of the expertise that participants and practitioners own. This approach allows all individuals involved to engage in a mutual process of exchanging and translating knowledge. A female community sport coach explained that no matter with whom you interact, she preferred *a two-way exchange of knowledge* and stated:

> It is the problem of adults. It is not because you successfully finished education that you know everything better. I can even learn from others and others can learn from me. Whatever their age, background . . . everybody can learn something from each other. I'm convinced that treating young people in this way pays off.
>
> (coach, female, 30 years, personal development)

In Chapter 3, a reflective method will be described as an example to show how a two-way exchange of knowledge in a goal-setting process can take place. The practitioners mentioned the importance of setting and adapting well-defined goals and expectations in accordance with the aspirations, values and ambitions of the participants (Debognies et al. 2019; Van der Veken et al. 2019, 2020a) and specific life circumstances (Sabbe et al. 2019b). One participant explained as follows:

> I don't always attend community sport, sometimes I do, sometimes I don't. Often, I come home and then I have to take care of my siblings. I really like the fact that community sport is something I can attend when I don't have other things in the way and that they don't judge me for that.
>
> (participant, female, 12 years, social cohesion)

This was in line with how a practitioner viewed this, when he stated:

> I mean, you can't expect them to be there every week. If a girl of 12 years old, who's been responsible her entire life for her family because her mom is single and works around the clock to provide for her family – if these girls are responsible for their brothers and sisters all day, you can't expect them to be here every Wednesday afternoon. Even if that means that the project doesn't run smoothly because of that.
>
> (coach, male, 33 years, social cohesion)

According to Noddings (2013), outcome-related expectations should not be set against a pre-established ideal, and caregivers (such as community sport coaches) should be perceptive and pay attention to individuals' own needs and aspirations because this is crucial for successful caring. In that sense, the customisation of 'growing opportunities' to the life circumstances of participants becomes an important precondition when asking the active agency of participants. However, such idea often clashes with views wherein 'responsibility is forced upon participants as a fixed concept, based upon predetermined indicators' (Sabbe et al. 2019a: 11–12). One respondent argued:

> The view of policy, namely that participants get the same opportunities as everyone else and that it is their responsibility to take those chances, is counteractive [in relation to the customised approach of community sport]. It simply is untrue as well. Getting the same opportunities, sounds great right, however, sometimes kids reside in life circumstances through which they cannot fully grasp those chances.
>
> (coach, male, 33 years, social cohesion)

Moreau et al.'s (2018) analysis of DesÉquilibres showed that one of the programme's key components relate to the fact that participants are stimulated to take charge of and are responsible for their own developmental trajectory. Considering an individual's agency seems to be very effective because working with fixed pre-defined goals might exclude individuals who differ most from the desired outcome (Haudenhuyse et al. 2012).

Creating an experiential learning context

Experiential learning is considered here as a sufficient condition that allows young people to actively engage in growing opportunities through (1) the provision of hands-on learning opportunities and (2) reflective practices. The development of caring relationships is considered to be necessary and a crucial first step towards facilitating experiential learning when working with young people in a community sport context. Community sport practitioners are, for instance, careful not to counteract self-initiated goals and actions as they perceive this individual agency as a prerequisite for fostering the engagement of participants in growing opportunities.

A common practice within community sport programmes with regard *to hands-on learning experiences* are the opportunities for young people to take up volunteer and leadership roles. It has been noted that adapting these opportunities to young people's abilities and gradually increasing the responsibilities youngsters can take are crucial to experience success and gain perceived self-efficacy. One coordinator told us about his approach and mentioned:

> If there are young people that take up some leadership, take some initiative, you can align the leadership opportunities towards the person's capabilities. You can start with very small challenges. Let the person take pictures during the activities for several times, or checking the timetables of the buses, handing out refreshments and fruit. . . . Such small responsibilities. And if that goes well and the young person feels good at it, you can gradually involve the participant more.
> (coordinator, male, 30 years, personal development)

Previous research underlines the personal benefits gained by young people through volunteering and community service in sport contexts, which include an increase in self-efficacy, leadership skills, pro-social identity, social connectedness and human capital (Eley and Kirk 2010; Hellison 1995; Kay and Bradbury 2009). Such hands-on learning opportunities have also been found to be beneficial to young people in vulnerable situations who have given up on school but maintain an interest in sport as an arena for achievement or prestige (e.g. Hellison 1995). Other examples of hands-on learning experiences are related to participants' involvement in (coaching) courses or specific opportunities created for participants during the community sport activities themselves as reported here by one participant:

> To let one help another. . . . Yes, that is meaningful. . . . To be granted a role, and to mean something to someone. For example, by performing an exercise together.
> (participant, female, 36 years, health)

The process wherein participants engage themselves in a meaningful role within the community (e.g. through voluntary work), referred to by practitioners as 'local grounding', regenerates young people's social status, feelings of belonging to the neighbourhood and positive acknowledgement and affirmations of community residents towards participants (Sabbe et al. 2018). Chapters 3 and 4 elaborate on the hands-on learning opportunities provided within two different community sport programmes in Flanders.

A second approach relates to the assistance provided during *reflective practices*. While hands-on learning can be a form of experiential learning, it does not necessarily involve participants to reflect on their developmental experiences. Experiential learning is the process of learning through reflection on behaviour or actions. According to the experiential learning theory, hands-on learning experiences comprise the first stage of the learning cycle (i.e. the concrete experience) (Kolb and Fry 1975). While hands-on learning opportunities are a common practice in community sport programmes, there are a number of providers who also work on the following stages of the learning cycle (i.e. reflective practice). Chapter 3 elaborates on the guidance during reflective practices within one specific community sport programme. Assisting in reflective practices with young people appears to be challenging for practitioners and is not something that happens automatically. Furthermore, practitioners expressed the challenge of adopting such reflective practice themselves on an individual level, with regard to their own actions and/or their relationship with participants as well as on a collective level, with regard to mechanisms at an organisational level (see Chapter 5).

Although both hands-on learning opportunities and reflective practices are common assets of community sport programmes, it should be noticed that experiential learning is often a slow process, that evolves usually in very slight, fragile and non-linear ways (Spaaij et al. 2016), requiring intellectual engagement from participants and those assisting them and regular practice (Nols 2018). In Chapter 5 more insight is provided about different approaches that foster critical reflection with and amongst practitioners on organisational, network and policy level as part of the conditions that shape strategies of structural work within community sport programmes.

Developing an enlarged and diversified social network

The third sufficient condition is shaped through contextual practices that intend to foster structural strategies (i.e. strategies focused on reducing the powers of exclusion) which lead to changes in the life conditions of these young people. A first contextual practice that community sport programmes set up are *anti-stigma interventions*. Community sport programmes have been working to transform stigma by establishing encounters and initiating dialogue between participants and the communities they live in. Community sport aims to influence the recognition of participants by using the positive branding of the community sport organisation itself. In doing so, the organisation attains to become a meaningful actor within the community and to transfer that constructive image to that of the participants (e.g. by using visual prompts such as logos, t-shirts and flags that express the organisational identity of community sport) (Sabbe et al. 2018). Such interventions are illustrated in the following quote:

> People see everything. Moreover, they see that we are doing a great job. It makes them realise that these youngsters can be trusted.
> (coach, male, 24 years, social cohesion)

It appears to be crucial for community sport practitioners and participants to display the disjuncture between prejudice in relation to certain behaviours, such as irregular attendance of participants, and the underlying reasons for these behaviours (e.g. taking care for young/old family members). One important critique relates to the presumed deficiency approach in relation to young people in vulnerable situations. There is extensive research evidence in the SfD field that problematises a deficiency approach and links this to neo-liberal ideologies that focus on the responsibilities of individuals to overcome their own 'underdevelopment' (Darnell 2012; Hayhurst 2009; Hartmann and Kwauk 2011). In fact, interventions in which encounters are set up and dialogue is initiated between participants and the communities they live in have an educational value for members of the local community, representatives of (potential) partner organisations and policymakers as they might lead to a more nuanced view about young people in socially vulnerable situations. In that sense, the above standing quote, for example, illustrates how the intervention of community sport does not change the behaviour of participants towards what is socially desirable but rather that their positive behaviours are more easily recognised within the wider community.

The second contextual practice relates to building *interorganisational partnerships* with the objective to open doors towards other individuals or organisations that have the ability and knowledge to support and help participants with challenges that they face in their lives. A coordinator mentioned in this context that:

> What often happens is that participants talk about their personal problems with me. I listen and try to provide good advice. But I'm not a social worker and in some cases I say 'look that's A [street worker] and B [welfare worker] who are sitting over there. If I was you, I would go and talk to one of these fantastic individuals . . . they will definitely help you.' If I'm the one that gives them this kind of advice, an advice from their coach to whom they look up to, to whom they listen, that they respect, then they will more easily do so. They are not taking such steps by themselves.
>
> (coordinator, male, 29 years, personal development)

Under ideal circumstances, partnerships with other key stakeholders (e.g. schools and youth work organisation) would partially enable sustainable and adapted support in order to facilitate structural changes for these young people. However, in reality, partnerships between community sport programmes and partner organisations often consist of providing these young individuals with additional volunteer opportunities or opportunities to take on responsibility. Not surprisingly, in interorganisational relationships, trust is also a key component that affects the effectiveness and relates to the mutual confidence in the abilities and intentions of the actors in the partnership (Willem and Lucidarme 2014). For any relationship between different partners, trust takes time to develop and needs to grow through a process of mutual learning or through shared accomplishments (Parent and Harvey 2009). It seems obvious that building sustainable and effective partnerships is challenging for community sport programmes due to the frequent staff changes and short-term projects including diverse objectives and different target groups. A more in-depth description of the challenges for working towards structural changes, inter alia, through the formation of networks, is provided in Chapter 5.

Conclusion

The first research phase of the CATCH project consisted of an in-depth cross-case comparison involving nine different community sport programmes in Flanders, the Northern Dutch-speaking part of Belgium. This research phase resulted in an evidence-informed framework, including necessary and sufficient conditions, for fostering social inclusionary outcomes through community sport. Our framework is built upon similarities across cases and themes. It is, however, important to mention that each community sport context is shaped by a unique set of contextual assets or practices leading to a context-specific set of necessary and sufficient conditions to work towards social inclusionary objectives.

Chapters 3, 4, and 5 elaborate on the action-oriented research in which interventions were developed and tested in close collaboration with community sport practitioners. Chapter 3 describes an existing training course emphasising that soft-skill development for young volunteers in local community sport programmes was redesigned. Chapter 4 focuses on the development and organisation of a training programme for community sport coaches with a focus on motivational coaching. Chapter 5 elaborates on opportunities for structural work in community sport (i.e. implementing strategies focused on reducing powers of exclusion).

Note

1 Broadly speaking, the target group of the CATCH research project was focused on young people from socially vulnerable situations aged between 14 and 25 years. The in-text description of the participating young people shows that we reached out to a much broader age category, resulting from the characteristics of community sport. Community sport practices typically use an accessible, flexible, informal, people-centred approach to lower the thresholds to participation.

References

Bailey, R. (2008) 'Youth sport and social inclusion', in: N. Holt (ed) *Positive youth development through sport*, London: Routledge, pp. 85–96.
Brewer, J. (2000) *Ethnography*, Buckingham: Open University Press.
Bryman, A. (2012) *Social research methods*, Oxford: Oxford University Press.
Coalter, F. (2007) *A wider social role for sport: Who's keeping the score?*, London: Routledge.
Coalter, F. (2013) *Sport for development: What game are we playing?*, London: Routledge.
Crabbe, T. (2005) *Getting to know you: Engagement and relationship building: First interim national positive futures case study report*, London: Positive Futures.
Crabbe, T. (2007) 'Reaching the "heard to reach": Engagement, relationship building and social control in sport based social inclusion work', *International Journal of Sport Management and Marketing*, 2(1–2), 27–40. DOI: 10.1504/IJSMM.2007.011388
Crabbe, T. (2008) 'Avoiding the numbers game: Social theory, policy and sport's role in the art of relationship building', in: M. Nicholson and R. Hoye (eds) *Sport and social capital*, Oxford: Elsevier Butterworth-Heinemann, pp. 21–37.

Crabbe, T., Slater, I. and Woodhouse, D. (2006) *Knowing the score. Positive futures case study research: Final report*, London: Positive Futures.

Curtis, A.C. (2015) 'Defining adolescence', *Journal of Adolescent and Family Health*, 7(2), 2.

Darnell, S. (2012) *Sport for development and peace: A critical sociology*, London: Bloomsbury Academic.

Debognies, P., Schaillée, H., Haudenhuyse, R. and Theeboom, M. (2019) 'Personal development of disadvantaged youth through community sports: A theory-driven analysis of relational strategies', *Sport in Society*, 22(6), 897–918. DOI: 10.1080/17430437.2018.1523144

DiCocco-Bloom, B. and Crabtree, B.F. (2006) 'The qualitative research interview', *Medical Education*, 40(4), 314–321. DOI: 10.1111/j.1365-2929.2006.02418.x

Eley, D. and Kirk, D. (2010) 'Developing citizenship through sport: The impact of a sports-based volunteer programme on young leaders', *Sport, Education and Society*, 7(2), 151–166. DOI: 10.1080/1357332022000018841

Hartmann, D. and Kwauk, C. (2011) 'Sport and development: An overview, critique, and reconstruction', *Journal of Sport and Social Issues*, 35(3), 284–305. DOI: 10.1177/0193723511416986

Haudenhuyse, R. (2012) *The potential of sports for socially vulnerable youth*, Published doctoral dissertation, VUBPress, Brussels.

Haudenhuyse, R., Theeboom, M. and Coalter, F. (2012) 'The potential of sports-based social interventions for vulnerable youth: Implications for sport coaches and youth workers', *Journal of Youth Studies*, 15(4), 437–454. DOI: 10.1080/13676261.2012.663895

Hayhurst, L. (2009) 'The power to shape policy: Charting sport for development and peace policy discourses', *International Journal of Sport Policy*, 1(2), 203–227. DOI: 10.1080/19406940902950739

Hellison, D. (1995) *Teaching responsibility through physical activity*, Champaign, IL: Human Kinetics.

Jones, I., Brown, L. and Holloway, I. (2013) *Qualitative research in sport and physical activity*, London: Sage.

Kay, T. (2009) 'Developing through sport: Evidencing sport impacts on young people', *Sport in Society*, 12(9), 1177–1191. DOI: 10.1080/17430430903137837

Kay, T. and Bradbury, S. (2009) 'Youth sport volunteering: Developing social capital?', *Sport, Education and Society*, 14(1), 121–140. DOI: 10.1080/13573320802615288

Kelly, L. (2011) 'Social inclusion through sports-based interventions?', *Critical Social Policy*, 31(1), 126–150. DOI: 385442 10.1177/0261018310385442

Kolb, D.A. and Fry, R. (1975) 'Towards an applied theory of experiential learning', in: C. Cooper (ed) *Theories of group process*, London: John Wiley, pp. 33–57.

Madden, R. (2010) *Being ethnographic*, London: Sage.

Meier, M. and Saavedra, M. (2009) 'Esther Phiri and the Moutawakel effect in Zambia: An analysis of the use of female role models in sport-for-development', *Sport in Society*, 12(9), 1158–1176. DOI: 10.1080/17430430903137829

Moreau, N., Lévesque, J.T., Molgat, M., Jaimes, A., Parlavecchio, L., Chanteau, O. and Plante, C. (2018) 'Opening the black box of a sports-based programme for vulnerable youth: The crucial role of social bonds', *Qualitative Research in Sport, Exercise and Health*, 10(3), 291–305. DOI: 10.1080/2159676X.2018.1430060

Morgan, D. (1988) *Focus groups as qualitative research*, London: Sage.

Nicholls, S. (2009) 'On the backs of peer educators: Using theory to interrogate the role of young people in the field of sport-for-development', in: R. Levermore and A. Beacom (eds) *Sport and international development*, Basingstoke: Palgrave Macmillan, pp. 156–175.

Noddings, N. (2013) *Caring: A relational approach to ethics and moral education*, New York: Teachers College.

Nols, Z. (2018) *Social change through sport for development initiatives: A critical pedagogical perspective*, Published doctoral dissertation, VUBPress, Brussels.

Parent, M. and Harvey, J. (2009) 'Towards a management model for sport and physical activity community-based partnerships', *European Sport Management Quarterly*, 9(1), 23–45. DOI: 10.1080/16184740802461694

Pawson, R. (2001) *Evidence based policy, vol. 1, in search of a method*, ESRC UK Centre for Evidence Based Policy and Practice, Working Paper 3, London: Queen Mary University of London.

Pawson, R. (2006) *Evidence-based policy: A realist perspective*, Thousand Oaks, CA: Sage.

Sabbe, S., Bradt, L., Roets, G. and Roose, R. (2019b) 'Revisiting the notion of cohesion in community sport: A qualitative study on the lived experiences of participants', *Leisure Studies*, 38(2), 274–287. DOI: 10.1080/02614367.2019.1579853

Sabbe, S., Bradt, L., Spaaij, R. and Roose, R. (2018) 'Community sport and social cohesion: In search of the practical understandings of community sport practitioners in Flanders', *Community Development Journal*, 55(2), 258–276. DOI: 10.1093/cdj/bsy046

Sabbe, S., Roose, R. and Bradt, L. (2019a) 'Tipping the balance back towards emancipation: Exploring the positions of Flemish community sport practitioners towards social control', *Sport in Society*, 22(6), 950–965. DOI: 10.1080/17430437.2019.1565384

Schaillée, H. (2016) *More than just a game? The potential to foster positive youth development among disadvantaged girls*, Published doctoral dissertation, VUBPress, Brussels.

Schaillée, H., Spaaij, R., Jeanes, R. and Theeboom, M. (2019) 'Knowledge translation practices, enablers, and constraints: Bridging the research-practice divide in sport management', *Journal of Sport Management*, 33(5), 366–378. DOI: 10.1123/jsm.2018-0175

Schaillée, H., Vyncke, V., Debognies, P., Sabbe, S. and Steenberghs, E. (2017) 'Buurtsport, een onvoorwaardelijk aanbod: Een springplank voor sociale inclusie [Community sport: An unconditional offer: A springboard for social inclusion]', *Vlaams Tijdschrift voor Sportbeheer*, 259, 108–113.

Spaaij, R. (2011) *Sport and social mobility: Crossing boundaries*, London: Routledge.

Spaaij, R., Oxford, S. and Jeanes, R. (2016) 'Transforming communities through sport? Critical pedagogy and sport for development', *Sport, Education and Society*, 21(4), 570–587. DOI: 10.1080/13573322.2015.1082127

Van der Veken, K., Lauwerier, E. and Willems, S. (2020a) 'How community sport programs may improve the health of vulnerable population groups: A program theory', *International Journal for Equity in Health*, 19(74). DOI: 10.1186/s12939-020-01177-5

Van der Veken, K., Lauwerier, E. and Willems, S. (2020b) 'To mean something to someone: Sport-for-development as a lever for social inclusion', *International Journal for Equity in Health*, 19(1), 11. DOI: 10.1186/s12939-019-1119-7

Van der Veken, K., Willems, S. and Lauwerier, E. (2019) 'Health promotion in socially vulnerable youth: Sport as a powerful vehicle?', *Health Promotion Practice*, 22(2), 275–286. DOI: 10.1177/1524839919874751

Van Hove, G. and Claes, L. (2011) *Qualitative research and educational sciences: A reader about useful strategies and tools*, Edinburgh: Pearson Education Limited.

Van Poppel, M. (2015) *Benchmark Buurtsport: Buurtsport in Vlaanderen anno 2014* [*Benchmark community sport: Community sport in Flanders in the year 2014*], Belgium: Flemish Institute of Sport Management and Recreation Policy.

Weiss, C.H. (1995) 'Nothing as practical as good theory: Exploring theory-based evaluation for comprehensive community initiatives for children and families', in: J. Connell, A. Kubisch, L. Schorr and C.H. Weiss (eds) *New approaches to evaluating community initiatives: Concepts, methods, and contexts*, New York: The Aspen Institute, pp. 65–92.

Willem, A. and Lucidarme, S. (2014) 'Pitfalls and challenges for trust and effectiveness in collaborative networks', *Public Management Review*, 16(5), 733–760. DOI: 10.1080/14719037.2012.744426

Yin, R.K. (1994) *Case study research: Design and methods*, 2nd edn, Thousand Oaks, CA: Sage.

Yin, R.K. (2004) *The case study anthology*, London: Sage.

Part 2
Thematic insights into community sport and social inclusion

3 Reflective practices in a volunteer community sport coach training programme

Dorien Brosens, Hebe Schaillée, Marc Theeboom and Pieter Debognies

Introduction

A limited amount of research has underlined that community sport can contribute to the personal development of young people in socially vulnerable situations (e.g. Debognies et al. 2019; Super et al. 2018; Whitley et al. 2016). For instance, Whitley et al. (2016) reported that by participating in community sport programmes, young people increase their ability to show respect and care for others, and leadership, interpersonal or teamwork skill. According to Super et al. (2018), community sport coaches have an important role in stimulating the personal development of these young people by offering fun sport activities, creating little moments of success, creating opportunities to experience success and increasing young people's ability to identify the skills that they can use to manage situations. This is in line with the first phase of the *community sport for AT-risk youth: Innovative strategies for promoting personal development, health and social CoHesion* (CATCH) project that demonstrated that community sport coaches can stimulate young people in socially vulnerable situations to take up volunteer and leadership roles by creating a context in which young people can show active engagement. This can lead to successful experiences and can increase participants' perceived self-efficacy (see Chapter 2). However, this first phase also revealed that while such hands-on learning experiences can be a form of experiential learning, it does not necessarily involve participants to reflect on their behaviour or actions. Experiential learning is the process of learning through reflection on behaviour or actions (see Chapter 2). Super et al. (2018) underlined that stimulating critical reflection is an essential aspect in the personal development of young people in socially vulnerable situations as it enables young people to better understand sport-specific situations and to identify strategies they can use to deal with it. In their study, young people's reflection was stimulated when community sport coaches asked questions, instead of providing instructions and feedback, through which the participants became more self-conscious and responsible. These questions enabled the participants to reflect on situations and actions, through which they were able to better understand how sport environments work.

DOI: 10.4324/9780429340635-5

Studies that focused on the development of professional sport coaches showed that the use of tools, models and frameworks facilitated coaches' dialogue and reflection (Jacobs et al. 2016; Voldby and Klein-Dossing 2019) and thus contributed to the reflective practice. Examples in the study of Voldby and Klein-Dossing (2019) were printed posters with questions such as 'what were the positive/negative effects from your experiment?', 'what did you learn from your experiment?' and included a model with different levels of reflections. It is also valuable to understand how reflective practices can be used for young people who aim to become voluntary community sport coaches. Therefore, this chapter focuses on the use of reflective practices as a mechanism to stimulate the personal development of young people in socially vulnerable situations who undertake a training programme to become a voluntary community sport coach. This chapter describes the action research we set up in a community sport organisation in Flanders to realise that aim.

Reflective practice

Reflective practice is considered as an approach that helps individuals to explore their decisions and experiences, aiming to better understand and manage themselves and their sport practice (Anderson et al. 2004). Mezirow (1990) underlined that having experience does not necessarily result in learning. Learning only occurs when people make sense of that experience by giving it an interpretation, so that the decisions they make afterwards can be based on these interpretations. According to Paterson and Chapman (2013), reflection is thus a vital part of a learning experience. It is a complex process which addresses the whole person, ranging from personal perceptions, emotions, behaviours, their interactions, its impact on the situation to the impact of the context on all of these (Knowles et al. 2014). Several academics underlined that by examining their own work and whole self, individuals become more able to understand, change and improve what they do (Dixon et al. 2016), their practice and the situation in which it occurs (Knowles et al. 2014).

The value of reflective practice has been recognised not only in teacher education programmes (Kis and Kartal 2019; Lamb and Aldous 2016) and nursing (Mansah et al. 2014; O'Neill et al. 2019) but also in the field of professional sport coaching (Jacobs et al. 2016; Voldby and Klein-Dossing 2019) and community sport coaching (Van der Veken et al. 2019). Different reflective methods can be used, for instance (Knowles et al. 2014):

- written journals: using specific frameworks and questions to stimulate the reflective writing process;
- visual sociology: using photographs, video images or drawings;
- recorded narratives: using digital voice recordings made during the action or immediately after;
- reflective conversations: focused and structural conversations with critical friends.

Research context: a voluntary community sport coach training programme

City Coach is a short-term training programme for young people in socially vulnerable situations between 15 and 25 years to prepare them to work as a voluntary community sport coach. The training programme, which was first organised in 2013, is provided by the municipal sport service of the city of Antwerp. Between 2013 and 2018, 120 young people participated in the programme. It consists of four days, followed by an internship of four hours. During the internship, participants are required to organise sport and play activities for children and need to apply the knowledge and skills gained from the training programme. At the end, an evaluation interview takes place. Once the training and internship have been completed successfully, participants can take up a role as a voluntary community sport coach in Antwerp. As the community sport organisation was struggling with how they could improve reflective practice within their training programme, the researchers suggested to set up a participatory action research.

A pre-intervention study was set up to get more insight into the challenges the organisation experienced in stimulating reflection among its participants. Two types of data were collected:

1 **Documentation.** Staff members of the training programme provided the researchers with relevant documentation, consisting of the project plan of City Coach for 2016–2017, a 'Sportfolio', a YouTube movie about the programme, access to a shared folder on Google Drive, etc. The Sportfolio contained reflective exercises which were used during the training programme and is considered as a type of a written journal (Knowles et al. 2014).
2 **Participatory observations, informal conversations and field notes** were collected during the first City Coach training of 2018 by the fourth author. The aim was to get insight into how reflective practice was implemented and to observe participants' actual responses. Observations were structured by means of a general checklist. The informal conversations took place with participants and trainers. Field notes were kept in a research diary and focused on the challenges in stimulating reflection and potential areas to improve reflection among the participants.

All data were subjected to inductive analysis (i.e. data driven). MaxQDA, a qualitative software programme designed for doing analyses, was used.

Three challenges on which the intervention could build

The project plan for 2016–2017 described City Coach as a practice and competence-oriented learning and experiencing course which was considered as a possible step towards other training programmes such as 'movement animator' organised by the Vlaamse Trainersschool (i.e. Flemish Training School) or animator in youth work. According to the plan, during the training programme, participants:

1   learn to prepare and guide a sport or physical activity (under supervision),
2   are stimulated to self-reflect and describe their own learning points.

The pre-intervention phase revealed that two features of the training programme are used to realise these outcomes. A first central feature of the voluntary community sport coach training programme was the course content, which has (1) a theoretical component and (2) a practical component. The project plan underlined that 20 per cent of the programme consisted of theory. Central themes were for instance didactics, how to prepare and guide sport and physical activities, how to be creative in using space, time and materials, how to deal with different target groups and being aware of and dealing with safety issues. The other 80 per cent consisted of hands-on learning activities. By preparing and guiding sport and physical activities, participants learnt to put the theory into practice. The hands-on learning activities enabled participants to understand the theory when preparing and guiding sport or physical activities, feel able to prepare and guide such activities, and learn from it. These were considered as strong points of the training programme. During the first course of 2018, participants were encouraged to take action and experiment with the theoretical aspects in their role as a voluntary community sport coach. In an observation note, the researcher wrote down that a trainer considered the power of the practical component, including experiential learning, as:

> That you have to say to the participants that they do not have to try to do everything well from the first time. They better have ten unsuccessful experiences *(hands-on learning activities)* than succeed from the first time. Every time when something turns out to be unsuccessful, they will have very useful experiences for the future.
>
> (observation notes, course 1, day 2)

Besides focusing on the theoretical and practical component, the training programme also concentrated on six key competences (i.e. second central feature of the volunteer community sport training programme): being able to get in contact with others, handling feedback, possessing good reflective abilities, showing empathy, taking initiative and teamwork.

Although possessing good reflective abilities was one of the key competences, the project plan for 2016–2017 emphasised this not merely as an outcome but also as a mean to develop other competences. After each practical exercise, a reflective conversation took place with the aim of stimulating self-reflection and getting this competence into the thinking and handling pattern of participants.

During the first day, a trainer who guided the training programme told participants that the six competences are essential for their future, for instance in the search for a (voluntary) job. The competences were introduced by spreading six papers with information throughout the sporting hall. While participants passed by the papers, the trainer asked what they thought these competences meant and added additional information. It was observed that this way of working was too theoretical for many participants. In addition, the researcher noted that it was not clear which exercise focused on which of the competences through which the competences did not have a central place anymore during the other course days, except for reflection. Although several efforts were made to stimulate reflection of participants at the end of each practical exercise during the other course days, several difficulties were observed.

A first difficulty was that the post-activity reflective conversations took place in one group with all 21 participants. The researcher noticed several times that there was no safe climate and that 'there was a giggly atmosphere'. Several times people are called 'donkey' or 'stupid' by other participants through which they were not encouraged to say something (observation notes, course 1, day 2). Literature suggests that the larger a group, the more challenging it is to create group cohesion and trust (McGart and Higgins 2006). Larger groups (≥10 participants) seem to have a negative influence on participants' wellbeing. Participants of such groups also feel less comfortable to express themselves compared to participants of smaller groups (5–7 participants) (Schaub-de Jong 2012). The first challenge of this action research thus consisted of reducing the group size during the reflective conversations.

A second observed difficulty was that the reflective conversations solely focused on the content of the sport activity (e.g. goal, materials used, explanation and rules of play), while limited attention was paid to the key competences, how the participants have put them into practice or could develop them. The researcher noted in his diary: 'It seems that the competences have a less important place than content-related aspects' (observation notes, course 1, day 2). The second challenge deriving from this observation was thus to focus more on the development of the key competences during the reflective conversations.

After the second course day, the researcher expressed his concerns to the trainers guiding the training programme about the way reflection was done as more attention could be paid to how reflection could be used as a mean to develop the other competences. The researcher and trainers decided to limit the group size for the post-activity reflective conversations to seven participants. Three trainers were present and able to guide one reflective group each. Participants felt safer and were encouraged to give concrete examples of how they practiced the competences during the training programme through which in-depth reflection could be stimulated. However, there were huge differences between the concrete examples illustrated by the participants. Many of them strayed off and focused on the content-related aspects of the sport activities instead of reflecting on their own learning process related to the six key competences. The researcher wrote in his research diary: 'The reflection at the end starts with focusing on the competences, but frequently shifts towards a technical evaluation about the rules of play and things that have not gone so well during the activity' (observation notes, course 1, day 4). This resulted in the need for more guidance and concrete reflective methods. After the first course, the researcher expressed that, based on other studies, reflective methods (e.g. written journals and visual sociology – see Knowles et al. 2014) could possibly make the reflective conversations more focused on the key competences and less on the technical aspects of the sport and physical activities. It would make the participants' personal development with regard to the key competences more visible. Such a tool could be the Sportfolio. Although the City Coach project plan for 2016–2017 has put the Sportfolio forward as a central tool to work on and keep track of the evolutions made regarding the six key competences, it was not used at all during this first course of 2018. This observation led to the third challenge of providing more guidance during the reflective conversations and making use of reflective methods to support this guidance.

In sum, the pre-intervention phase enabled us to identify three challenges. These challenges were understood as ways to improve the programme's efficiency and effectiveness. During the action research, an intervention was set up that addressed these challenges. Before describing the intervention, first the action research itself is presented.

Participatory action research

According to Kemmis and McTaggart (2005), participatory action research involves a spiral of different self-reflective cycles consisting of planning, acting and observing, reflecting and revised planning. The use of this spiral has been applied in previous studies related to sport and physical activities (Keegan 2016; Robinson et al. 2019). For instance, Keegan (2016) used the spiral to enhance her own teaching and the learning experiences of students in physical education. We also applied the spiral of self-reflective cycles of Kemmis and McTaggart (2005) during our action research to improve the reflective practices employed within the training programme. During 2018, four courses were organised. Before and during the first course, the pre-intervention context of the training programme was analysed and the three challenges on which the action research would build were formulated. This was necessary to get to know the training programme (i.e. pre-intervention). The three following courses corresponded to three self-reflective cycles of planning, acting and observing, reflecting and revised planning as described by Kemmis and McTaggart (2005) (i.e. intervention) (see Figure 3.1).

The decision-making responsibilities about the action research were shared among the action research team, which consisted of three researchers and two professional staff members of the municipal sport service. Together, they agreed on the goal and the different steps of the action research.

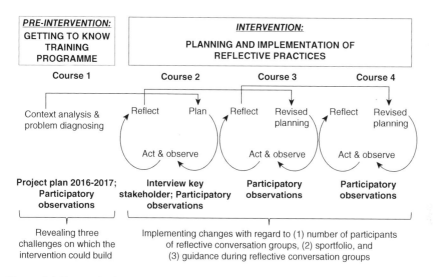

Figure 3.1 Research phases

Intervention

The action research focused on how to deal with the three challenges that came out of the pre-intervention phase: i.e. (1) reducing the group size during the reflective conversations, (2) focusing more on the development of the six key competences during the reflective practices and (3) providing more guidance during the reflective conversations supported by the use of reflective methods. In this respect, changes were planned regarding: (1) the number of participants during the reflective conversation groups, (2) the Sportfolio and (3) guidance during the reflective conversation groups. The Sportfolio and reflective conversation groups are considered as reflective methods.

Two types of data were collected during the intervention phase:

1 **Participatory observations, informal conversations and field notes** were collected during the second, third and fourth City Coach training of 2018. All observations were conducted by the fourth author. In addition, also informal conversations took place with participants and trainers involved in the training programme. Reflective observation notes were kept in a research diary and focused on success factors and potential areas for improvement to increase participants' reflective abilities.
2 **Interview with a relevant stakeholder outside the voluntary community sport coach training programme.** An individual interview with a staff member of the municipal centre for integration was conducted as this person supported several organisations to systematically implement reflective tools. The aim was to gain insight into the reflective methods used by this centre and see what could be learned from it for the voluntary

52 *Dorien Brosens et al.*

community sport coach training programme. This interview took place in March 2018 and was afterwards subjected to inductive analysis using MaxQDA.

Table 3.1 presents an overview of the changes implemented during the second, third or fourth City Coach course of 2018 to increase participants' reflective abilities. The challenges deriving from the pre-intervention phase were used as starting points and supplemented with insights from previous studies to further improve the efficiency and effectiveness of the City Coach course. In line with the self-reflective cycle (Kemmis and McTaggart 2005), the planned changes were implemented. Observations were made, which allowed the action research team to evaluate these changes and decide how to revise planning for the following courses.

Table 3.1 Changes planned and implemented in the second, third and fourth City Coach course of 2018

Central components	*Second course (April 2018)*	*Third course (July/August 2018)*	*Fourth course (September 2018)*
Number of participants per reflective conversation group	Five to six participants.	Two to three participants.	Four participants.
Sportfolio	Re-implemented as a reflective method, including mountain exercise* and 42 behavioural indicators for measuring the key competences.	The mountain exercise was adapted, and rubrics* were introduced for measuring 19 behavioural indicators related to the key competences.	The mountain exercise and rubrics were maintained.
Guidance during the reflective conversation groups	Three reflective groups, each guided by one trainer, to reflect on participants' experiences with the hands-on learning activities and exercises included in the Sportfolio. Coming together at the end of each course day.	Idem. Coming together at the start of the course day and once again later during the day.	No additional changes.

* These concepts are explained in part 'changes to the Sportfolio'.

In the following sections, we describe the changes that were planned and implemented regarding the three central components throughout the second, third and fourth City Coach course of 2018.

Changes to the number of participants per reflective conversation group

From the second course of 2018, the maximum number of participants of the training programme was limited to 16. By limiting the total number of participants, the action research team hoped that the trainers would be able to give enough possibilities to every participant to experiment with developing and organising sport and physical activities (i.e. hands-on learning experiences) and also – and mainly – to create small reflective conversation groups to stimulate self-reflection among the participants. During each course, participants were divided into three groups for the reflective conversations which were each guided by one trainer. Knowles et al. (2014) consider reflective conversations as focused and structural conversations with critical friends. In the second course, each reflective conversation group consisted of five to six participants, in the third course two to three and in the fourth course four participants. The size of the reflection groups differed according to the number of enrolled participants. The observations revealed that the smaller the group, the better the trainers were able to provide individual feedback and support. The reflective discussion groups were created as safe places that challenged the participants to make and discuss the exercises included in the Sportfolio, so that they could think about and demonstrate the progress they made on the key competences. Although the trainers recognised the importance of small groups to realise high-quality reflections, they were confronted with limited resources. Smaller groups implied more trainers and thus a higher organisational cost.

Changes to the Sportfolio

Major changes have been implemented regarding the Sportfolio. In the past, a Sportfolio was used through in which the participants could demonstrate the progress they made on each of the key competences. The action research team implemented the Sportfolio as a type of written journal, in which specific frameworks and questions were used to stimulate the reflective writing process (Knowles et al. 2014). Between courses 1 and 2, it was planned to implement an adapted version of the Sportfolio. The initial Sportfolio provided participants' definitions of the key competences and the possibility to indicate which aspects of these competences they already had based on behavioural indicators (yes/no). Following the interview with the key stakeholder, it was planned to involve the participants in formulating one goal they wanted to reach and indicating the behavioural indicators they needed to improve to reach that goal. This gave participants more agency, which was considered as a prerequisite for fostering personal development in our study.

54 Dorien Brosens et al.

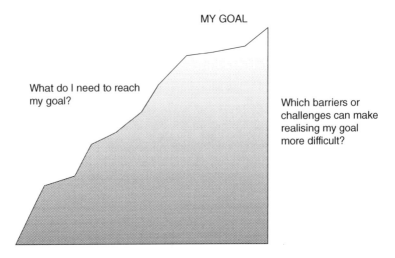

Figure 3.2 Mountain exercise

For this aim, we created an adapted Sportfolio that enabled the participants (1) to reflect on their own goal, (2) to get to know the six key competences and how they could recognise them, (3) to gain insight into the competences they already had based on a self-assessment of behavioural indicators and (4) to stimulate the participants to formulate the challenges they would come across to reach their goal.

In order to act upon this, a practical exercise was introduced in the second course. Making use of the visualisation of a mountain, participants were invited to set a goal they wanted to reach by participating in the training programme (see Figure 3.2).

The action research team considered the mountain exercise as a type of visual sociology, which was a reflective method (Knowles et al. 2014). On the left side of the mountain, participants could write the aspects they needed to reach this goal (e.g. having certain knowledge, people that can help or support them), or opportunities. On the right side, they could write possible barriers or challenges they would possibly face in reaching this goal. During the second course, it was observed to be difficult for many participants to formulate a concrete goal and the goals did not always relate to a role of a community sport coach. From the third course, the participants were presented four different roles of a community sport coach (i.e. game leader, guider, organiser or trainer). They had to choose one as the goal they wanted to reach. The observations revealed that because the participants had to choose a role of a community sport coach as a goal, this exercise was more concrete compared to the previous course where no specific guidelines were provided about the type of goal they needed to formulate. As it turned out that not all participants were well informed about the final end goal of the training programme, in this way, the trainers helped the young people in direction setting (Pawson 2006).

After formulating the goal, participants were invited to think about the key competences they needed to reach their goal. By assessing themselves on behavioural indicators, participants gained insight into which indicators they could improve during the training programme. In the second course, participants could self-assess these competences by using 42 behavioural indicators (ranging from 'I can improve this' to 'I am very good in this' on a bar) which were included in the Sportfolio. These indicators were an arbitrary list composed by the professionals of City Coach over the years. Examples of behavioural indicators were 'I listen to other people', 'I have respect for others', 'I do not hurt or insult others', and 'I think about the consequences of my actions'.

On the basis of this self-assessment, the participants needed to decide which behavioural indicators they wanted to improve to reach the goal they had set. Observations, however, revealed that not all indicators were clearly formulated and sometimes caused confusion. In addition, filling in the indicators was perceived as a time-consuming process within the limited amount of course days. It turned out that not all participants filled in all the indicators. As a result, this exercise was adapted during the third and fourth course to make it less time-consuming and visually more attractive. To realise this, two steps were implemented.

In a first step, the action research team had a critical look at the 42 behavioural indicators related to the key competences and decided to reduce the number of indicators, ultimately resulting in 19. Following the interview with the key stakeholder outside City Coach, it was planned to make use of rubrics to help participants to assess themselves on the indicators. For each of the 19 behavioural indicators, three or four possible answer categories were formulated. The key stakeholder was involved in formulating these answer categories because of his experience in working with rubrics. For instance, for the behavioural indicator 'making yourself understandable', the answer categories were adapted as follows:

A) I do not think about what I want to say in advance. It does not matter how others see me.
B) Sometimes I think about what I want to say and hope that the others understand me.
C) Beforehand, I think carefully about what I want to say and how I am going to say it.

In a second step, the participants were instructed to pick out two behavioural indicators they wanted to improve to reach their goal, starting from the self-assessment. Through facilitating this self-directed goal-setting approach, trainers supported participants' direction setting (Pawson 2006). For instance, if the goal of a participant was to become a trainer, it was essential to have good listening skills. If participants selected level B for 'listening to others', they were challenged to think how they could reach level C and to formulate a concrete action to realise that. The trainers took up a coaching role during the realisation of the actions (Pawson 2006). During the second course, the participants only had to formulate a goal and select behavioural indicators which they wanted to improve, without making them more concrete by formulating actions. Making use of the behavioural indicators was considered as positive by the trainers. They had the feeling that these helped the participants to gain insight into the extent to which they already managed the competences and in deciding which two indicators they wanted to improve to reach their goal. In the end, all participants formulated two concrete actions which they wanted to perform during the training programme. The trainers stimulated the young people to effectively perform these actions during the course days.

During the City Coach course, rubrics were used as an instructional tool to stimulate reflection (Cheng and Chan 2019). Previous studies that have investigated the use of rubrics have demonstrated that rubrics are useful for stimulating people's self-regulation as it helps them in their goal setting, planning, self-monitoring and self-reflection (Wang 2017). Although the rubrics helped the trainers in stimulating participants to formulate actions to realise a goal the participants set earlier in the training programme, it might be that the participants were influenced by the social desirability bias, in which they wanted their responses to be viewed favourably by the supervisors. Rubrics could also be used by teachers – or supervisors – as a formative evaluation tool (Hunt et al. 2016). These two manners of using rubrics came together in the reflective rose that was created and put into practice after the fourth course of 2018 (see description of the post-intervention phase).

Changes to guidance during the reflective conversation groups

The action research revealed that guiding the participants during the reflective conversations was essential. Central in the Sportfolio was the mountain exercise. The participatory observations demonstrated that this exercise was done in small groups of five to six participants at the end of the first course day during the second course of 2018. Each group had a trainer who supported them in formulating their goal (i.e. a way of direction setting – Pawson 2006), the possible opportunities and barriers to reach this goal. For some participants, this exercise turned to be easier than for others. As noted in the research diary:

> I saw that there are big differences between persons. Some could quickly decide what they wanted to do and why. . . . But on the other hand, there was also a boy who said that he wanted to reach 'something' by participating in City Coach. I asked him what he wanted to reach, but it was difficult for him to indicate what he really wanted.
>
> (observation notes, course 2, day 1)

Additional efforts were made by the trainers to support the participants who experienced difficulties in completing the mountain exercise. This was, among others, the case for participants who did not really understand the end goal of the training programme. For example, one participant said he joined the programme because his nephew told him that it would look good on his CV. From the third course, participants were stimulated not only to set a goal and select the behavioural indicators they wanted to improve but also to make them more concrete by formulating two concrete actions.

The role of the trainers had many similarities with 'mentoring as direction setting' and 'mentoring as coaching' as described by Pawson (2006). Direction setting in the context of the training programme implied that the trainers helped participants in goal setting (e.g. by providing four different roles of a community sport coach) and formulating concrete actions to reach those goals. Coaching referred to trainers who supported young people in performing their actions and stimulating them to actively participate in the reflective conversation groups to think about the progress they made. During these conversations, it was observed that the trainers paid attention to several aspects related to experiences (e.g. describing learning experiences, expressing feelings related to these experiences, what was good and bad and what could have been done differently). However, there were no concrete guidelines the trainers followed during these reflective conversations. Posing such questions was essential as according to Mezirow (1990), learning experiences do not necessarily result in developmental outcomes. Learning only happens when people can make sense of their experiences. The trainers had an essential role in stimulating participants to reflect about the development of their competences. Some participants found it easier to reflect on their own competences while others experienced difficulties to go beyond organisational aspects.

Another observation related to the timing of the reflective conversations. During the second course, the reflective conversations took place at the end of each course day. The researcher observed that it was difficult for several participants to stay focused at the end of each day because they were tired. From the third course, the day started with a reflective conversation group where the formulated goals and actions were repeated and where it was discussed what each participant would do to reach those goals and actions during the day. Later during the day, the groups came together again to reflect about the actions that were taken during the day and the progress the participants made regarding the key competences.

Post-intervention

After the fourth course, the researcher and trainers discussed the potential use of a 'reflective rose' as an additional visual reflection method. From 2019, participants rated themselves on a digital indicator scale. Afterwards, their answers were automatically transformed into the rose, through which participants got an overview

58 *Dorien Brosens et al.*

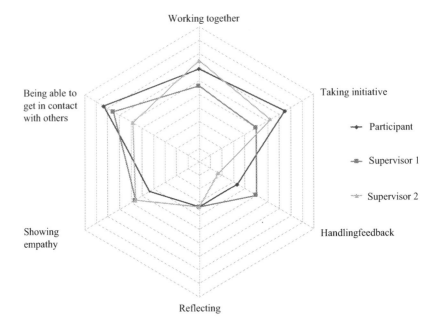

Figure 3.3 Reflective rose

of how well they felt they have these six competences. Figure 3.3 provides an example of a reflective rose that was created during an internship in 2019.

Both the participant (see instructional tool) and supervisors (see evaluation tool) assessed the participant on the behavioural indicators, after which the tool was used as the start of a reflective conversation. However, as this was only implemented after the end of our action research, it would be interesting to investigate the experiences of participants and supervisors in using the reflective rose.

Discussion

Reflective practice in a voluntary community sport coach training programme

Our action research focused on improving reflective practice in an existing training programme for young people in socially vulnerable situations who aimed to become voluntary community sport coaches. As mentioned in Chapter 2, reflection is a central component of experiential learning mechanism that stimulates participants' personal development. The purpose of this chapter was to investigate how reflective practice was implemented and could further be improved within the context of a voluntary community sport coach training programme. It also described the challenges and changes, as well as the different phases. These phases were context analysis and problem diagnosis (i.e. pre-intervention), and three self-reflective cycles of planning, acting and observing, reflecting and revised planning (i.e. intervention) (Kemmis and McTaggart 2005). The self-reflective cycles were an effective method for structuring our intervention and are in line with previous research in the field of sports (Keegan 2016; Robinson et al. 2019). It was a process of trial and error to find ways to improve reflective practice within the City Coach course. The challenge within these types of training programmes is that these are dynamic entities that need to be flexible to changes (e.g. new partnerships) and are embedded in a social reality (e.g. number of participants) that influences how the intervention is implemented and how various actors in that reality respond to it. In what follows, we elaborate on three major findings from this action research that relate to the content of the training programme.

Firstly, offering experiential learning opportunities turned out to be essential to stimulate reflective practice among youths participating in City Coach. By preparing and guiding sport and physical activities, participants learn to transform the theory they get during the training programme into practice, resulting in experiences that might contribute to one's personal development. However, Mezirow (1990) underlined that hands-on learning experiences do not necessarily result in developmental outcomes. Learning only occurs when young people make sense of an experience by giving it an interpretation and make decisions starting from this interpretation. Reflecting on their behaviours and actions is necessary to learn (see experiential learning – Chapter 2). In the City Coach course, experiential learning is fostered through reflective exercises but still might be further improved by, for instance, structurally implementing the six reflection stages described by Gibbs (1988) in the training programme. Our research reveals that the trainers challenged the participants to describe their experiential learning experiences (i.e. stage 1 of Gibbs reflective cycle model), express their feelings and thoughts related to these experiences (i.e. stage 2), and think about what was good and bad (i.e. stage 3). In addition, stage 4 has also been applied to a limited extent as the trainers encouraged participants to make sense out of their experiences and link it to previous experiences in other contexts. During reflection stage 5, the trainers and participants think together about what the participant could have done differently. However, introducing a systematic approach (e.g. list of specific questions) by taking into account these six stages might further improve the developmental gains of the City Coach participants and consequently the efficiency and effectiveness of the course. Ongoing attention also needs to be paid to reflection about the development of the competences of the participants and not to limit the reflection to organisational aspects of the sport activities. Some participants found it easier to reflect on their own competences while others could not go beyond organisational aspects. The last stage of Gibbs' reflective cycle (1988) was not fully implemented in the City Coach course. This would have been the case if participants made an action plan about what they would do in case they were confronted with a similar situation in another context (e.g. school). Nevertheless, it has been practiced the other way around. Trainers stimulated participants to give examples of how they used their competences in other contexts.

Secondly, the informal conversations we had with participants revealed that they had different predispositions to reflect on their actions. However, our research revealed that combining group-based reflective conversations with other reflective tools such as written journals (e.g. Sportfolio) and visual methodologies (e.g. mountain exercise and reflective rose) stimulated the personal development of all participants. This is in line with previous research that states that combining different reflective methods are effective to stimulate people's development (Knowles et al. 2014). Making use of such reflective methods allowed the trainers of City Coach to keep the participants focused on the key competences instead of straying off to other issues. The observations revealed that by reflecting, participants had a better understanding of specific situations which enabled their capacity to identify strategies they could use to deal with challenges they encountered. Such advantages related to reflective practice have also been recognised in recent research of Super et al. (2018). According to Dixon et al. (2016), people become more able to understand, change and improve what they do by examining their own work and whole self (Dixon et al. 2016). Also, our participants better understood their learning process as the trainers of the training programme supported participants in setting their goal for the training programme, formulating opportunities and possible barriers to reach this goal, letting young people reflect about the competences they needed to improve to reach the goal and formulating concrete actions. The support of the trainers provided young people agency in goal setting, which was considered a prerequisite for fostering personal development in our study. Reflection can thus be considered as a mechanism to stimulate personal development of young people in socially vulnerable situations (see also Chapter 2).

Thirdly, our research reveals that a small group size for these reflective conversations is essential to create a sense of safety and an open atmosphere. The importance of small groups is also reflected in the literature (McGart and Higgins 2006; Schaub-de Jong 2012). Nevertheless, optimising reflective practice in the training programme was sometimes challenging. This can mainly be attributed to the challenges in finding appropriate reflective methods and exercises for the target group in terms of, for instance, the time spent on the reflective practice. In addition, the influence of the trainers in stimulating participants to actively reflect and learn from their experiences, the tensions between the group size and cost prize for the organisation, and difficulties in following the participants after they finished the training programme was experienced as challenging.

Action research design

A group of researchers and staff members of a municipal sport service were actively involved in the action research by designing and implementing the intervention. This enabled to share planning and decision-making responsibilities among the different actors involved and made the intervention more practice driven (see also Chapter 4) and adapted to the local situation. In the beginning, time was spent to getting to know the City Coach programme, which was a first and essential phase to improve the way reflective practice was implemented in this course. Throughout the rest of the action research, the team strived for an open communication, with respect for each one's own perspective but with the aim to implement changes that were commonly approved by the entire team. It happened that members of the action research team had different meanings about the changes they wanted to implement in the training programme. An example were the different meanings about the reflective exercises they wanted to include in the Sportfolio, in this case, time needed to be taken to discuss the different meanings and come to an agreement. In addition, including young people in socially vulnerable situations in the development of and involvement in the whole research project would have been valuable as well. Previous action research showed that young people can effectively be involved as members of an action research team (Luguetti et al. 2017). Spaaij et al. (2018) also recognise power as an essential dimension in participatory research and state that in most sport-for-development studies, researchers experience difficulties in relinquishing power and control over the research process. Considering the explanatory nature of our research, we deliberately chose to focus on the perspectives of the research team and practitioners. Consequently, we are aware that involving some former participants in making decisions about the design, planning, implementation and evaluation of the different steps would have increased their level of involvement and power to share their perspectives on how to improve the reflective practices in the City Coach programme.

Participant perspectives have been further explored in an evaluation study of the training programme we set up after the completion of the intervention (Tassignon 2020) that is described in this chapter. This evaluation aimed to gain insight into participants' perceptions related to the use and implementation of the reflection tool (i.e. Sportfolio) in the City Coach programme. Driven by a realist perspective, the study of Tassignon (2020) assumed that participants' perceptions are diverse as a programme operating in certain conditions can work for some and not for others. Q-methodology was used to ascertain the individual perceptions of 16 participants regarding the Sportfolio. The COM-B model of behavioural change by Michie et al. (2011) was employed to focus on participants' perceived levels of capability (i.e. knowledge, skills and abilities), opportunities (i.e., contextual influences) and motivation (i.e., automatic and reflective brain processes which direct our decisions and behaviours) when using the Sportfolio. While the majority of the participants indicated that ample opportunities were provided to the use the Sportfolio and felt capable and motivated to work with it, results also showed that some participants experienced difficulties with regard to multiple aspects of the tool (e.g. ability to engage in certain exercises, perceived lack of guidance during the exercises). Two indicators were related to the perceived difficulties. Firstly, the participants that perceived more difficulties were significantly younger than the average participant. The second one related to the fixation on competences participants still needed to improve, which might have caused the low degree of motivation and perceived incapable when employing the Sportfolio. City Coach trainers need to be aware of these aspects, particularly for the younger participants who enrol in the programme as they seem to benefit from more individual guidance and support when using the Sportfolio.

References

Anderson, A.G., Knowles, Z. and Gilbourne, D. (2004) 'Reflective practice for sport psychologists: Concepts, models, practical implications, and thoughts on dissemination', *The Sport Psychologist*, 18(2), 188–203. DOI: 10.1123/tsp.18.2.188

Cheng, M. and Chan, C. (2019) 'An experimental test: Using rubrics for reflective writing to develop reflection', *Studies in Educational Evaluation*, 61, 176–182. DOI: 10.1016/j.stueduc.2019.04.001

Debognies, P., Schaillée, H., Haudenhuyse, R. and Theeboom, M. (2019) 'Personal development of disadvantaged youth through community sports: A theory-driven analysis of relational strategies', *Sport in Society*, 22(6), 897–918. DOI: 10.1080/17430437.2018.1523144

Dixon, M., Lee, S. and Ghaye, T. (2016) 'Strengths-based reflective practices for the management of change: Applications from sport and positive psychology', *Journal of Change Management*, 16(2), 142–157. DOI: 10.1080/14697017.2015.1125384

Gibbs, G. (1988) *Learning by doing: A guide to teaching and learning methods*, Oxford: Oxford Brookes University.

Hunt, K., Gurvitch, R. and Lund, J.L. (2016) 'Teacher evaluation: Done to you or with you?', *The Journal of Physical Education, Recreation & Dance*, 87(9), 21–27. DOI: 10.1080/07303084.2016.1226215

Jacobs, F., Claringbould, I. and Knoppers, A. (2016) 'Becoming a "good coach"', *Sport Education and Society*, 21(3), 411–430. DOI: 10.1080/13573322.2014.927756

Keegan, R. (2016) 'Action research as an agent for enhancing teaching and learning in physical education: A physical education teacher's perspective', *The Physical Educator*, 73(2), 255–284. DOI: 10.18666/TPE-2016-V73-I2-6236

Kemmis, S. and McTaggart, R. (2005) 'Participatory action research: Communicative action and the public sphere', in: N.K. Denzin and Y.S. Lincoln (eds) *The sage handbook of qualitative research*, Thousand Oaks, CA: Sage, pp. 559–603.

Kis, S.K. and Kartal, G. (2019) 'No pain no gain: Reflections on the promises and challenges of embedding reflective practices in large classes', *Reflective Practice*, 20(5), 637–653. DOI: 10.1080/14623943.2019.1651715

Knowles, Z., Gilbourne, D., Cropley, B. and Dugdill, L. (2014) 'Reflecting on reflection and journeys', in: Z. Knowles, D. Gilbourne, B. Cropley and L. Dugdill (eds) *Reflective practice in the sport and exercise sciences: Contemporary issues*, London: Routledge, pp. 3–15.

Lamb, P. and Aldous, D. (2016) 'Exploring the relationship between reflexivity and reflective practice through lesson study within initial teacher education', *International Journal for Lesson and Learning Studies*, 5(2), 99–115. DOI: 10.1108/IJLLS-11-2015-0040

Luguetti, C., Oliver, K.L., Kirk, D. and Dantas, L. (2017) 'Exploring an activist approach of working with boys from socially vulnerable backgrounds in a sport context', *Sport, Education and Society*, 22(4), 493–510. DOI: 10.1080/13573322.2015.1054274

Mansah, M., Coulon, L., Brown, P., Reynolds, H. and Kissiwaa, S. (2014) 'Tailoring dementia care mapping and reflective practice to empower assistants in nursing to provide quality care for residents with dementia', *Australian Journal of Advanced Nursing*, 31(4), 34–44.

McGart, D. and Higgins, A. (2006) 'Implementing and evaluating reflective group sessions', *Nurse Education in Practice*, 6(3), 175–181. DOI: 10.1016/j.nepr.2005.10.003

Mezirow, J. (1990) 'How critical reflection triggers transformative learning', *Fostering Critical Reflection in Adulthood*, 1(20), 1–6.

Michie, S., van Stralen, M.M. and West, R. (2011) 'The behavior change wheel: A new method for characterizing and designing behavior change interventions', *Implementation Science*, 6(2), 42. DOI: 10.1186/1748-5908-6-42

O'Neill, L., Johnson, J. and Mandela, R. (2019) 'Reflective practice groups: Are they useful for liaison psychiatry nurses working within the emergency department?', *Archives of Psychiatric Nursing*, 33(1), 85–92. DOI: 10.1016/j.apnu.2018.11.003

Pawson, R. (2006) *Evidence-based policy: A realist perspective*, London: Sage.

Paterson, C. and Chapman, J. (2013) 'Enhancing skills of critical reflection to evidence learning in professional practice', *Physical Therapy in Sport*, 14(3), 133–138. DOI: 10.1016/j.ptsp.2013.03.004

Robinson, D.B., Robinson, I.M., Currie, V. and Hall, N. (2019) 'The Syrian Canadian sports club: A community-based participatory action research project with/for Syrian youth Refugees', *Social Sciences*, 8(6), 1–15. DOI: 10.3390/socsci8060163

Schaub-de Jong, M. (2012) *Facilitating reflective learning*, Doctoral dissertation, University of Groningen, Groningen.

Spaaij, R., Schulenkorf, N., Jeanes, R. and Oxford, S. (2018) 'Participatory research in sport-for-development: Complexities, experiences and (missed) opportunities', *Sport Management Review*, 21(1), 25–37. DOI: 10.1016/j.smr.2017.05.003

Super, S., Verkooijen, K. and Koelen, M. (2018) 'The role of community sports coaches in creating optimal social conditions for life skill development and transferability – a salutogenic perspective', *Sport Education and Society*, 23(2), 173–185. DOI: 10.1080/13573322.2016.1145109

Tassignon, F. (2020) *Evaluating a reflection tool for sports-based programmes targeting disadvantaged youth: Stakeholders perceptions*, Unpublished thesis, Vrije Universiteit, Brussel.

Van der Veken, K., Willems, S. and Lauwerier, E. (2019) 'Health promotion in socially vulnerable youth: Sport as a powerful vehicle?', *Health Promotion Practice*, 22(2), 275–286. DOI: 10.1177/1524839919874751

Voldby, C.R. and Klein-Dossing, R. (2019) '"I thought we were supposed to learn how to become better coaches": Developing coach education through action research', *Educational Action Research*, 28(3), 534–553. DOI: 10.1080/09650792.2019.1605920

Wang, W. (2017) 'Using rubrics in student self-assessment: Student perceptions in the English as a foreign language writing context', *Assessment and Evaluation in Higher Education*, 42(8), 1280–1292. DOI: 10.1080/02602938.2016.1261993

Whitley, M.A., Hayden, L.A. and Gould, D. (2016) 'Growing up in the Kayamandi township: II. Sport as a setting for the development and transfer of desirable competencies', *International Journal of Sport and Exercise Psychology*, 14(4), 305–322. DOI: 10.1080/1612197X.2015.1036095

4 Health promotion in the context of community sport

Illustration of a theory-informed approach to programme development and evaluation

Emelien Lauwerier, Karen Van der Veken, Kaatje Van Roy and Sara Willems

Health and prevention among at-risk young people

Health is not equally and fairly distributed, and those in socially vulnerable situations suffer more. Socio-economic inequalities in health emerge at a very young age already, influencing for example, low birth weight and infant mortality rates (Sidebotham et al. 2014; Weightman et al. 2012) and persist throughout childhood and adolescence into adult life. Early promotion and prevention tackling smoking, poor diet, physical inactivity, or alcohol use are important keys pertaining to better health. All CYP (i.e., children and young people) should have access to prevention as unhealthy behaviour has an early onset (Alamian and Paradis 2009; Mitchell et al. 2012; Monshouwer et al. 2012; Nader et al. 2008; Ortega et al. 2013), tends to persist into adulthood (Due et al. 2011) and therefore, increases the risk of morbidity and mortality at a later age (Djoussé et al. 2009).

Although it is widely recognised that health promotion must also primarily target at-risk groups, this is not easily attained. Current health promotion programmes still fail to impact at-risk youth for a number of reasons. A first reason may be that health promotion programmes tend to overlook the social/structural factors that impede health in vulnerable youth (Mohajer and Earnest 2009). Young people at highest risk for poor health often come from families struggling with their own problems and living in poor, underserved and often-violent surroundings. In defining main determinants of health, Dahlgren and Whitehead (1991) stress the importance of multiple layers of influence. Personal behaviour factors, such as smoking habits or physical inactivity, interact with higher-level negative influences, such as interactions with peers and immediate community, and also families' living and working conditions, access to essential goods and services, and even the wider socio-economic and cultural environment. These health risk factors and risk conditions may typically affect high-risk groups more, leading to the observed social inequities in health. One example is social position. Higher educated people and those having more occupation and economic resources typically have more power and opportunities to live a healthy life compared to those who are less privileged

DOI: 10.4324/9780429340635-6

(Link and Phelan 1996). Another example is the prevalence of risk behaviour and health problems at a young age. Illness in childhood – more common among those living in at-risk situations – may have long-term consequences for health in later life. Likewise, risky health behaviour during adolescence, such as smoking, is related to poor socio-economic circumstances later on. A second reason is that most prevention programmes tend to address health issues as problems. Typically, a population at risk is assessed on the basis of the presence of a problem not on the basis of its potential. A different approach is to build prevention activities that promote strengths, assets and protective factors that facilitate healthy youth development (Pittman et al. 2003). This requires new prevention programmes that focus on individual strengths and address factors that predispose a young person to multiple risks. Illustrative are youth development programmes that focus on installing protective factors or resources in youth's social environment. Such programmes may achieve greater improvements in outcomes among at-risk youth compared to those that focus on minimising risk (Resnick 2005; Wilson et al. 2007). A third reason relates to the setting in which prevention programmes are mostly implemented. Specifically, it can be observed that youth prevention programmes are often achieved in school contexts. However, school-based programmes might not prove evenly effective for all youths or at least not for all youth subgroups. For example, anti-smoking interventions seem to work better for adolescents with a low socio-economic background when spread through informal social networks (peers) instead of through school (Mercken et al. 2012).

Therefore, while it is clear that increasing the possibilities for a healthy and positive childhood is one of the well-accepted challenges with the aim of reducing social inequities in health and the promotion of better health for all (World Health Organisation 2005), questions remain regarding how to develop and set up prevention that is more equitable and able to reach at-risk youth. Improving not only the access to these services but also tailoring them to the circumstances in which these CYP grow up might contribute considerably to reducing inequities in health (Spencer et al. 2019). In the next section, we tackle community sport programmes as a new and possible powerful lever for health promotion among at-risk youths.

Community sport as a lever for health promotion

There is growing interest in the use of sport as a delivery platform for prevention messages (Eime et al. 2008; Geidne et al. 2013; Van der Veken et al. 2019). Participation in sports may aid at-risk youth to open the gate for health promotion (Fraser-Thomas et al. 2005; Gould and Carson 2008). In Belgium, the first community sport programmes date back to the late 1990s. Community sport was launched with the specific purpose of using sports as a vehicle to tackle issues such as education, employment, community involvement and also health promotion (Haudenhuyse et al. 2012).

The idea of sport coaches as deliverers of health messages is not new, and programmes have been developed and are available for a number of health behaviours such as healthy diet and/or physical activity (Dubuy et al. 2014; Kelly et al. 2010) and alcohol or smoking prevention (King et al. 2010; Hilland et al. 2014; Romeo-Velilla et al. 2014). The possibility to build trusted relationships is seen as an important precondition towards achieving positive change (Langan et al. 2013; Petitpas et al. 1999). For CYP at risk, coaches may be regarded as positive role models (Coatsworth and Conroy 2006). The extent to which sport coaches are trained in delivering health messages is a crucial part of programme effectiveness (Almand et al. 2013). Given the multiplicity of roles and profiles of coaches often involved in community sport programmes, training towards efficient delivery of health promotion may be a challenging endeavour. There are several elements that contribute to the complexity (Craig et al. 2008):

- The complex set of skills required by those delivering the programme (e.g. present as a positive role model, provide information, tailor information to the needs of CYP at-risk, communicate in a clear and non-victimising way);
- The number of groups or organisational levels targeted by the programme (e.g. coaches, staff, local policymakers and other stakeholders);
- The number and variability of intended outcomes (e.g. health behaviour, skills, attitudes, knowledge);
- The degree of flexibility or tailoring of the programme that is permitted.

The core of complex interventions is that these are characterised by unpredictability, emergence and non-linear outcomes (Moore et al. 2015). If the aim is, in the end, to evaluate the effectiveness of programmes, some difficulties may arise. Evaluation is inescapably concerned with cause and effect. If we want to implement a prevention programme in a target population of at-risk youth, for example, we want to know to what extent the program will lead to better health outcomes. In order to be able to interpret programme effects, however, a clear vision is needed on the underlying assumptions through which a programme has its effects. Therefore, the process of programme development itself needs serious consideration and detailed descriptions are needed on the theoretical assumptions of a programme and how these have been translated into concrete programme elements. In the next section, we describe how we used theory to develop and operationalise the causal assumptions of a programme with the aim of promoting health of CYP at risk within the context of community sport. Also, we explain the need for process evaluation preceding effect evaluation studies to understand the extent to which and how implementation, theoretical assumptions and context shape programme outcomes.

The importance of theory in the development and evaluation of complex programmes

Intervention mapping as a tool for programme planning

In the past decades, a programmatic approach has become visible in the field of health education and promotion, and several comprehensive planning tools have been developed. One of these is intervention mapping (IM; Bartholomew et al.

2006, 2011, 2016). IM is a protocol for systematic theory- and evidence-based planning for behaviour change (Bartholomew et al. 2001). The protocol consists of six steps: (1) conducting a needs assessment or problem analysis; (2) creating matrices of change objectives by combining behaviour with its determinants; (3) selecting theory-based programme methods and translation of these methods into practical applications; (4) designing an integrated programme plan and materials; (5) planning for the adoption, implementation and sustainability of the programme and 6) generating an evaluation plan. The completion of one step creates an end product that can be used as a guide for the subsequent step. Three perspectives guide IM: a multi-theory approach, an ecological approach, and a participation perspective (Kok 2014).

A multi-theory approach

At different points during programme development and planning, the protocol insists on using theories. Theories can inform selection of the target behaviour to be tackled by the programme. Theories can further inform the selection of behaviour change techniques. Existing taxonomies on behaviour change techniques (e.g. Abraham and Michie 2008; Bartholomew et al. 2001, 2006, 2016) help to select those techniques that have the best potential to change one or more determinants of behaviour of the target group. Theories can also be used to create a logical sequence for the programme plan.

An ecological approach

IM acknowledges that humans and human behaviour are part of a complex system. Therefore, changing a target group's behaviour also involves changing the relevant environmental conditions surrounding the target group. In some cases, it may be more convenient to tackle environmental conditions instead of individual-level determinants. The highest chance of effective behaviour change can be expected from a programme that targets multiple levels of influence, but, of course, this is extremely difficult to achieve. A single-level intervention is simpler, easier to achieve and allows planners and researcher to gain in-depth understanding about a single influencing factor.

A participation perspective

A third perspective is concerned with the involvement of all relevant stakeholders during programme development. Stakeholder involvement is paramount to programme success. Members of the target, intended implementers, decision makers and others should be involved, for instance, in deciding on the content and format of a programme and the way of implementing a programme. When insufficiently done, programme development and implementation is likely to fail due to, for example, inappropriate choice of programme methods and materials and/or inadequate implementation (Kok 2014).

Process evaluation as a way to progress towards programme refinement

As stated earlier, complex interventions have many underlying causal assumptions and we discussed IM to be a valuable heuristic planning tool to allow focusing on the assumptions that need to be addressed in order to create a programme that works in a given context. A major step within IM is evaluation. Process evaluation is at hand to evaluate whether and how a programme succeeds in tackling its assumptions. In other words, to test whether the implementation of a programme and its selected ingredients (theory of change) have led to the desired change (Craig et al. 2008). Realist science (Pawson and Tilley 1997) is interesting in order to underpin process evaluation. It emphasises the contextual contingency of underlying mechanisms of change that produce certain effects. There are at least two important insights from this approach that may help to guide keen evaluation. Firstly, participants of a programme are no passive recipients but interact with the programme. Therefore, the effects of a programme are effects of these interactions rather than of the programme itself (Pawson and Tilley 1997). Secondly, context affects implementation and outcomes. Context means anything outside the programme itself that may hinder or positively influence its effects (Moore et al. 2015). Based on a realist approach, an evaluation plan should then allow uncovering mechanisms of change in relation to the context in which the programme was developed and implemented. Process evaluation also comes with examining programme delivery itself, namely the quality (fidelity and acceptability) and quantity (dose) of what was implemented in practice, as well as the extent to which the programme reached the intended users or target population (reach) (Steckler and Linnan 2002).

Current chapter

This chapter provides an exemplar of how to approach the development and process evaluation of a health-promoting programme from a pre-existing programme theory. We use the IM protocol and describe several steps: (1) the identification of the needs of all stakeholders regarding the set-up of a health-promoting programme; (2) the statement of the programme aims; (3) the selection of the methods and techniques for behaviour change; (4) the design of the programme plan and materials; (5) the construction of the plan for implementation and (6) the construction of the process evaluation plan.

Methods

Case study

The programme aims at improving the health of CYP in socially vulnerable situations attending in the context of a community sport practice in Bruges, Flanders. In Flanders, Belgium, around 22 per cent of Flemish municipalities provide such practices (Van Poppel 2015). These are usually subsidised by local governments and mostly directed towards the social inclusion of disadvantaged groups, in particular vulnerable CYP (Haudenhuyse and Theeboom 2015). In Bruges, community sport operates under the supervision of the Bruges' Public Centre for Social Welfare, coordinating the social services in the city. Its activities run within the four most deprived neighbourhoods of the city which are characterised by high numbers of single-parent families, children with learning difficulties, unstable housing conditions and low employability rates. It consists of open-air activities primarily focused on young children and teenagers from unprivileged and often poor areas that are run on a daily basis by two main coordinators and several sport coaches. The majority of the coaches are practitioners in training. Those practitioners follow an employment and education trajectory, with the ultimate goal of employment, either within the (community) sport sector or other domains. Their profile is characterised by several vulnerabilities, including longer-term unemployment, disruptive childhoods, school dropout, poverty, financial debts, problematic substance use (e.g. alcohol, drugs), poor housing, major psychological problems (e.g. depression, psychosis) and/or language issues. The education trajectory they follow is met through short-term training courses and/or longer-term courses by, for instance, obtaining a high school or bachelor's degree.

IM steps

The case study applied the steps of IM as indicated previously. A community participatory design approach (Minkler and Wallerstein 2003) was used to progress across steps 2 to 5 and as such to co-create and implement the programme. To this end, a participatory design group consisting of both researchers and practitioners was set up and met regularly. Next, we describe how we approached through all steps of IM, and specific strategies of the participatory approach are described whenever relevant. Within this chapter, plans for implementation and evaluation are provided. The specific (process) evaluation results are described elsewhere (Lauwerier et al. 2020).

Step 1 (*identifying community needs*). A planning group was set up consisting of target group representatives (coaches), programme deliverers (staff) and policymakers within the context of the specific case study. The goal was to dissect the needs and views of all stakeholders regarding health promotion. To this end, we used the data as obtained within the first research phase of the CATCH project (Van der Veken et al. 2020). In this phase, street soccer teams from three small to medium Flemish cities targeting youngsters and adults in homeless situations were observed and we gathered data from training moments, leisure moments, teambuilding activities, staff meetings and national and local tournaments. Also, semi-structured interviews were performed with coordinators, coaches and social partners (n = 22) as well as participants (n = 10). Partners ranged from social workers, youth workers and centres for social welfare to drug rehabilitation centres and homeless shelters. Lastly, two focus group interviews with coordinators, coaches and partners (respectively, n = 6; n = 7) were held. In analysing the data, we applied the method of grounded theory (Glaser and Strauss 1967) involving the systematic development of a theory or agglomerate of interrelated concepts. Data were collected iteratively, sourcing from (participatory) observations and semi-structured interviews. Consecutive focus groups served to validate the data obtained. The resulting programme theory was an illustration of how individual and environmental factors related to health.

Step 2 (stating programme aims). Step 2 of IM determines the goals for the programme, specifying what the target population has to do or change as a result of the programme. These goals were discussed in co-design. Data obtained within step 1 as well as theory (e.g. mentoring theory of Pawson 2006) informed the development of programme goals. A final set of measurable outcomes ('change goals') were defined.

Step 3 (selecting methods and applications for behaviour change). The objective of step 3 is to generate the core of the programme. The main idea behind this step is to link the change goals to effective *methods* and to translate these into practical *applications*. The participatory design group formulated preliminary ideas for methods. The researchers complemented these with current evidence on effective behaviour change methods from existing taxonomies (Bartholomew et al. 2011; Kok et al. 2016). Behaviour change methods are general techniques or processes that have been shown to be able to change one or more influencing factors of behaviour of an at-risk group or environmental agents. Taxonomies summarise the evidence for a method regarding effective behaviour change based on several behavioural and/or social science theories (Abraham and Michie 2008).

Step 4 (designing the programme plan). The main aim of step 4 is to build the programme in terms of content, scope and sequence, making use of the methods and applications selected in step 3. The Health Action Process Approach (HAPA) model (Schwarzer 2008), explaining human behaviour change in terms of a transition from motivation (e.g. 'Do I want to perform this behaviour') to volition ('How do I succeed in translating my intention to change my behaviour into action?'), was taken as the backbone for constructing the programme sequence. The final programme was drafted through iterative brainstorm and discussion among the members of the participatory design group. The applications of step 3 were taken as a starting point. We were also able to integrate material from other training curricula (e.g. videos, teasers and assessments) that shared some similarities regarding topics or themes.

Step 5 (constructing the implementation plan). The fifth step consists of the identification of implementers; the development of implementation and maintenance scope, sequence and instruction; the planning of activities to motivate and train implementers; and the planning of logistics including staffing or materials. Resulting deliverables are a list of persons who will implement the programme and procedures, and materials that are needed for implementation (e.g. training sheets and protocols).

Step 6 (constructing the evaluation plan). In the sixth step, evaluation is decided on (e.g. design, indicators and measures, and questions). This case study summarises the set-up of a process evaluation plan describing the underlying theory of change, context and implementation of the programme. Detailed reporting of results is available elsewhere (Lauwerier et al. 2020).

Results

Step 1 (identifying community needs)

An extensive data collection period led to the formulation of a programme theory describing why, how and when community sport may act as a lever for promoting health of CYP at-risk. The results are described in more detail elsewhere (Van der Veken et al. 2020), but its main assumptions are given below. We used assumptions from this programme theory, the backbone for programme development.

- Central in the programme theory was the idea of mechanisms for change, being triggers for intended outcomes when certain conditions are met. These mechanisms included the creation of a safe experiential learning environment (M1), installing a positive group dynamic (M2), motivational counselling (M3) and creating opportunities for personal goal setting and realisation (M4).
- Mechanisms are only promoted on the premise of contextual boundaries which obviously differ throughout the trajectory towards goal setting and health promotion. Among the main necessary conditions include a context that is sufficiently safe and mature (C), trusting relationships between coach and participant and among participants (C), presence of role models (C), development of self-esteem and self-efficacy (C) and constructive group dynamics (C).
- The interaction between mechanisms and contextual conditions gives rise to certain outcomes (O). Outcomes are most easily thought of as observable changes such as the adoption of new behaviour but also include less easily observable changes, such as a sense of safety within the environment and interpersonally while performing community sport, self-awareness about one's own behaviour and knowledge about exercise and health-related behaviour, mental space (i.e. acceptance of oneself and one's situation and openness to a community sport environment), a sense of belonging (i.e. feeling related to the group and coaches) while performing community sport, a positive self-esteem (i.e. a sense of autonomy to be oneself, also while performing physical exercise and healthy behaviour) and perceived self-efficacy (i.e. a sense of competence that one can perform and maintain physical exercise and undertake actions towards healthy behaviour and skills demonstrating the ability to be physically active and set health goals).

The result of step 1 was a formulation of the general aim of the programme, which was decided on in co-design with the stakeholders, being to increase coaches' capabilities and skills to build connection with CYP at-risk and improve their health. This would provide them with transferable skills that could improve employability successes, also in other domains than community sport.

Step 2 (stating programme aims)

A total of 24 specific aims in terms of behavioural actions (i.e. what change in behaviour is aimed for after the programme has been implemented?) were selected. These were used to state specific programme aims or change goals, specifying not only 'what' the intended change in behaviour is but also 'how' this change is achieved. Examples of change goals include: coaches (1) 'are aware of the importance' (how) to 'stimulate roles and responsibility among CYP' (what); (2) 'express advantages of' (how) 'acting as a role model regarding healthy behaviour (what); (3) 'express confidence' (how) that they can be a role model during sport activities (e.g. no smoking, healthy snacking, acting relaxed, sufficient sleep)' (what); and (4) 'show skills' (how) in 'providing a health-promoting climate (e.g. through the provision of healthy snacks, etc.)' (what). A selection of actions and change goals is presented in Table 4.1.

Step 3 (selecting the methods and applications for behaviour change)

A number of different methods were applied given the variety of actions and change goals. Table 4.2 presents selected examples of change goals, their linkage

Table 4.1 Selected actions for coaches and related change goals: examples regarding self-efficacy/skills

Actions (coaches)	Change goals (coaches)
Stimulate participants to get to know one another and the coach	Express confidence that they can properly use tools and techniques for getting to know each other, also in groups that seem difficult to manage at first sight.
Stimulate participants to identify strengths within themselves	Express confidence that they can stimulate participants to become aware of strength and realisations Show skills in stimulating participants to become aware of strengths and realisations
Identify sources of conflict timely and are able to prevent escalation of conflict	Express confidence that they can identify sources of conflict and prevent escalation Show skills in identifying sources of conflict and prevention of conflict during assistance of sport activities
Reflect on their level of health-promoting behaviour and set self-goals	Express confidence that they can self-monitor their behaviour and set goals, even when they are tired, busy, etc. Show progress towards at least one goal during the course of the programme

Table 4.2 A selection of goals aimed for after the programme (change goals), their linkage with a theoretical method and a translation into programme components (applications)

Change goal (coaches)	Method(s)	Application
Describe the importance of healthy living in feeling and being healthy and can give a list of health behaviours (PA, sleep, nutrition, non-smoking, etc.) Coaches are aware of the need to self-monitor own lifestyle behaviour and the importance of setting goals in working towards better health	Persuasive communication	Through awareness exercises, based on brainstorm, discussions and small assignments in between sessions, coaches acknowledge the need for monitoring (own) risky lifestyle behaviour(s)
Express advantages of acting as a role model compared to educating youths on health behaviour	Modelling	Coaches and peers share examples on acting as a role model and the effect they have on youth during discussion moments
Express confidence that they can identify sources of conflict and prevent escalation	Active learning	Coaches learn to identify sources of conflict and how to react using role-plays
Show progress towards at least one goal during the course of the programme	Feedback	During individual sessions, coaches are given information regarding the extent to which they accomplished personal goals (or not) and its possible impact

with theoretical methods and how these are translated into programme components (applications).

Step 4 (constructing the programme plan)

The programme was developed through continuous researcher–practitioner collaboration. The final programme included ten 4-hour sessions, observational activities and one individual session in between (for a detailed report, see Van der Veken et al. 2019). The programme covered topics such as health promotion, healthy living, positive coaching, communication, and team dynamics and conflict. Several methods for behaviour change were used. In the first series of sessions, methods were used to raise awareness on health, lifestyle and the merits of health promotion among CYP attending sport activities. To this end, several strategies were adopted such as group sessions moderated by one or two tutors with game-wise activities, information, reflection and discussion exercises, and a peer visit to a community sport practice within a different city in Flanders. Later sessions focused on attitude shifting, self-efficacy and skill building and were designed to encourage coaches and staff to discuss health-promoting behaviour and help them to build skills and apply health-promoting actions during activities. To work on the coaches' attitudes, we used methods such as direct experience, self-re-evaluation and modelling, and to change self-efficacy and skills, we used goal setting, action planning, guided practice, verbal persuasion and modelling. During these later sessions, we again made use of group sessions moderated by one or two tutors consisting of games, information, discussion and reflection moments, role plays and structured observation tasks (e.g. peer observation and expert observation while coaching). In between and after group sessions, several individual sessions were planned. After a first series of four group sessions, two individual sessions were planned with a job coach, with whom coaches were already acquainted and had regular encounters with regard to their personal (work) trajectory. Aims of these sessions were to encourage elaborated thinking regarding their health status and personal health goals, and the set-up of a personal action plan. At the end of the programme, the job coach planned to have at least one follow-up session discussing the coaches' own progress towards living healthy, as well as their concerns in applying skills to promote health among youths attending sport activities.

Step 5 (planning for implementation)

The implementation plan was built in co-creation through iterative discussions with the participatory design group. As this group proceeded through each and every step from the beginning of development of the programme, implementation and sustainability of the programme was taken as one of the starting points. The program was designed to be delivered by one to two tutors being practitioners of the community sport practice itself. Researchers co-assisted through the first enrolment of the programme. This continuous researcher–practitioner collaboration allowed for a co-learning process that values and integrates different ways of knowing. The scope, sequence and script of every session were written out and discussed beforehand among the participatory design group.

Step 6 (planning for evaluation)

The aim of the evaluation plan was to explore the underlying theory of change and implementation of the programme, and a process evaluation design was adopted to this end. Multiple process measures were integrated into the design based on the Medical Research Council (MRC) guidelines for evaluating complex interventions (Moore et al. 2015). Measurable outcomes included programme feasibility and quality of implementation (i.e. reach, dose, fidelity, acceptability), and the supposed theory of change, i.e. what in the programme leads 'how' and 'under which circumstances' to 'which effects' (e.g. 'what is changed over the course of the programme leading to some of the supposed impact', 'what elements in the context seem to be making a difference'). Table 4.3 provides an example of

Table 4.3 Process evaluation components and associated questions, indicators and sources/timing

Components	Question	Indicator	Source/timing
Reach	Do the intended participants come into contact with the programme and how? Are any participants left behind/not taking part?	Number of intended participants who followed the programme; number of participants who dropped out of the programme	Document logs of meetings between the project team (PT) and deliverers/staff prior to and during the programme Observation of deliverers/staff and participants/coaches interacting with the programme
Dose	Is the programme being delivered as a whole? Is there something being omitted and why is that?	Number of sessions and duration of sessions that are delivered; sequencing of the programme	Document logs Observation of programme sessions
Fidelity	Was the programme implemented as intended?	Appraisal on how messages are linked to theoretical methods and mechanisms of change as proposed in the programme theory	Observation of programme sessions
Acceptability	Was the programme acceptable to participants?	Perception of users and deliverers on the acceptability of the programme	Observation of programme sessions Interviews with coaches and deliverers
Theory of change	How does the delivered programme produce change? How does context affect implementation and outcomes?	Perception of users and deliverers on key changing factors and on influencing or hindering context factors on delivery and outcomes of the programme	Interviews with participants/coaches and deliverers/staff after the programme (max within 8 weeks) Focus group interview with deliverers/staff and stakeholders (local youth welfare organisations, public service for social welfare, job placement and experts on Flemish community sport practice) at one week following the programme

the linkage between process evaluation components, questions and measures, and sources that we used for performing the process evaluation. Details on the process evaluation (plan) are described elsewhere (Lauwerier et al. 2020).

Discussion

This chapter provides an exemplar of how to approach the development and evaluation of a health-promoting programme from a pre-existing programme theory. We present a case study and describe our approach of developing and testing a health-promoting programme within the specific context of a sport-for-development practice in Bruges, Flanders. We used the IM protocol to develop the programme and construct an implementation and evaluation plan. As we wanted to investigate the underlying theory of change and process of implementation, the last step consisted of the description of how we conducted a process evaluation.

Detailed description of programme planning is rare in the field of health promotion practice (Michie et al. 2009), but it is of utmost importance as such descriptions add to the development of culturally grounded interventions. Also, knowledge on the theory of change of an existing programme may help to interpret their effectiveness. We consider it a strength to have used the IM protocol (Bartholomew et al. 2001, 2006, 2011, 2016) in designing the programme and setting up the implementation and evaluation plans, for a number of reasons. Firstly, the IM protocol starts with a thorough contextual analysis among different groups of stakeholders involved in programme design and/or implementation. We built on the data obtained within an extensive first phase of data collection during the CATCH project, which resulted in a programme theory describing the mechanisms as well as context factors leading to better health outcomes for CYP in socially vulnerable situations. This led to the selection of the main courses of actions for change, as well as an idea of how change should be accomplished. By bringing in and cooperatively discussing the initial programme theory within the context of a specific community sport practice in Bruges, Flanders, a programme was co-created and plans for implementation and evaluation co-developed. This brings us to a second and related strength, being the fact that we followed a participatory approach. As mentioned previously, we started programme design with the set-up of a planning group, involving members of the target group (i.e. coaches), implementation partners (i.e. staff) and local policymakers. This planning group decided on the needs for a programme, its scope and breath and was consulted with regard to broader implementation and dissemination. Also, a participatory design group, consisting of both researchers and staff, determined how to progress through each and every step of the IM protocol. This makes the designed programme practice driven, referring to continuous participation of and reflection with local stakeholders, as well as theory driven, referring to the systematic stepwise approach and selection of theory-based methods for the programme. Our participatory design approach clearly adds to the general validity of the study; however, it also comes with challenges because community involvement is of course a complex endeavour (see also, Spaaij et al. 2018). It requires continuous collaborative efforts between academics and community partners while recognising the strengths of each and allowing for shared leadership and decision-making (Minkler and Wallerstein 2003). The participatory approach described in this chapter is a good starting point and might allow researchers and practitioners to build further on the ideas and cumulate knowledge and good practice. Thirdly, the explicit use of theory was essential. Both implicit theorising, referring to the depth of knowledge derived from empirical data and observation, and explicit theories and models were inspirational and used in the process of programme development and testing. Fourthly, within the IM protocol, evaluation is explicitly bound with programme development. The current chapter described the set-up of a process evaluation plan. Besides implementation (is the programme delivered as planned and delivered at all?), process evaluation measures should also contain detailed reporting on the theory of- change underlying the programme. This helps programme developers to make choices on how to adapt a programme while preserving its essential working elements. Bowing on well-described examples is helpful in the context of limited time and money for development.

Reflecting in more detail about the process evaluation plan within this chapter, a few remarks are of interest to the reader. Firstly, we described a case study approach, which allows for an in-depth analysis of the theory of change underlying coaches' role in using sport for improving the health of at-risk youth. We followed a programme theory perspective (Pawson 2006), assuming that interventions carry about not one but several theories/mechanisms leading to its effects, under specific circumstances. Following this approach, the results can be deep and rich but, of course, are mainly limited to the theories/mechanisms of the particular programme theory under study. We may have missed mechanisms/contextual influencing factors that are also important with regard to the successes of a health-promoting programme within a community sport context. This includes for instance (local) policy decisions or macroeconomic factors regarding housing or finances. Also, certain groups may be more prone to encounter negative peer pressure or may live in precarious family situations that negatively impact agency to take control over one's health and life. Recent theories emphasise the influence of such environmental influencing factors on motivation to perform healthy behaviour and on behaviour change as such (Michie et al. 2011). Future research is needed to identify these factors within the context of community sport, as well as their interaction with more proximate context factors and individual agentic determinants. Secondly, we used a systematic approach to design our process evaluation plan, using the MRC guide (Moore et al. 2015). The hearing of multiple stakeholders and the use of different data collection methods (observations, interviews, focus group and self-reports) allow understanding more of the complexity of the inner workings of the community sport programme. However, interviews may not be best suited for interviewees who in general may find it difficult to express their experiences in spoken language. We may want to consider other data collection tools as well, such as coding of video-recorded interactions. A third remark pertains to the challenges of the participatory process as mentioned previously. It is noticeable that the programme was co-constructed up until the phase of the evaluation.

The choice of measurement instruments such as observation and interview guides was taken independent from stakeholders. It would be worthwhile to co-construct evaluation frame and measures, leaving control regarding monitoring and evaluation to community stakeholders and increasing the chance of successfully embedding these methods in practice. A last remark concerns the limits of the evaluation plan discussed. As we were interested in implementation and theory-of-change, the focus was put on process evaluation. We do not report on the actual impact of the programme or effect, and other designs are needed to evaluate this.

This chapter describes a feasible way of developing and evaluating a health-promoting programme based on a pre-existing programme theory within a community sport context. Our approach has taught us that a team of local stakeholders and researchers is of great value in combining context-specific experiences with theoretical insights of more general validity. IM provides a feasible framework in doing so. It is highly valuable that the resulting programme is practice driven; a planning group and participatory design group were responsible for the original plan as well as the implementation into practice. Because of their experience in the field, local stakeholders are best suited to tailor programme content to the needs of the target group, as well as to suggest implementation plans and strategies so that the programme would fit with their routines. Researchers may guarantee that the plans are in accordance with the theoretical strategies and fit with the original aims of the programme. However, working according to IM still is challenging as it may require more time than is usually available in practice. We advocate for the detailed reporting of the development of programmes as well as (evidence regarding) their theory of change so that the field may benefit from these examples and adapt the programmes to the particularities of different contexts while preserving the main working ingredients.

References

Abraham, C. and Michie, S. (2008) 'A taxonomy of behavior change techniques used in interventions', *Health Psychology: Official Journal of the Division of Health Psychology, American Psychological Association*, 27(3), 379–387. DOI: 10.1037/0278–6133.27.3.379

Alamian, A. and Paradis, G. (2009) 'Clustering of chronic disease behavioral risk factors in Canadian children and adolescents', *Preventative Medicine*, 48(5), 493–499. DOI: 10.1016/j.ypmed.2012.03.014

Almand, L., Almand, M. and Saunders, L. (2013) *Coaching sport for health: A review of literature*, London: Sports Coach.

Bartholomew, L.K., Markham, C.M., Ruiter, R.A.C., Fernàndez, M.E., Kok, G. and Parcel, G.S. (2016) *Planning health promotion programs: An intervention mapping approach*, 4th edn, San Francisco, CA: Jossey-Bass.

Bartholomew, L.K., Parcel, G.S., Kok, G. and Gottlieb, N.H. (2001) *Intervention mapping: Designing theory and evidence-based health promotion programs*, Mountain View, CA: Mayfield Publishing.

Bartholomew, L.K., Parcel, G.S., Kok, G. and Gottlieb, N.H. (2006) *Intervention mapping: Designing theory- and evidence-based health promotion programs*, San Francisco, CA: Jossey-Bass.

Bartholomew, L.K., Parcel, G.S., Kok, G., Gottlieb, N.H. and Fernández, M.E. (2011) *Planning health promotion programs: An intervention mapping approach*, 3rd edn, San Francisco, CA: Jossey-Bass.

Coatsworth, J.D. and Conroy, D.E. (2006) 'Enhancing the self-esteem of youth swimmers through coach training: Gender and age effects', *Psychology of Sport and Exercise*, 7(2), 173–192. DOI: 10.1016/j.psychsport.2005.08.005

Craig, P., Dieppe, P., Macintyre, S., Michie, S., Nazareth, I. and Petticrew, M. (2008) 'Developing and evaluating complex interventions: The new medical research council guidance', *British Medical Journal*, 337, a1655. DOI: 10.1136/bmj.a1655

Dahlgren, G. and Whitehead, M. (1991) *Policies and strategies to promote social equity in health*, Stockholm, Sweden: Institute for Futures Studies.

Djoussé, L., Driver, J.A. and Gaziano, J.M. (2009) 'Relation between modifiable lifestyle factors and lifetime risk of heart failure', *The Journal of the American Medical Association*, 302(4), 394–400. DOI: 10.1001/jama.2009.1062

Dubuy, V., De Cocker, K., De Bourdeaudhuij, I., Maes, L., Seghers, J., Lefevre, J., De Martelaer, K., Brooke, H. and Cardon, G. (2014) 'Evaluation of a real-world intervention using professional football players to promote a healthy diet and physical activity in children and adolescents from a lower socio-economic background: A controlled pretest-posttest design', *BMC Public Health*, 14, 457. DOI: 10.1186/1471-2458-14-457

Due, P., Krolner, R., Rasmussen, M., Andersen, A., Damsgaard, M.T., Graham, H. and Holstein, B.E. (2011) 'Pathways and mechanisms in adolescence contribute to adult health inequalities', *Scandinavian Journal of Public Health*, 39(6), 62–78. DOI: 10.1177/1403494810395989

Eime, R.M., Payne, W.R. and Harvey, J.T. (2008) 'Making sporting clubs healthy and welcoming environments: A strategy to increase participation', *Journal of Science and Medicine in Sport*, 11(2), 146–154. DOI: 10.1016/j.jsams.2006.12.121

Fraser-Thomas, J.L., Côté, J. and Deakin, J. (2005) 'Youth sport programs: An avenue to foster positive youth development', *Physical Education and Sport Pedagogy*, 10(1), 19–40. DOI: 10.1080/1740898042000334890

Geidne, S., Quennerstedt, M. and Eriksson, C. (2013) 'The youth sports club as a health-promoting setting: An integrative review of research', *Scandinavian Journal of Public Health*, 41(3), 269–283. DOI: 10.1177/1403494812473204

Glaser, B. and Strauss, A. (1967) *The discovery of grounded theory: Strategies for qualitative research*, Chicago: Aldine Publishing Company.

Gould, D. and Carson, S. (2008) 'Life skills development through sport: Current status and future directions', *International Review of Sport and Exercise Psychology*, 1(1), 58–78. DOI: 10.1080/17509840701834573

Haudenhuyse, R. and Theeboom, M. (2015) 'Buurtsport en sociale innovatie: Een tweede start voor buurtsport in Vlaanderen? [Community sport and social innovation: A second start for community sport in Flanders?]', in: M. Theeboom, R. Haudenhuyse and J. Vertonghen (eds) *Sport en Sociale Innovatie* [*Sport and social innovation*], Brussels: VUBPress, pp. 191–208.

Haudenhuyse, R., Theeboom, M. and Coalter, F. (2012) 'The potential of sports-based social interventions for vulnerable youth: Implications for sport coaches and youth workers', *Journal of Youth Studies*, 15(4), 437–454. DOI:10.1080/13676261.2012.663895

Hilland, T.A., Beynon, C.M., McGee, C.E., Murphy, R.C., Parnell D, Romeo-Velilla, M., Stratton, G. and Forweather, L. (2014) 'Training sports coaches to tackle tobacco:

Formative evaluation of the smokefree sports campaign', *International Journal of Health Promotion and Education*, 53(1), 2–16. DOI: 10.1080/14635240.2014.915758

Kelly, B., Baur, L.A., Bauman, A.E., Smith, B.J., Saleh, S., King, L.A. and Chapman, K. (2010) 'Health promotion in sport: An analysis of peak sporting organisations' health policies', *Journal of Science and Medicine in Sport*, 13(6), 566–567. DOI: 10.1016/j.jsams.2010.05.007

King, K.A., Dowdall, M.P. and Wagner, D.I. (2010) 'Coaches' attitudes and involvement in alcohol prevention among high school athletes', *Journal of Community Health*, 35, 68–75. DOI: 10.1007/s10900-009-9190-4

Kok, G. (2014) 'A practical guide to effective behavior change: How to apply theory- and evidence-based behavior change methods in an intervention', *The European Health Psychologist*, 16(5), 156–170. DOI: 10.31234/osf.io/r78wh

Kok, G., Gottlieb, N.H., Peters, G.-J.Y., Mullen, P.D., Parcel, G.S., Ruiter, R.A.C., Fernández, M.E., Markham, C. and Bartholomew, L.K. (2016) 'A taxonomy of behaviour change methods: An intervention mapping approach', *Health Psychology Review*, 10(3), 297–312. DOI: 10.1080/17437199.2015.1077155

Langan, E., Blake, C. and Lonsdale, C. (2013) 'Systematic review of the effectiveness of interpersonal coach education interventions on athlete outcomes', *Psychology of Sport and Exercise*, 14(1), 37–49. DOI: 10.1016/j.psychsport.2012.06.007

Lauwerier, E., Van Poel, E., Van der Veken, K., Van Roy, K. and Willems, S. (2020) 'Evaluation of a program targeting sports coaches as deliverers of health-promoting messages to at-risk youth: Assessing feasibility using a realist-informed approach', *PLoS One*, 15(9), e0236812. DOI: 10.1371/journal.pone.0236812

Link, B.G. and Phelan, J.C. (1996) 'Understanding sociodemographic differences in health – the role of fundamental social causes', *American Journal of Public Health*, 86(4), 471–473. DOI: 10.2105/ajph.86.4.471

Mercken, L., Moore, L., Crone, M.R., De Vries, H., De Bourdheaudhuij, I., Lien, N., Fagiano, F., Vitória, P.D. and Van Lenthe, F.J. (2012) 'The effectiveness of school-based smoking prevention interventions among low- and high-SES European teenagers', *Health Education Research*, 27(3), 459–469. DOI: 10.1093/her/cys017

Michie, S., Fixsen, D., Grimshaw, J.M. and Eccles, M.P. (2009) 'Specifying and reporting complex behaviour change interventions: The need for a scientific method', *Implementation Science*, 4(40). DOI: 10.1186/1748-5908-4-40

Michie, S., van Stralen, M.M. and West, R. (2011) 'The behaviour change wheel: A new method for characterising and designing behaviour change interventions', *Implementation Science*, 6, 42. DOI: 10.1186/1748-5908-6-42

Minkler, M. and Wallerstein, N. (2003) *Community based participatory research for health*, San Francisco, CA: Jossey-Bass.

Mitchell, J., Pate, R., Beets, M. and Nader, P. (2012) 'Time spent in sedentary behavior and changes in childhood BMI: A longitudinal study from ages 9 to 15 years', *International Journal of Obesity*, 37, 54–60. DOI: 10.1038/ijo.2012.41

Mohajer, N. and Earnest, J. (2009) 'Youth empowerment for the most vulnerable: A model based on the pedagogy of Freire and experiences in the field', *Health Education*, 109(5), 428–438. DOI: 10.1108/09654280910984834

Monshouwer, K., Harakeh, Z., Lugtig, P., Huizink, A., Creemers, H.E., Reijneveld, S.A., De Winter, A.F., Van Oort, F., Ormel, J. and Vollebergh, W.A.M. (2012) 'Predicting transitions in low and high levels of risk behavior from early to middle adolescence: The TRAILS study', *Journal of Abnormal Child Psychology*, 40(6), 923–931. DOI: 10.1007/s10802-012-9624-9

Moore, G.F., Audrey, S., Barker, M., Bond, L., Bonell, C., Hardeman, W., Moore, L., O'Cathain, A., Tinati, T., Wight, D. et al. (2015) 'Process evaluation of complex interventions: Medical research council guidance', *British Medical Journal*, 350, h1258. DOI: 10.1136/bmj.h1258

Nader, P.R., Bradley, R.H., Houts, R.M., McRitchie, S.L. and O'Brien, M. (2008) 'Moderate-to-vigorous physical activity from ages 9 to 15 years', *The Journal of the American Medical Association*, 300(3), 295–305. DOI: 10.1001/jama.300.3.295

Ortega, F.B., Konstabel, K., Pasquali, E., Ruiz, J.R., Hurtig-Wennlöf, A., Mäestu, J., Löf, M., Harro, J., Bellocco, R., Labayen, I. et al. (2013) 'Objectively measured physical activity and sedentary time during childhood, adolescence and young adulthood: A cohort study', *PLoS One*, 8(4), e60871. DOI: 10.1371/journal.pone.0060871

Pawson, R. (2006) *Evidence-based policy: A realist perspective*, London: Sage.

Pawson, R. and Tilley, N. (1997) *Realist evaluation*, London: Sage.

Petitpas, A.J., Giges, B. and Danish, S.J. (1999) 'The sport psychologist-athlete relationship: Implications for training', *The Sport Psychologist*, 13(3), 344–357.

Pittman, K., Irby, M., Tolman, J., Yohalem, N. and Ferber, T. (2003) *Preventing problems, promoting development, encouraging engagement: Competing priorities or inseparable goals?*, Washington, DC: The Forum for Youth Investment, Impact Strategies, Inc. Available HTTP: www.forumfyi.org (accessed 17 December 2019)

Resnick, M. (2005) 'Healthy youth development: Getting our priorities right', *Medical Journal of Australia*, 183(8), 398–400. DOI: 10.5694/j.1326-5377.2005.tb07101.x

Romeo-Velilla, M., Beynon, C., Murphy, R.C., McGee, C., Hilland, T.A., Parnell, D., Stratton, G. and Foxweather, L. (2014) 'Formative evaluation of a UK community-based sports intervention to prevent smoking among children and young people: Smokefree sports', *Journal of Sport for Development*, 2(3), 1–10.

Schwarzer, R. (2008) 'Modeling health behavior change: How to predict and modify the adoption and maintenance of health behaviors', *Applied Psychology: An International Review*, 57(1), 1–29. DOI: 10.1111/j.1464-0597.2007.00325.x

Sidebotham, P., Fraser, J., Fleming, P., Ward-Platt, M. and Hain, R. (2014) 'Patterns of child death in England and Wales', *Lancet*, 384(9946), 904–914. DOI: 10.1016/S0140-6736(13)61090-9

Spaaij, R., Schulenkorf, N., Jeanes, R. and Oxford, S. (2018) 'Participatory research in sport-for-development: Complexities, experiences and (missed) opportunities', *Sport Management Review*, 21, 25–37. DOI: 10.1016/j.smr.2017.05.003

Spencer, N., Raman, S., O'Hare, B. and Tamburlini, G. (2019) 'Addressing inequities in child health and development: Towards social justice', *BMJ Paediatrics Open*, 3(1), e000503. DOI: 10.1136/bmjpo-2019-000503

Steckler, A. and Linnan, L. (2002) *Process evaluation for public health interventions and research*, San Francisco, CA: Jossey-Bass.

Van der Veken, K., Willems, S. and Lauwerier, E. (2019) 'Health promotion in socially vulnerable youth: Sports as a powerful vehicle?', *Health Promotion Practice*, 22(2), 275–286. DOI: 10.1177/1524839919874751

Van der Veken, K., Lauwerier, E., & Willems, S. (2020) 'How community sport programs may improve the health of vulnerable populations: a program theory', *International Journal for Equity in Health*, 19(1). DOI: 10.1186/s12939-020-01177-5

Van Poppel, M. (2015) *Benchmark Buurtsport: Buurtsport in Vlaanderen anno 2014 [Benchmark community sport: Community sport in Flanders in the year 2014]*, Belgium: Flemish Institute of Sport Management and Recreation Policy.

Weightman, A.L., Morgan, H.E., Shepherd, M.A., Kitcher, H., Roberts, C. and Dunstan, F.D. (2012) 'Social inequality and infant health in the UK: Systematic review and meta-analyses', *BMJ Open*, 2(3), e000964. DOI: 10.1136/bmjopen-2012-000964

Wilson, N., Dasho, S., Martin, A.C., Wallerstein, N., Wang, C.C. and Minkler, M. (2007) 'Engaging young adolescents in social action through photovoice: The youth empowerment strategies (YES!) project', *Journal of Early Adolescence*, 27, 241–261. DOI: 10.1177/0272431606294834

World Health Organization (2005) *The European health report 2005 – public health action for healthier children and populations*, Geneva. Available HTTP: www.euro.who.int/__data/assets/pdf_file/0004/82435/E87325.pdf (accessed 11 September 2020)

5 Facilitating conditions for establishing social cohesion through structural approaches in community sport

Shana Sabbe, Lieve Bradt and Rudi Roose

Introduction

Community sport has been introduced into Western society because, compared to white, highly educated, heterosexual groups, vulnerable young people are underrepresented in regular sport clubs (Hylton and Totten 2008). Of critical importance is that the exclusion of young people from regular sport participation is argued to be a symptom of the broad social vulnerability of young people. This social vulnerability points at the broader disconnection between young people and societal institutions (Haudenhuyse 2012; Vettenburg 1998). According to scholars, social vulnerability, therefore, refers to a broad process of social exclusion (see Chapter 1) (Levitas et al. 2007). In other words, the underrepresentation of vulnerable young people in regular sport points at their exclusion from broad mainstream networks and amenities in society, such as their families, the labour market, education, health care, justice and social work (Haudenhuyse et al. 2013). Hence, these young people are often referred to as young people in NEET: not in education, employment or training (Haudenhuyse et al. 2013). At the basis of this disconnection lies the accumulation of youngsters' negative experiences with mainstream institutions, which may lead to feelings of incompetence, failure, rejection and a lower self-image (Andrews and Andrews 2003). As a result, these young people are less likely to profit from the potential benefits of a healthy interaction with mainstream services, in comparison to other young people (Haudenhuyse 2012). These processes of exclusion, however, are often fuelled by the ideas which underpin these institutions (e.g. assumptions regarding vulnerable young people's deficits) (Haudenhuyse 2012; Haudenhuyse et al. 2013; Vettenburg 1998). Community sport practices take this social vulnerability of young people as a ground for intervention. In Flanders, for example, community sport practices take vulnerability rates (based on indicators such as demography, accommodation, education and employment) as a point of departure to select their target groups or to select the geographical areas in which they develop their practices. By taking social vulnerability as a ground of intervention, community sport not only aims to create equal participation opportunities, it also attempts to provide an answer to the distorted, interactional component in the relationship between

DOI: 10.4324/9780429340635-7

vulnerable young people and societal institutions and aims for social inclusion (Haudenhuyse 2012).

In order to address the issue of social vulnerability, community sport claims to develop itself as a social intervention (Hartmann 2003). Such development resides from the sport-plus philosophy (Coalter 2006), in which sport is used as a means rather than an end (Bailey 2005). As scholars have stated that there is a limit to what sports can do to address complex social issues (Spaaij et al. 2013), this has led to the idea that, particularly for young people in socially vulnerable situations, the establishment of non-sport objectives is more important than the achievement of merely sport objectives (Coalter 2006; Haudenhuyse et al. 2013). In this chapter, we focus on social cohesion as a third objective within our operationalisation of social inclusion, as mentioned in Chapter 1. Literature shows that social cohesion is believed to be a desirable social objective for community sport (Ekholm 2016; Kelly 2011), as it is seen as a potential lever to combat broad and complex issues such as social vulnerability and exclusion (Berger-Schmitt 2000).

> [It] is a concept that includes values and principles which aim to ensure that all citizens, without discrimination and on an equal footing, have access to fundamental social and economic rights. Social cohesion is a flagship concept which constantly reminds us of the need to be collectively attentive to, and aware of, any kind of discrimination, inequality, marginality or exclusion.
> (Council of Europe 2001: 5)

In this vein, social cohesion is considered a key ingredient for strong and healthy societies (Kearns and Forrest 2000; Novy et al. 2012). Especially in Flanders, social cohesion seems to be a pinnacle objective for community sport, in comparison to other social objectives such as health and personal development. As mentioned in Chapter 1, a survey in 2014 among all Flemish local authorities showed that 90 per cent of community sport programmes which claim to contribute to non-sport objectives aim at improving social cohesion primarily (Van Poppel 2015).

The shaping of social cohesion in post-welfare states

Notwithstanding the importance of social cohesion as an objective for community sport practices, social cohesion is claimed to be a rather contested notion (Bailey 2005; Chan et al. 2006). Social cohesion is often referred to as a 'concept of convenience', referring to its pragmatic, chameleon-like and often instrumental use (Chan et al. 2006).

> In other words, how social cohesion is to be defined depends to a large extent on the substantial problem(s) the researcher or policymaker is focusing on. . . . Social cohesion is largely a 'catchword' for incorporating the most pressing social issues of the day: unemployment, poverty, discrimination, exclusion, disenchantment with politics, together with any problems that a policymaker fit.
> (Chan et al. 2006: 288)

Within the current context of the post-welfare state, however, this dynamic, relational and messy (Stead 2017) character of social cohesion might become dangerous, as it might render social cohesion more vulnerable for an increased focus on private obligations at the expense of attention for collective responsibilities (Lorenz 2016).

During the mid-1970s, post-World War II welfare states transitioned from a politics of redistribution, implying that state interventions are focused on labour market qualifications, creating equal opportunities, securing social order and tackling social inequality by compensating for losses in times of economic crisis (Morel et al. 2012), to post-welfare states, under the influence of neoliberal critique (Kessl 2009). The emergence of post-welfarism became steered by neoliberal principles of privatisation, marketisation and consumerisation (Brown 2017). As a result, European western welfare states have become more dominantly oriented towards a free market-based idea of economic growth, wherein the state would have less responsibility. A strong focus on social security would make place for more corporate competitiveness and inequality would be considered the ultimate motivation to become economically active (Morel et al. 2012). This shift from welfare to post-welfare states has heightened the focus on human capital, individual autonomy, choice and responsibility (Kessl 2009; Lorenz 2016). Underpinning this focus is the assumption that all individuals are able to lead successful lives as free, rational, resilient, self-reliant and active citizens despite structural barriers in society (Brown 2017). In that sense, social cohesion seems to have become conditioned by economic and neoliberal values, such as personal responsibility and obligation. In that sense, it has been argued that post-welfarism enables the deconstruction of collective values (Lorenz 2013) as social responsibilities become translated into private concerns (Lorenz 2016) and social problems into an individual lack of skills (Kessl 2009). Following from this, the objective to establish social cohesion on the basis of principles such as social justice, human rights, collective responsibility and respect for diversity (International Federation of Social Workers 2014) has become constrained (Lorenz 2013, 2016).

The withdrawal of the state and the decreased support of governments suggests an increased focus of post-welfare states on the community as a place to address social issues and to install values such as 'participation, active citizenship and collective action' (Jordan 2013: 172) through the use of community development programmes (Forde and Lynch 2015), such as community sport practices.

Between instrumental and structural approaches

Dominance of instrumental approaches

A critical concern regarding the increased role of community-based interventions to (re-)create structures of social cohesion is that these interventions are often steered top-down, rather than bottom-up, due to their financial dependency on the state (Craig 2007). Consequently, such interventions become mobilised to focus on social issues, which the state deems important. On this, Forde and Lynch

(2015: 35) argue: 'The reform and modernisation of welfare systems involves greater reliance on voluntary and community provision of services, decentralisation of services, increased formalisation of relationships in and between welfare-providing organisations, and greater monitoring and inspection.' This leaves little room for critical community-based practices, due to the position of such practices as passive recipients of policy (Forde and Lynch 2015). The privatisation of welfare provision furthermore pushes social practitioners in their controlling role, as if they were social entrepreneurs (Fret 2007), rather than a role in which they could oversee the provision of rights (Lorenz 2013). Blackshaw and Crabbe (2004: 82) as cited in Sabbe et al. (2019b: 5) argue:

> Rather than being emancipatory the welfare services today constitute a second-rate and repressive regime, which have recourse to the expert and governmental 'gaze' of those employed by the state: the DSS officer [Diplomatic Security Service], the community sport development worker, the GP [General Practitioner], the social worker, the probation officer, and so forth that collectively 'police' the 'flawed consumer'.

In the specific practice of sport-based interventions, Spaaij (2009) argues that these practices often create the illusion of providing non-state interventions whilst actually being tentacles of a top-down governance strategy.

Within sport-based practices, this is believed to debouch in the dominance of instrumental approaches above critical, political and structural approaches (Coakley 2011; Darnell et al. 2016; Hartmann and Kwauk 2011; Nols 2018). However, such dominant approaches are challenged in many ways through alternative, critical, politicised and structural perspectives (see Coakley 2011; Darnell et al. 2016; Hartmann and Kwauk 2011).

The main critique upon instrumental approaches is that, within such approach, social objectives are often subjected to a 'displacement of scope' (Haudenhuyse et al. 2013: 8), wherein broader macro-level changes are confused and replaced with or given form through micro-level outcomes. In relation to social cohesion, this means that it is narrowed down to increasing young people's social capital in order to prevent undesirable behaviour (Haudenhuyse et al. 2013) and to teach youngsters 'attributes needed to achieve personal success' (Coakley 2011: 1). Through such approach, socially vulnerable young people are portrayed as 'anti-social others' (Kelly 2011: 136) and public targets of dangerousness (Crabbe 2009). In other words, such approaches contribute to a discourse wherein vulnerable young people are 'responsibilised' and 'adulterised' (Kelly 2011: 129) and, wherein, the problem of social vulnerability is made non-structural and apolitical (Oosterlynck et al. 2017). Such de-politisation in which the focus lays solely on the individual emanates from a 'reductive analysis of these complex processes, where individual deficits and "self-exclusion" are highlighted and structural inequalities de-emphasized' (Kelly 2011: 145). Such reduction might obscure the structural understanding of the root causes of inequality and vulnerability, such as social division and power inequality (Crabbe 2009). Furthermore such discourses are expected to feed approaches which 'reinforce and reproduce the social status quo' (Hartmann and Kwauk 2011: 292) rather than changing it. In other words, within such an instrumentalised approach, community sport practices are mainly concerned with improving young people's individual knowledge, skills and resilience and perhaps risk to become blind for the needed eradication of the structural exclusion mechanisms which young people in vulnerable situations are facing (Crabbe 2009; Ekholm 2016; Kelly 2011). At the core of the issue lies the fact that, whereas community sport takes the social vulnerability of participants as a legitimate reason to intervene in their lifeworld, the objectives believed to tackle this vulnerability, such as social cohesion, become detached from this original intention, due to this use of instrumental approaches.

A plea for structural approaches

Based on this dominance of instrumental approaches, scholars plea for the instalment of 'a socio-pedagogical shift' (Haudenhuyse et al. 2013: 480), referring to the development of a more structural understanding of and approach to the social vulnerability of young people (Coakley 2011; Darnell et al. 2016; Hartmann and Kwauk 2011).

> [A]ny form of youth work, including sports-based social interventions, should not be seen as a versatile instrument for social inclusion or integration of socially vulnerable young people, but needs to be understood as part of social life, and therefore inevitably a co-carrier of processes of, for example, social vulnerability. This understanding means a socio-pedagogical shift from the attention for individual well-defined outcomes, towards assuring social rights and equal access to socio-economical provisions for young people through sports-based social interventions.
> (Haudenhuyse et al. 2013: 480)

In other words, structural approaches align with Veit-Wilson's (1998: 45) 'strong' discourse on social inclusion (as described in Chapter 1), where we 'aim at solutions which reduce the powers of exclusion' rather than a 'weak' discourse wherein 'the solutions lie in altering these excluded peoples' handicapping characteristics and enhancing their integration into dominant society'.

In the next section, we focus on the empirical research (see Chapter 2) that was undertaken from the objective to contribute to such 'socio-pedagogical shift' (Haudenhuyse et al. 2013) and thus to a more structural understanding and approach to social cohesion in the context of community sport. This objective was steered by the social work perspective we adopted throughout this research, wherein the 'realisation of human rights, social justice and social change' (Roose et al. 2016: 1022) is a key ambition.

Research perspectives

In order to install a 'socio-pedagogical shift' (Haudenhuyse et al. 2013: 480) in the practice of community sport, scholars argue for a re-socialisation of research. In that vein, it could be argued that the dominant focus of sport-based research on linking expected results to certain inputs of particular programmes (Coalter 2007) and the lack of attention for processes of and within community sport programmes (see Chapter 1) hinders the instalment of such structural approaches. Scholars have argued that sport-based social interventions, as such, remain black or magical boxes (Coalter 2007; Haudenhuyse et al. 2013). In the light of this socio-pedagogical shift, Haudenhuyse et al. (2013) argue that this dominant focus on outcomes, rather than processes, fails to acknowledge the complexity of young people's life circumstances, often marked by a broad and structural process of exclusion. Especially with regard to the objective of social cohesion, there seems to be a lack of empirical research on the meaning of social cohesion. Stead (2017: 4) elaborates: 'For all that has been written about social cohesion, relatively little attention has been paid to the on-the-ground-dimension, of its emergence, to the local places where these translations occur'. For example, in the specific context of community sport, contemporary research on social cohesion is largely confined to 'anecdotal evidence' (Schulenkorf 2010: 3), suggesting that the available data are both scarce and non-rigorous (Beutler 2008). Scholars therefore argue that research should focus on unravelling the perspectives and experiences of those actors involved in community sport (Haudenhuyse et al. 2013). Answering to this question through research is deemed important, especially regarding the objective of social cohesion, as it has been argued that social cohesion only becomes meaningful when enacted through 'the multiple interpretations and practices of multiple, situated actors' (Stead 2017: 6). Given the fact that there seems to be a lack of empirical research to the on-the-ground dimensions of social cohesion (Stead 2017), we aimed at exploring how community sport practitioners understand and define social cohesion within their daily practices. This implies that this research took to 'on-the-ground-dimension' (Stead 2017: 4) of social cohesion as a starting point. Doing so enabled the uncovering of complexities, ambiguities and paradoxes within the concept of social cohesion rather than searching for a pre-defined, solid, one-dimensional definition.

In order to uncover the 'on the ground understandings' regarding social cohesion and how to establish this within community sport, a two-phase research approach (aligning with the broader set-up of the *community sport for AT-risk youth: Innovative strategies for promoting personal development, health and social CoHesion* (CATCH) project) was used. In phase 1, interviews with practitioners involved in the organisation of community sport (N = 34) were undertaken. The group of interviewees consisted of community sport practitioners (n = 16), local partners (n = 17) and one ex-practitioner. The semi-structured interviews were structured around four main questions: (1) 'What are you seeking to achieve when taking social cohesion as an objective of community sport?', (2) 'What are the expected effects of the establishment of social cohesion and why is it important to strive towards these effects?', (3) 'How and to what extent does community sport currently contribute to social cohesion?' and (4) 'Which mechanisms and conditions influence this contribution to social cohesion?'

Throughout this first phase, it became clear that a more in-depth exploration of strategies of structural work together with practitioners was needed, as the practitioners pinpointed this as an important challenge in relation to the objective of social cohesion. Therefore, the second phase of the research focused on uncovering strategies of structural work (i.e. strategies focused on reducing the powers of social exclusion) by conducting a single-case study in one practice in Flanders (see Sabbe et al. 2019a for an extended overview of findings). During a seminar of the Flemish Institute of Sport Management and Recreation Policy, the researcher questioned practitioners on their willingness to participate in the second phase of the research, which would focus on exploring this structural role. In total, 12 practices showed their interest in participating. The researcher selected a case on the basis of one indicator: the extent to which the initiative intended to contribute to the issue at stake, enacting a structural approach within their practice (meaning that this practice had strong ambitions to combat and therefore reduce the powers of social exclusion). In order to make this selection, the practices were elaborately discussed with the Flemish Institute of Sport Management and Recreation Policy and the coordinators of the respective projects were contacted to discuss their ambitions regarding their structural role. One practice, in particular, already explicitly and formally made structural work part of their strategic organisational objectives and was therefore selected for our study. The case study consisted of a document analysis of vision statements and operating reports, participatory observations during five case meetings (which are gatherings where community sport practitioners can discuss their struggles, concerns and questions regarding specific cases and can give form to their structural role), nine semi-structured interviews with practitioners steered by the questions – (1) 'How do practitioners implement structural approaches (i.e. strategies focused on reducing the powers of exclusion) in their daily practice?', (2) 'How do the individual trajectories of community sport practitioners relate to the development of this structural role?' and (3) 'How can methods, such as case meetings, contribute to the development of this structural role?' – and one focus group with the community sport practitioners and coordinator of the case.

In the next section, we give an overview of our findings regarding structural community sport strategies in Flanders. In doing so, we first refer to the results from both research phase 1 and 2. Thereafter, we specifically shed light upon the facilitating conditions which were identified by practitioners across phases 1 and 2 in order to adopt such structural approaches within community sport. We will illustrate our findings with quotations, accompanied by the respondents' function, age (for some of the respondents this information was not available) and gender.

Findings

Understanding social cohesion 'on the ground': untapped potential

The results of the interviews in phase 1 reveal that developing structural approaches (i.e. strategies that focus on combating exclusionary mechanisms that participants of community sport practices are facing, such as advocating for young people's access to public spaces in the neighbourhood) remain a rather distant ambition for community sport practitioners (see Sabbe et al. 2018 for an extended overview of the findings). As such, practitioners feel that it is quite impossible to actually develop or install such approaches.

> You could say we are a like a drop of water on a hot plate. The only thing we can do is distract youngsters from their situation and that is valuable as well. We do not have the ambition . . . or else we are not in a position to change anything and moreover we don't have the means to do so.
> (coordinator, woman, 29 years)

In shedding light upon this impossibility, our findings partially confirm the critique of scholars that structural approaches to social cohesion in community sport remain largely undeveloped. Still, the empirical data display a tension between this perceived impossibility and the ambitions of practitioners in relation to installing structural approaches.

> We really strive to change something about their situation. I think this should be the starting point. Moreover, there should be a rock-solid belief that we can do so.
> (coordinator, man, 32 years)

This tension nuances the critique of scholars regarding the undeveloped character of structural approaches as it displays the structural potential of community sport through practitioners' structural understandings and ambitions. This potential, however, remains untapped due to two main challenges: (1) practitioners' inability to translate structural ambitions into a day-to-day approach (due to the external pressure from policymakers and/or the internal lack of experience, expertise and knowledge to do so) and (2) practitioners' inability to find concepts which might give language to these ambitions and actions.

Structural community sport strategies: inside-out and outside-in

The findings in phase 2 of the research uncovered a dominance of structural strategies directed to establish change outside of the organisation of community sport, for example, towards policy and partner organisations. From these strategies, which we refer to as outside-in strategies, the signalling of mechanisms which detriment the equal opportunities of young people to external actors was identified by practitioners as the most tangible outside-in strategy. For example, on the inaccessibility of regular sport practices (e.g. classic sport club) for young people in socially vulnerable situations, practitioners signalled the following:

> They [partner] don't question themselves enough. They look for causes of their problems in the conviction that 'our groups [community sport groups] cannot get to their camps; our people did not make a reservation for their halls'.... It's a white middle-class service ... Taking into account the feeling that this service is a 'closed house', I argue that we should do more to tackle this and to get this signal out there.
>
> (practitioner, man)

The findings further uncover that whilst outside-in strategies are very well developed, strategies directed at creating changes within the own organisation are underdeveloped. Taking the example of accessibility here again, our data display how community sport itself can become a source of exclusion due to the power imbalance between participants and practitioners. One of the practitioners reflected upon a conversation with a participant:

> I was tired of it and then I acted in a wrong way, I was mad and then I told her [a participant]: 'I am sick of it, it's been like this for months on end and if you keep acting like this, then don't bother coming to the activities no more.' ... and then I just left.
>
> (practitioner, woman)

Given such self-inflicted moments of exclusion, practitioners argued for the necessity of developing strategies which address these. We referred to such strategies as inside-out strategies (e.g. by reflecting on participant–practitioner relationships and by creating processes of shared decision-making which can lead to societal change). According to practitioners, such strategies are underdeveloped on an organisational level and remain limited to the individual reflections of practitioners upon such processes of exclusion.

In the following section, we specifically address the conditions which we, based on the findings from both phase 1 and phase 2 of our research, identify as being facilitating in order to enable community sport practices to give form to such strategies of structural work.

Facilitating conditions

The different facilitating conditions we identified can be structured on three levels: (1) organisational level, (2) network level and (3) policy level.

Organisational level

The first facilitating condition relates to the challenges of community sport practitioners in relation to (1) translating their structural ambitions into a day-to-day approach (partially due to the lack of experience, and expertise and knowledge on an organisational level) and (2) finding concepts to give language to these structural ambitions and actions.

Throughout the different interviews it became clear that practitioners are in need of more reflection on an organisational level in order to overcome the abovementioned challenges. More specifically, reflection amongst practitioners might enable the development of inside-out strategies of structural work, in which the position and role of the practitioners become a topic of discussion, particularly regarding the ways in which community sport practices might contribute to social inequality and exclusion of vulnerable young people.

Therefore, the practitioners argue that collective reflection and meaning-making is needed on an organisational level, especially because organisations are often consumed with the 'work of the day' and organisational-technical issues (e.g. which activities should be provided) or are only focused on success stories.

> We always have to talk about our successes, but there is a need to talk about the stories where we completely failed.
>
> (practitioner, man)

As such, the findings indicate that such reflection should become an inherent part of the organisation, next to the mere provision of sport activities. Furthermore, collectively reflecting upon the 'failures' of practitioners (without judging them) might help practitioners to develop structural strategies whilst still leaving space for experimenting with and changing such strategies based on the collective insights retrieved through reflection processes.

Network level

Throughout the chapter, we have referred to the ways in which instrumental and structural approaches seem to stand in a tense relationship with each other. As instrumental and individual approaches are often intertwined, this might create the idea that also structural and individual approaches are opposite to each other. However, our findings reveal that individual approaches (e.g. creating cross-cultural interactions, creating feelings of belonging to the broader neighbourhood, enhancing the positive recognition of participants and making participation sustainable) do not necessarily hinder establishing more structural approaches.

For example, practitioners in our research stressed that creating belonging (an objective often linked to social cohesion) did not only imply creating individual feelings of belonging with participants but also entailed a structural process that needed to be promoted externally, through the positive affirmations of community residents and societal institutions.

In fact, practitioners urge for the reconnection of individual and structural approaches through the collaboration of actors on a network level, especially given the fact that developing individual as well as structural approaches cannot be expected from the single practice of community sport. As one of the respondents in our study argued:

> We are dealing with complex problems that relate to anything and everything. We are convinced that external actors such as youth welfare workers and community workers can respond to this and answer these issues to a certain extent, through collaboration with multiple partners.
>
> (coordinator, man)

Collaboration on a network level with other practices is essential in this. We illustrate this on the basis of one example regarding the relationship between community sport and regular sport practices (e.g. classic sport club). A huge part of community sport's 'DNA' is built up around the fact that community sport provides an alternative approach to regular sport provisions (Crabbe 2009; Haudenhuyse et al. 2013). Community sport is, in certain situations, expected to 'getting target groups, especially socially vulnerable groups, to [regular] sport and exercise' (Van Poppel 2015: 8, own translation). However, our data show that community sport can provide outcomes for participants which regular sport cannot, revealing the unique potential of community sport on its own.

> Community sport has to be a solid and structural practice in society.... Community sport has to remain being a practice that lowers thresholds and that provides direct access. Because if participants dropout of regular sports, they will still need a place to go.
>
> (practitioner, man)

Therefore, practitioners urge that a more effective and stronger connection between community sport and regular sports might be found in a more reciprocal relationship wherein they could inspire and guide each other. As such, community sport would not merely become a 'light' version of regular sports, with the sole purpose of getting young people from community sport to regular sport, but would be able to inspire and guide regular practices towards higher accessibility and towards approaching the needs of vulnerable participants.

Policy level

Throughout this research, the findings reveal the challenges of practitioners in dealing with the pressure from local policy to conform to pre-structured and often individualised indicators. Such top-down influence, for example, portrays in what practitioners refer to as a 'marketisation of youth work'.

> In recent years, a marketisation of youth work has occurred wherein you have to work with a tender, which means that a job is written out for every organisation in the field to sign into. Often, the critical factors to decide who gets the job are pinpointed on who has the cheapest price. So the decision is 60% dependent on the price and 40% on the content. . . . Moreover, what I notice is that local governments want results right away.
>
> (coordinator, man, 33 years)

In contrast to these pre-structured and individualised indicators, our findings display how social cohesion takes a long time to establish, asks for shared efforts and, furthermore, demands the 'right' political willingness. Acknowledging this complexity on a policy level is essential in striving for a more structural approach in the practice of community sport.

A first step towards doing so, according to the practitioners, might be found in a better collaboration between practitioners and policymakers. More dialogue might provide opportunities for practitioners and policymakers to create shared insights, a common language, shared indicators of success, more suitable accountability strategies, etc. Moreover, this might prevent practitioners of shaping structural strategies under the radar of policymakers. Our research illustrates such underground strategies in the ways in which practitioners sell their programmes to policymakers by highlighting instrumental output (e.g. number of participants reached, duration of participation, performance rates and employment trajectories), whereas their core ambitions (e.g. enabling social change) remain unseen and underground.

> If I would have to convince a policy maker of the effectiveness of community sport, I would stress that community sport keeps socially vulnerable young people away from the streets, from exercising criminal activities, from exercising vandalism. I think, in a sense, we do such things although it is not the core of our practice.
>
> (practitioner, man, 30 years)

According to practitioners, another important step towards acknowledging this complexity can be found in tackling top-down models of funding. The complexity of social cohesion as described here suggests that social cohesion does not let itself be captured in the (often too) simplistic and linear logics of policy rationales or in pre-structured, individual-level indicators (e.g. number of participants reached, duration of participation, performance rates and employment trajectories) nor can social cohesion be traced back to the mere efforts of community sport. Instead, eradicating social vulnerability asks for an approach in which continuity is created, especially given the background of community sport participants who have often been sent 'from the cupboard to the wall'. This continuity, however, can be challenging in contexts where community sport projects receive a project-based and/or temporary funding (e.g. based on the term of legislature of a local government) of community sport projects.

> Sometimes the pressure is really high when working in a project-based way whilst there is not yet a relationship of trust with the participants. I really believe in the benefits of working in a project-based way, however you can't expect too much too soon, not from the participants and not from the practitioner, who has been dropped into the project for only three months.
> (coordinator, man, 33 years)

Also accountability strategies are often imposed upon community sport practices in a top-down way. Our data speak volumes on that.

> We need to increasingly account for what we are doing, why are you doing this? how many young people are you reaching? how much does this cost? We need difficult and hard evidence. If we want to organise certain projects we get questions: is that necessary? should we do that? Everything becomes questioned and we just hope we can keep up with it.
> (coordinator, woman, 45 years)

In order to give practitioners the possibility to work towards structural approaches within community sport, practitioners state that a shift from top-down strategies to bottom-up strategies of accountability is needed. Bottom-up strategies allow the creation of space, mandate and power for community sport practices to experiment with elements of the programme that are deemed valuable by community sport participants and practitioners first and foremost (e.g. unconditionality). Such bottom-up accountability strategy then becomes steered by the dialogue and negotiations between participants, practitioners and policymakers rather than a one-way stream of questions, expectations and regulations.

> How I see it, when a project is writing out bottom-up, the city needs to give it form on the basis of dialogue with young people themselves.
> (coordinator, man, 33 years)

Discussion

This chapter aimed to give insight into how community sport practices can enact structural strategies as a way to establish social cohesion and which conditions are facilitating to do so. The findings confirm the statement that social cohesion essentially is a complex, dynamic, relational and messy objective (Stead 2017). In comparison to other objectives, which have more clear-cut indicators for success, social cohesion has no terminus or endpoint. Following from this complexity is that a structural approach to social cohesion is a slow-burn process rather than a short-term realisation. In light of the facilitating conditions, the practitioners argued the necessity of 'collective reflection' and 'collaboration' on multiple levels (organisation, network and policy). We argue that developing community sport practices as 'fora for controversy and public debate' (Bouverne-De Bie et al. 2019) might provide a way to accommodate these conditions. At the heart of such a forum function lies the creation of dialogue and discussion. Creating fora is about debating 'the relation between the definition of the problem, the goals which are set and the methods to be used' and 'taking a stance towards societal developments, from a perspective of human dignity and social justice' (Bouverne-De Bie et al. 2019). Creating such a forum might provide an answer to the facilitating condition of 'collective reflection' and 'collaboration'.

Firstly, creating fora might provide a way to 'learn through reflection' and to develop a 'reflective practice' (Ruch 2005: 171). The idea of reflective practices suggests the process of systematically reflecting as a way to grasp practitioners' practical skills and intuitive or tacit knowledge. Especially in the context of Flanders, this is important given the background of many practitioners as 'experts by experience', meaning that community sport practitioners themselves come from socially vulnerable background and have not received professional training (Sabbe et al. 2019a). Such reflection can help practitioners to theorise their practice on the basis of their experiences and to act in relation to the formed theory (Ruch 2005). Learning through reflection allows for the creation of theory on the basis of knowledge that is relative, situated and uncertain (Ruch 2005). On the idea of 'learning through reflection', Vlaeminck (2005: 33) states:

> Theory and research do not necessarily have to precede practice. Oftentimes, theory is implicitly present and integrated in the practice. Every usable theory has to be adjusted in the practice due to the many unforeseen obstacles and insecurities. Such reflection upon a practice contributes to theory formation and the improvement of research and practice.

Secondly, creating fora means that community sport has a role in continuously debating the life circumstances of participants, in addressing the ways in which instrumental approaches are not sufficient to better these life circumstances and in developing alternative strategies. In that vein, we argue that the quest of scholars to install 'a socio-pedagogical shift' (Haudenhuyse et al. 2013: 480) requires that community sport practitioners consider themselves as social policy actors (De Corte and Roose 2018; Lorenz 2016) rather than executers of policy. In their role as social policy actors, community sport practitioners might be able to connect individual and structural approaches. De Corte and Roose (2018: 10) refer to such role as establishing 'linkages between their task of providing individual treatment to citizens and a more structural approach to realize broader social reforms'. Lorenz (2013, 2016) furthermore describes this social policy role as the renegotiation of the relationship between the private domain of autonomy and individual responsibility and the public domain of solidarity, equality and democracy.

An important condition for connecting individual and structural objectives, however, is that individual objectives become part of a structural and wholesale approach which implies striving for social change whilst simultaneously focusing on individual change (Lundy 2011). Creating such wholesale project (Lundy 2011) with strong individual and structural approaches asks for the involvement of external actors (i.e. regular sport clubs, policymakers, social partners and community residents) to collaborate with community sport. In other words, our research displays that the development of a 'socio-pedagogical shift' (Haudenhuyse et al. 2013: 480) should be called for as a collective endeavour and learning process rather than being put upon community sport as an exclusive task. After all, the social vulnerability of young people displays not only within the domain of sport but also within the labour market, education, health care, justice and social work.

Note

1 This chapter is based upon the doctoral dissertation Sabbe, S. (2019) *Community Sport and Social Cohesion: A Social Work Perspective*. Doctoral Dissertation, Ghent University: Faculty of Psychology and Educational Sciences.

References

Andrews, J.P. and Andrews, G.J. (2003) 'Life in secure unit: The rehabilitation of young people through the use of sport', *Social Science and Medicine*, 56(3), 531–550. DOI: 10.1016/S0277-9536(02)00053-9

Bailey, R. (2005) 'Evaluating the relationship between physical education, sport and social inclusion', *Educational Review*, 57(1), 71–90. DOI: 10.1080/0013191042000274196

Berger-Schmitt, R. (2000) *Social cohesion as an aspect of the quality of societies: Concept and measurement*, Manheim: Centre for Survey Research and Methodology.

Beutler, I. (2008) 'Sport serving development and peace: Achieving the goals of the United Nations through sport', *Sport in Society*, 11(4), 359–369. DOI: 10.1080/17430430802019227

Blackshaw, T. and Crabbe, T. (2004) *New perspectives on sport and 'deviance': Consumption, performativity and social control*, New York: Routledge.

Bouverne-De Bie, M., Coussée, F., Roose, R. and Bradt, L. (2019) 'Social pedagogy and social work', in F. Kessl, W. Lorenz, H. Otto and S. White (eds) *European social work: A compendium*, Berlin: Verlag Barbara Budrich.

Brown, K. (2017) *Vulnerability and young people: Care and control in policy and practice*, Bristol: Policy Press.

Chan, J., To, H.P. and Chan, E. (2006) 'Reconsidering social cohesion: Developing a definition and analytical framework for empirical research', *Social Indicators Research*, 75(2), 273–302. DOI: 10.1007/s11205-005-2118-1

Coakley, J. (2011) 'Youth sports: What counts as "positive development?"', *Journal of Sport and Social Issues*, 35(3), 306–324. DOI: 10.1177/0193723511417311

Coalter, F. (2006) *Sport-in-development: A monitoring and evaluation manual*, London: UK Sport.

Coalter, F. (2007) *A wider social role for sport: Who's keeping the score?*, London: Routledge.

Council of Europe (2001) *Promoting the policy debate on social cohesion from a comparative perspective*, Report No. 1, Germany: Council of Europe.

Crabbe, T. (2009) 'Getting to know you: Using sport to engage and build relationships with socially marginalised youth', in: R. Levermore and A. Beacom (eds) *Sport and international development*, Houndmills: Palgrave Macmillan, pp. 176–197.

Craig, G. (2007) 'Community capacity building: Something old, something new. . . ?', *Critical Social Policy*, 27(3), 335–359. DOI: 10.1177/0261018307078846

Darnell, S.C., Chawansky, M., Marchesseault, D., Holmes, M. and Hayhurst, L. (2016) 'The state of play: Critical sociological insights into recent "sport for development and peace" research', *International Review for the Sociology of Sport*, 53(2), 133–151. DOI: 10.1177/1012690216646762

De Corte, J. and Roose, R. (2018) 'Social Work as a policy actor: Understanding social policy as an open-ended democratic practice', *European Journal of Social Work*, 23(2), 227–238. DOI: 10.1080/13691457.2018.1462768

Ekholm, D. (2016) *Sport as a means of responding to social problems: Rationales of government, welfare and social change*, Doctoral dissertation, Linköping University, Linköping.

Forde, C. and Lynch, D. (2015) *Social work and community development*, London: Palgrave Macmillan.

Fret, L. (2007) 'Als zorg commercie wordt [When care becomes commerce]', *Alert*, 33(3), 5–8.

Hartmann, D. (2003) 'Theorizing sport as social intervention: A view from the grassroots', *Quest*, 55(2), 118–140. DOI: 10.1080/00336297.2003.10491795

Hartmann, D. and Kwauk, C. (2011) 'Sport and development: An overview, critique, and reconstruction', *Journal of Sport and Social Issues*, 35(3), 284–305. DOI: 10.1177/0193723511416986

Haudenhuyse, R. (2012) *The potential of sports for socially vulnerable youth*, Published doctoral dissertation, VUBPress, Brussels.

Haudenhuyse, R., Theeboom, M. and Nols, Z. (2013) 'Sport-based interventions for socially vulnerable youth: Towards well- defined interventions with easy-to-follow outcomes?', *International Review for the Sociology of Sport*, 48(4), 471–484. DOI: 10.1177/1012690212448002

Hylton, K. and Totten, M. (2008) 'Community sports development', in: K. Hylton (ed) *Sports development: Policy, process and practice*, London: Routledge, pp. 77–117.

International Federation of Social Workers (IFSW) (2014) *Global definition of social work*. Available HTTP: www.ifsw.org/global-definition-of-social-work/ (accessed 9 March 2019).

Jordan, B. (2013) 'Associations, communities and nations: The solidarities and services sustaining human capabilities', in: H. Otto and H. Ziegler (eds) *Enhancing capabilities: The role of social institutions*, Opladen: Barbara Budrich Publishers, pp. 171–178.

Kearns, A. and Forrest, R. (2000) 'Social cohesion and multilevel governance', *Urban Studies*, 37(5–6), 995–1017. DOI: 10.1177/0042098012444890

Kelly, L. (2011) 'Social inclusion through sports-based Interventions?', *Critical Social Policy*, 31(1), 126–150. DOI: 10.1177/0261018310385442

Kessl, F. (2009) 'Critical reflexivity, social work, and the emerging European post-welfare states', *European Journal of Social Work*, 12(3), 305–317. DOI: 10.1080/13691450902930746

Levitas, R., Pantazis, C., Fahmy, E., Gordon, D., Lloyd, E. and Patsios, D. (2007) *The multi-dimensional analysis of social exclusion*, Bristol: University of Bristol.

Lorenz, W. (2013) 'Recognising the face of the other: Difference, identity and community', *International Journal of Social Welfare*, 22(3), 279–286. DOI: 10.1111/ijsw.12027

Lorenz, W. (2016) 'Rediscovering the social question', *European Journal of Social Work*, 19(1), 4–17. DOI: 10.1080/13691457.2015.1082984

Lundy, C. (2011) *Social work, social justice and human rights: A structural approach to practice*, 2nd edn, New York: University of Toronto Press.

Morel, N., Palier, B. and Palme, J. (2012) *Towards a social investment welfare state? Ideas, policies and challenges*, London: The Policy Press.

Nols, Z. (2018) *Social change through sport for development initiatives: A critical pedagogical perspective*, Published doctoral dissertation, VUBPress, Brussels.

Novy, A., Swiatek, D.C. and Moulaert, F. (2012) 'Social cohesion: A conceptual and political elucidation', *Urban Studies*, 49(9), 1873–1889. DOI: 10.1177/0042098012444878

Oosterlynck, S., Schuermans, N. and Loopmans, M. (2017) *Place, diversity and solidarity*, London: Routledge.

Roose, R., Roets, G., Schiettecat, T., Pannecoucke, B., Piessens, A., Van Gils, J., Op de Beeck, H., Vandenhole, W., Driessens, K., Desair, K. et al. (2016) 'Social work research as a practice of transparency', *European Journal of Social Work*, 19(6), 1021–1034. DOI: 10.1080/13691457.2015.1051950

Ruch, G. (2005) "'Self-ish' spaces: Reflective practice and reflexivity in contemporary child care social work practice and research in the U.K', in: L.M. Stoneham (ed) *Advances in sociology research*, vol. 2, New York: Nova Science Publishers, pp. 165–192. DOI: 10.1111/j.1365-2206.2005.00359.x

Sabbe, S., Bradt, L., Spaaij, R. and Roose, R. (2018) 'Community sport and social cohesion: In search of the practical understandings of community sport practitioners in Flanders', *Community Development Journal*, 55(2), 258–276. DOI: 10.1093/cdj/bsy046

Sabbe, S., Bradt, L., Spaaij, R. and Roose, R. (2019a) '"We'd like to eat bread too, not grass": Exploring the structural approaches of community sport practitioners in Flanders', *European Journal of Social Work*, 24(1), 162–174. DOI: 10.1080/13691457.2019.1618792

Sabbe, S., Roose, R. and Bradt, L. (2019b) 'Tipping the balance back towards emancipation: Exploring the positions of Flemish community sport practitioners towards social control', *Sport in Society*, 22(6), 950–965. DOI: 10.1080/17430437.2019.1565384

Schulenkorf, N. (2010) 'Towards sustainable community development through sport and events: A conceptual framework for sport-for-development projects', *Sport Management Review*, 15(1), 1–12. DOI: 10.1016/j.smr.2011.06.001

Spaaij, R. (2009) 'Sport as a vehicle for social mobility and regulation of disadvantaged urban youth', *International Review for the Sociology of Sport*, 44(2–3), 247–264. DOI: 10.1177/1012690209338415

Spaaij, R., Magee, J. and Jeanes, R. (2013) 'Urban youth, worklessness and sport: A comparison of sports-based employability programs in Rotterdam and Stoke-on-Trent', *Urban Studies*, 50(8), 1608–1624. DOI: 10.1177/0042098012465132

Stead, V. (2017) 'Doing "social cohesion": Cultural policy and practice in outer metropolitan Melbourne', *Critical Social Policy*, 37(3), 1–20. DOI: 10.1177/0261018316681283

Van Poppel, M. (2015) *Benchmark Buurtsport: Buurtsport in Vlaanderen anno 2014* [*Benchmark community sport: Community sport in Flanders in the year 2014*], Belgium: Flemish Institute of Sport Management and Recreation Policy.

Veit-Wilson, J. (1998) *Setting adequacy standards*, Bristol: Policy Press.

Vettenburg, N. (1998) 'Juvenile delinquency and the cultural characteristics of the family', *International Journal of Adolescent Medicine and Health*, 10(3), 193–210. DOI: 10.1515/ijamh.1998.10.3.193

Vlaeminck, H. (2005) *Het Gebruik van Casuïstiek in het Sociaal Werk* [*The use of casuistry in social work*], Gent: Academia Press.

Part 3

Broader perspectives on community sport and social inclusion

6 The evolution of evaluation

From the black box to programme theory

Fred Coalter

Introduction

Scriven (1994) provides a useful broad framework for understanding the development of and the variety of approaches to evaluation. This outlines three main approaches – black box, grey box and white box evaluations – which can also be viewed in chronological terms.

From the black box perspective, a programme is regarded as an undifferentiated unit – i.e. a black box – about whose components nothing is known (Rossi and Wright 1984). Astbury and Leeuw (2010: 364) state that 'when evaluators talk about the black box "problem" they are usually referring to the practice of viewing social programs primarily in terms of effects, with little attention paid to how those effects were produced'. This approach dominated the 'Golden Age' of evaluation (Rossi and Wright 1984) in the 1960s and early 1970s in the USA. During this period, widespread and federally mandated evaluation was undertaken of the social programmes in the War on Poverty-Great Society initiatives, with evaluation dominated by the randomised, controlled experimental paradigm (Rossi and Wright 1984). The key limitation of such an approach was that it 'could not explain why programmes worked or failed' (Weiss 1987: 44). As we will see, this funder-favoured outcome measuring 'black box' approach is still prevalent in sport for development (SfD).

In *grey box evaluations*, 'one can simply discern the components, although not their principles of operation' (Scriven 1994: 5). This is broadly similar to descriptive logic models, which describe the contents – the inputs, outputs and outcomes – of programmes but do not fully reveal the *principles of the operation* of the programme.

White box evaluations are 'rarely possible although frequently assumed to be an essential part of evaluation' (Scriven 1994: 77). This goes beyond the descriptive grey box approach and refers to a theory of change perspective, which seeks to identify the processes and inner workings, connections and operations of programme components. Such an approach seeks to explore the mechanisms via which the programme achieves its outcomes. There are a number of approaches in this perspective and we will outline these later in the chapter.

DOI: 10.4324/9780429340635-9

The black box

We have noted that Rossi and Wright (1984) refer to the 1960s and early 1970s in the USA as the 'Golden Age' of evaluation. This was related to the increasing complexity of national and local government, the widespread expansion of social programmes and the desire to assess their efficiency and effectiveness (Rossi et al. 2004). The predominant methodology was strongly influenced by federal government's emphasis on a planning-programming-budgeting approach and an emphasis on cost-benefit analysis (Weiss 1972). This resulted in an evaluation methodology dominated by a randomised controlled experimental approach. That this was a 'black box' approach is indicated by Weiss' (1987: 44) comment that although evaluations could measure limited outcomes and

> which people benefitted, and which categories did not. They were not well equipped to tell how programs managed to make an impact on people's lives or what factors prevented them from doing so. They could not explain why programs worked or failed.

This limitation was significant because 'the key lesson from the Golden Age is that the expected effects of social programs hover near zero' (Rossi and Wright 1984: 331). In this regard, Weiss (1987: 41) states that 'the news was dismaying. Nothing seemed to be working as expected. . . . Those of us engaged in evaluation research in the 1960s and 1970s were dismayed by the results. We seemed to be messengers of doom and gloom'. Weiss (1987) outlines several factors which explain such negative outcomes.

One of the most obvious weaknesses was *methodological* – control groups were not always randomly assigned. The comparison groups that served as controls were often more privileged than the programme participants, which therefore made programme impacts look weaker than they were. More generally Rossi and Wright (1984: 335) argue that 'randomised controlled experiments could only be done correctly under very limited circumstances and the demand for evaluation covered many programs that simply could not be assessed in this way'. Pawson (2006: 511–512) offers a more fundamental critique of the use of control groups:

> This is not the world at repose. There is no vacuum, because there is no such thing as a policy vacuum. Control groups or control areas are in fact kept very busy. All things already going on in a locality and everything happening simultaneously to an individual constitute 'the control'. So, it too will be crammed with other, concurrent policies and programmes, pounded by previous policies and programmes, stuffed with stakeholder interests, and surrounded by a full repertoire of contextual constraints. All is on the move, but under a different and unknown combination of forces in a different and unknown state of development.

The second issue was that measured outcomes were *politically imposed aspirations*. The original 'great expectations of Washington' were grandiose and unrealistic. Evaluations using these expectations as criteria against which programmes would be judged were using a yardstick that almost guaranteed failure. This reflects Pawson's (2004) comment that much social policy can be characterised as 'ill-defined interventions with hard-to-follow outcomes' and, as we will see, this remains an issue in SfD.

The implicit models of behaviour embedded in the evaluation were *simplistic and inadequate*. The variables included tended to be characteristics of the individual and one or two attributes of the programme (sometimes only one variable noting whether the respondent participated in the programme). Missing were all the variables of social context. As Weiss (1987: 43) argues 'to judge by the statistical models employed, evaluation studies tended to assume that the program itself would be powerful enough to cancel out all contrary influences in participants' lives'. Chen and Rossi (1989: 301) argue that

> black-box evaluations regard everything that occurs between random assignment and measurement of outcomes to be the treatment. It is this lumping together of a program and its delivery system that is the focus of one of the major criticisms of such evaluations.

More generally Pawson (2006: 52) argues that:

> In line with the fundamental assumption that the intervention itself is the causal agent, every attempt is made to neutralise the effects of human volition. . . . However, social programmes are active and not passive. . . . Human intentionality is not a confounding influence but the very medium through which such interventions work.

Although the evaluations could measure limited outcomes and which people benefitted and which categories did not, they were not well equipped to explain how programmes managed to make an impact on people's lives or what factors prevented them from doing so. They could not explain why programmes worked or failed. Chen and Rossi (1989: 301) refer to such approaches as 'atheoretical experimentation'.

In many cases, evaluations suggested that a reason for the paucity of programme results was that programmes were not well or consistently implemented. This raises the issue of *a lack of understanding of implementation theory* (Weiss 1995) – assumptions about how the programme had to be implemented to maximise effectiveness (we address this issue later in the chapter).

We now turn to an examination of the influence of the black box perspective on SfD.

Sport for development and the black box

Despite the clear limitations of the 'black box' approach, this perspective is common in SfD. Spaaij and Schaillee (2020: 1–2) state that 'research has long treated SfD as a black box, with little consideration of the (families of) mechanisms that might produce desired outcomes.' Reflecting this, Jones et al. (2017) in an integrative review of 185 articles on sport-based youth development literature found that a majority of articles (53 per cent) treated sport participation as a binary variable (i.e. youth play or do not play sport), with far less attention to the basic issues associated with participation, such as frequency (24 per cent), duration (18 per cent) or competition level (2 per cent). A majority of articles treated sport as a singular variable (49 per cent) rather than categorising by specific sports (31 per cent) or sport type (i.e. team versus individual) (20 per cent). Further, only 18 per cent outlined the logic or rationale for the programme and only 22 per cent provided a brief description of the sports programme (more than a sentence).

Jones et al. (2017: 2) argue that 'empirical research examining youth development through sport has been continuously critiqued for remaining outcome-oriented and focused almost exclusively on the individual'. This was also reflected in Schulenkorf, Sherry and Rowe's (2016: 30) integrated literature review of 437 articles in which 'two hundred twenty-five articles discussed sport as a concept, rather than specific sport activities'.

Lubans et al. (2012: 11), in a systematic review of 15 studies on the impact of physical activity programmes on social and emotional well-being in at-risk youth, concluded that 'knowledge regarding the mechanisms responsible for the effects of physical activity programmes on psychological well-being is limited'. Hermens et al. (2017: 14) in a review of 18 research articles on life skill development for vulnerable youth found little information regarding 'which elements of existing frameworks are conducive to life skill development in sports programs'. The review 'showed that sports programs serving socially vulnerable youth are settings in which socially vulnerable youth can develop life skills' but that 'as only five of the included studies investigated conditions that may be conducive to life skill development in the sports program, it is not possible to draw firm conclusions' about conducive conditions for life skill development (Hermens et al. 2017: 13).

On this basis, Jones et al. (2017: 14) raise a fundamental question about the limitations of much descriptive outcome-based research and the lack of analysis of process – 'without this information it is unclear if the evaluative criteria used by the researchers matched the programme model, or if the constructs being measured were an intended or unintended consequence of participation'.

Reflecting Weiss's analysis of the black box approach and Washington's 'grandiose and unrealistic' expectations, Harris and Adams (2015) suggest that many problems with which sport is charged with 'fixing' are poorly defined, lack clarity and are resistant to clear and agreed solutions. Such a situation can be explained by two factors. Firstly, SfD is characterised by an evangelism about the 'power of sport' both in policy rhetoric and among highly committed practitioners. For example, Coakley (2011: 307) argues that 'sport-related decisions and policies remain shaped primarily by unquestioned beliefs grounded in wishful thinking' and Kruse (2006: 8) refers to strong beliefs 'based on intuitive certainty . . . that there is a positive link between sport and development'. Among those who adopt an evangelical perspective – an intuitive faith in SfD – evidence is often required simply to confirm their beliefs. For example, Johan Koss, president of Right to Play, at a Next Step Conference in 2003 stated: 'We do not evaluate enough and so we invite people to do research into things like sport and development, sport and peace. We need to prove what we say that we do' (van Kampen 2003: 15). A further example is provided by a UNICEF report (2006: 4) which argued strongly for the need for more M&E but also referred to 'a shared *belief* [emphasis added] in the power of sport-for-development [and] a shared determination to find ways to document and objectively verify the positive impact of sport'. In this regard, Schulenkorf et al. (2016: 34) suggest that 'studies on the impact of SDP [Sport for Development and Peace] come as no surprise given the interest and need for organisers and communities to justify their programs' worth'. Such perspectives reduce the role of science to confirming what we already think that we know to be the case (Emler 2001) and view sport as a black or magic box, which produces measurable outcomes.

Secondly, the inflated promises made for SfD can be viewed as an area-specific example of a more general phenomenon in which the formulation of ambitious, wide-ranging, vague and ill-defined claims are a function of the processes of lobbying, persuasion, negotiation, alliance building and pragmatic opportunism that are part of all policy processes. However, this is greatly exaggerated in the marginal policy area of SfD. Weiss (1993: 96) emphasises the essentially political nature of much policy formulation, resource bidding and programme development arguing that:

> Because of the political processes of persuasion and negotiation that are required to get a program enacted, inflated promises are made in the guise of program goals. Furthermore, the goals often lack the clarity and intellectual coherence that evaluation criteria should have. . . . Holders of diverse values and different interests have to be won over, and in the process a host of realistic and unrealistic goal commitments are made.

The political and interest-based nature of policy making, the associated requirement for accountability and the clear limitations of the black box approach partly explain the rise in the use of logic models as a basis for programme design, evaluation and, most of all, accountability in the 1970s.

Logic models

Logic models are Scriven's (1994) grey box in which there is a graphical presentation of the components of a programme and the chronology of their appearance and implementation, with a basic structure of inputs, outputs and outcomes.

Clark and Anderson (2004: 7) argue that logic models were 'the first widespread attempt to depict program components so that activities matched outcomes'. Further, because of its graphical nature it enables all stakeholders to have a mental picture of what is going to happen (Wells and Arthur-Banning 2008). The approach began to be used widely in the 1970s, emerging from business and logistics planning. Gasper (2000: 21) argues that the approach was based on 'assumptions of relatively well-understood and controllable change, engineered via a "project" within or largely controlled by a single organisation. It centres attention on outputs and service delivery and on the achievement of intended effects by intended routes'.

Logic models provided a graphical illustration of programme components which helped all stakeholders to identify the nature of inputs, outputs/activities and presumed outcomes. Logic models have the following characteristics:

- They are output-led and describe core components of a programme and ILLUSTRATE *assumed* connections between each component.
- They provide a *descriptive framework* for planning, resource allocation, implementation, management and M&E (W.K. Kellogg Foundation 2004).
- They help to guide programme implementation. Wells and Arthur-Banning (2008: 195) suggest that 'during program implementation, logic models will help administrators and managers to maintain their focus and energy'.
- They establish targets, milestones and *necessary conditions*. For example, how many participants are recruited and retained, how many sessions were delivered and how many graduates achieved what outcomes?
- They identify where to monitor and assess the *implementation* of a programme.
- They provide the basis for *summative evaluation* (i.e. measuring the final outcomes or impacts of the programme).
- Perhaps most importantly, they provide a basis for accountability, as it indicates when and if promised actions were undertaken. For example, Gasper (2000: 22) suggests that 'distant busy funders and supervisors typically prefer a clear-cut simple description of a project. They consider it something definite against which recipients of public resources can be held accountable'.

Gugiu and Rodriguez-Campos (2007: 340) summarise logic models as follows:

> The purpose of a logic model is to provide stakeholders with a visual map or narrative description of how specific program components are related to the program's desired results. . . . Logic models serve numerous functions, including assisting evaluators to focus the evaluation on the principal elements of the program, providing staff and other stakeholders with a common understanding of program services and goals, identifying a set of performance indicators that may be used to develop a monitoring system and summarizing performance for funders and decision makers.

However, Gasper (2000: 21–22) identifies three types of sub-optimal log frames. Firstly, he refers to a 'logic-less frame' which is used only because external funders demand it and so it is then invented after a project is designed rather than used to guide the design by promoting logical thinking about the links from one level to the next higher one and about the role of external factors in affecting these connections. It is used to accommodate a pre-existing design. This is broadly similar to the Astbury and Leeuw's (2010: 375) critique that laying out the components of a programme and ordering them into some logical sequence amounts to little more than dissecting the 'operational logic' (i.e. how it is delivered) but not the 'conceptual logic' (i.e. an explanatory theory of a programme).

Secondly, there is a 'lack-frame' which is too simple, even for simple project designs. Not everything important can be captured. Finally, there is a 'lock-frame', which is one that tends to be fixed and not updated and is reduced to a 'box-ticking exercise' that reduces critical analysis and over-simplifies projects (Astbury and Leeuw 2010).

More generally, there have been substantial criticisms of the limitations of logic models.

Limitations of log frames

A logic model starts with *means* (i.e. what is done) and not ends (outcomes). It describes what the programme does and the nature of the outcomes which are *presumed*. It simply assumes that outcomes will follow from activities. Lee (2011) argues that means to ends thinking is designed to justify the specified means and that logic models are usually done for the sole purpose of justifying the funding of a programme or project – Gasper's (2000) logic-less frame. Consequently, logic models do not challenge managers to think broadly and creatively about their programmes. Lee (2011) therefore argues that logic models are not action oriented. They are depictions of a theory of how something is *supposed* to work. It is unlikely that they will generate ideas for improvement, because logic models are not designed to come up with new ideas and as such are very limited as tools for continuous improvement.

Descriptive logic models are based on *unexplained/assumed casual relationships* – especially regarding the causal relationships between outputs and outcomes. They do not capture the quality or detailed content of a programme (i.e. the *components/mechanisms/experiences* that lead to change). They do not explain *how* and *why* such outputs/activities are effective in achieving the desired outcomes. A logic model depicts *assumed* causal connections, not direct cause–effect relationships. These are simply working assumptions and it presents the operational logic and not the conceptual logic. Astbury and Leeuw (2010: 367) argue that 'a common mistake is for evaluators to conflate the term *mechanism* with programme activity. Mechanisms appear too frequently as unexplained "causal arrows"'.

Although logic models may provide a simplicity which has advantages for planning, monitoring and accountability, they tend to represent interventions as linear and relatively mechanistic and overplay the predictability of an intervention. For example, they tend to give the impression of steady change over time, whereas change may occur in jumps at certain points or problems may initially get worse before they get better (Public Health England no date). As Lee (2011: 2) argues:

> Logic models are built on the belief that the world is a place of clear causal relationships. . . . In the logic model world one thing leads to another in predictable or highly probable ways that can be written down in the form of a flow chart. . . . Logic models are incapable of representing the real world of uncertain causal relationships.

Power (1997: 288) suggests that the increased use of logic models was part of 'the audit explosion . . . the spread of a distinct mentality of administrative control'. Reflecting this, Gasper (2000: 126) argues that 'accountability considerations predominate . . . above learning considerations'. Therefore, this risks the use of logic models becoming a 'box-ticking exercise' that reduces critical analysis and oversimplifies projects (Astbury and Leeuw 2010).

One of the most frequent criticisms of logic models relates not to their analytical utility but to their frequent imposition by funders. Gasper (2000: 22) argues that

> Log frames are often only used when demanded by an external authority, because they require a high degree of consensus about what is feasible and valuable. When this consensus is missing then only the pressure of a dominant authority, the controller of funds may lead to it being declared.

Therefore log frames often reflect differential power relationships and 'accountability considerations predominate in ex post facto evaluation above learning considerations' (Gasper 2000: 26).

Sport for development and logic models

The logical framework/logic model approach was introduced in the 1990s by major development agencies including the UK Department for International Development and the US Agency for International Development, with the intention of promoting 'a very different view of development, where the focus was no longer on the aid agency but on the poor' (Kay 2012: 898). In his review of 15 SfD programmes, Levermore (2011: 341) concluded that the 'positivist logical framework ('log frame') approach' dominates contemporary development evaluation. He suggests that the logic model provides a methodology that 'aims to highlight a clear linkage between how far each component of the programme (such as inputs, outputs, immediate and wider objectives, risks/assumptions involved) assists in contributing to its objectives', with mainly outcome-oriented quantitative data collected, especially via surveys.

However, Kay (2011) emphasises the additional burden that such M&E requirements often place on SfD organisations and argues that the use of logic models has been regarded as problematic within international development. Kay (2012: 898) quotes Robb (2004) who argues that 'the log frame also emerged as the ideal instrument of control exemplifying systems that are too bureaucratic and upward-focused, predominantly reflect donor information needs and have little value to local users'. She also quotes Jassey's (2004) comment that 'its matrix acts more like a strait jacket than a useful development tool' – reflecting Astbury and Leeuw's (2010) contention that logic models risk becoming a 'box-ticking exercise' which reduces critical analysis and over-simplifies projects.

Kay (2012: 892) further illustrates these concerns by quoting Win's (2004) concerns about the constraining nature of imposed of logic models:

> We have to fit our visions, our way of thinking, into your template. Gone are our free expression, our long paragraphs and our way of seeing and interpreting our reality. We are now forced to express ourselves in a way that you understand and want.

This also reflects Lee's (2011) contention that logic models are (sometimes deliberately) intimidating to make some people look smarter than other people. Also, special interests or funders do not want logic model approaches questioned, as accountability is more central than learning (Gasper 2000). The result of this is often an imbalance between accountability and learning and programme development, with M&E being 'an imposition rather than a critical element of professional development' (Levermore 2011: 351).

We have already noted Jones et al.'s (2017: 14) concern about the limitations of much descriptive outcome-based research and the lack of analysis of process making the status of measured outcomes unclear. Because of this there is a need to 'connect individual outcomes with specific programme processes'.

Further, Whitley et al. (2018: 9), in a systematic review of 70 research studies in SfD, recommended that:

> organisations and researchers ... outline, adopt, and test intervention theories (i.e., programme theories), rather than focusing predominantly on intervention outcomes and benchmarks. The use of intervention theories (e.g. theories of change) was not common in this systematic review.

This brings us to the third element of Scriven's typology – the white box or theory-based evaluation (TBE).

Theory-driven evaluation

The perspectives included in this broad category seek to go beyond the black box view of programmes as undifferentiated units and the grey box logic model approach in which 'mechanisms appear too frequently as unexplained "causal arrows"' (Astbury and Leeuw 2010: 367).

Despite a variety of approaches and terminologies, the common aim of all perspectives is to identify the processes and inner workings, interconnections and operations of programme components and to explore the mechanisms via which the programme achieves its outcomes. They all seek to identify the theory of change or programme theory (i.e. the set of assumptions underpinning a programme about how it works and use it as a basis for evaluation). Chen and Rossi (1987: 102) argue that 'the theory-driven approach avoids the pitfalls of black-box evaluation and provides better understanding of the causal mechanisms underlying the relationship between treatment and effects'. This approach involves 'identifying the causal processes that theoretically intervene between program treatment and outcome'. (Chen 1990: 191). The Center for Theory of Change (no date) defines a theory of change as follows:

> A comprehensive description, illustration, and explanation of *how* and *why* a desired change is expected to happen in a particular context. It maps out what a programme does (its activities or interventions), the nature of such activities and *how* these lead to desired outcomes being achieved.

Weiss (1995), a key theorist of the theory of change perspective, outlines an approach which initially seems to combine and supplement elements of a logic model approach. Weiss (1995) makes a distinction between an implementation theory and programme theory (her definition of a theory of change combines both elements) (this is broadly similar to Astbury and Leeuw's (2010) distinction between 'operational logic' and 'conceptual logic'). Weiss (1998: 58) defines the implementation theory as:

> a theory about what is required to translate objectives into ongoing service delivery and program operation. The assumption is that that if the activities are conducted as planned, with sufficient quality, intensity and fidelity to plan, the desired results will be forthcoming.

This is like a theoretically informed logic model. However, the distinction between implementation theory and programme theory is necessary to counteract the crude oversimplification that assumes that *interventions* as outlined in the implementation theory change behaviour (the black box fallacy). Weiss (1998: 57) defines programme theory as 'the mechanisms that mediate between the delivery (and receipt) of the program and the emergence of the outcomes of interest'. This relates to the *processes that mediate* between programme components and the achievement of programme goals – these processes are largely cognitive and relate to participants' attitudes and behaviour in reaction to the resources and choices offered by the programme activities. She states that 'each stage of activity assumes an appropriate response from participants and the responses of participants condition the next stages of the program'. (Weiss 1998: 58). Consequently, for Weiss (1997: 460) 'the mechanism of change is not the program activities per se, but the response that the activities generate'. For Weiss (1997: 506)

> Implementation theory is useful when the purpose is ongoing feedback to program staff about how the intervention is operating. When the purpose is understanding how program effects are (or are not) being realised, the evaluation has to follow the logic of program theory.

Chen (1990: 43) uses a similar division between 'normative/prescriptive theory' and 'causative theory'. Normative theory provides theoretical guidance on how to design and implement a programme – what kinds of goals the programme should pursue, what kinds of interventions are required and what kinds of implementation procedures and processes are required. Causative theory specifies how the programme works and addresses issues such as what intervening and contextual factors could mediate the relationship between the treatment and the outcome. What kind of relationships exist between the treatment and outcomes? What kinds of intervening factors could be mediating the effects of the treatment on the outcome variables?

Such diverse questions and the emphasis on theoretical explanations means that theory-driven evaluation marks a shift from a debate about methods and methods-driven approaches to a theory-driven orientation in which no method is the 'gold standard' (Stame 2004).

Constructing a programme theory

Lipsey and Pollard (1989) state that programme theory can be developed from three distinct sources: (1) prior theory and research in the academic social sciences; (2) exploratory research directed towards discovering the underlying causal mechanisms of a programme. As Scriven's and others (e.g. Blamey and Mackenzie 2007) note, this is the least likely approach as it 'takes more time, money and effort than other modes of evaluation' (Weiss 1997: 511; Chen 1990). (3) Extraction of the stakeholders' implicit programme theory via in-depth dialogue.

Whilst all approaches use a mixture of (1) and (3), the relative emphasis varies between different researchers. For example, Weiss (1997: 503) who defines theory 'as a set of beliefs or assumptions that underlie action' tends to prioritise (3) – developing and prioritising the theoretical underpinnings held by programme designers and implementers. Weiss adopts such an approach partly because it is viewed as developmental and capacity building for designers and practitioners as 'by asking them to make their assumptions explicit it encourages them to think harder and deeper about the programs they design' (Weiss 1997: 517).

Unlike means-driven logic models, a theory of change starts with the ends (desired outcomes or impacts) of a programme and undertakes 'reverse mapping' as it works backwards to develop appropriate means (i.e. it bases activities on the desired outcomes or impacts and identifies rationales for and the chronology of activities and associated interim and final outcomes).

Chen (1990) and Chen and Rossi (1983) use a combination of (1) and (3) but give the evaluator a predominant 'educator' role (this approach is illustrated in Chapter 4). They are sceptical of the 'stakeholder approach' (3) because of vested interests and key stakeholders' perspectives and views which may overly emphasise the desirability rather than the plausibility of the programme. Chen and Rossi (1980: 110) argue that:

> It often happens that the administrators pick goals more on the basis of desirability or hope than possibility or understanding. Accordingly, official-goal-fixed approach evaluators who use administrators' statements of program goals as the limits within which to search for measurable effect variables may be on the wrong track in the first place.

Also the widespread absence of social science inputs to policy formulation means that 'conventional evaluation paradigms that accept program goal and treatment conceptions that derive from policymaker and administrator definitions are thus hitched to conventional, common-sense notions that may be quite wide of the mark' (Chen and Rossi 1980: 110).

Consequently, they propose a 'social science' approach in which 'the evaluator should use his (sic) own training, experience and expertise not only to help the stakeholders specify their theory, but also draw the attention of the stakeholders to the alternative ways of formulating theory' (Chen and Rossi 1989: 305) (this approach is illustrated in Chapters 3 and 4). Chen and Rossi (1980: 111) emphasise the value of objectivity and argue that:

> in our suggested approach, the evaluator should actively search for and construct a theoretically justified model of the social problem in order to understand and capture what a program really can do for a social problem – social science knowledge and theory become crucial in the evaluation process.

Consequently, 'program theory formulated from the perspective and understanding of both stakeholders and evaluators may enhance the sensitivity and usefulness of the evaluation' (Chen and Rossi 1989: 305) (this approach is illustrated in Chapter 4).

In terms of M&E, such perspectives shift evaluation from the outcome-oriented summative approaches of the black box and logic models to a formative approach. Firstly, Weiss (1997: 510) argues that the theory-based approach 'aims to surface the theoretical underpinnings of a program in advance and use the theories to help structure the evaluation'. Secondly, 'TBE [theory-based evaluation] aims to describe the actual mechanisms that are related to good outcomes'. Consequently, Weiss (1997: 501–502) argues that

> this approach ... offers a way in which evaluation can tell not only how much change has occurred, but also, if the sequence of steps appears as expected, how the change has occurred. If the posited sequence breaks down along the way, the evaluation can tell at what point the breakdown occurred.

For Weiss (1997: 514), the difference between TBE and the randomised controlled experimental approach is that:

> TBE can track the unfolding of events, step-by-step and this make causal attribution on the basis of demonstrated links. If this were so, evaluation would not need randomised control groups to justify its claims about causality.

Connell and Kubisch (1998: 3), of the Aspen Institute, a leading exponent of the theory of change approach, outlined three attributes of a good theory of change that stakeholders should confirm are present before committing to an evaluation:

> 1) It should be plausible. Do evidence and common sense suggest that the activities, if implemented, will lead to desired outcomes? 2) It should be doable. Will the economic, technical, political, institutional, and human resources be available to carry out the initiative? 3) It should be testable. Is the theory of change specific and complete enough for an evaluator to track its progress in credible and useful ways?.

Weiss (1995) outlines four major benefits of TBE: (1) It asks programme practitioners to make their assumptions explicit and to reach consensus with their colleagues about what they are trying to do and why. (2) It concentrates evaluation, attention and resources on key aspects of the programme. (3) As it concentrates on key mechanisms, it facilitates aggregation of evaluation results into a broader base of theoretical and programme knowledge. (4) Evaluations that address (and articulate) the theoretical assumptions embedded in programmes may have more influence on both policy and popular opinion. Weiss (1997) argues that policymakers 'like stories' and a theory of change is a story.

Learning and generalisation

One of the criticisms of traditional approaches to evaluation is that each programme is regarded as unique and evaluated in its own terms. With no analysis of process and mechanisms, it is not possible to generalise from the evaluation. For theory-driven analysis, mechanisms are the key to generalisability. For example, Weiss (1997: 510–511) argues that

> knowing the mechanism that works is even more important for other sites that want to adopt the successful program. It might not be possible for others to replicate all aspects of the programme, but when they know the essential levers, they can make the adaptation without fear of losing the key components that make the program effective.

As we will see, this emphasis on mechanisms, and their probably generic nature, as the basis for policy learning and generalisation is also central to the realist approach to evaluation.

Realist evaluation

Although this perspective is part of the broad theory-driven perspective, it differs from the theory of change perspective for three reasons: (1) it has a distinct epistemology, (2) its attitude to the role of theory and (3) it has a systematic framework of analysis. The framework is known as the context-mechanism-outcome (CMO) hypothesis, which provides the main structure for realist analysis. Within this framework 'the evaluator hypothesises in advance the mechanisms that are likely to operate, the contexts in which they might operate and the outcomes that will be observed if they operate as expected' (Westhorp 2014: 6). Consequently, the realist research question is not simply what works but w*hat works, for whom, in what respects, to what extent, in which context and how?* So, realism is not a research technique or method, but a logic of inquiry.

Pawson (2010b) rejects the 'successionist' approach to causation which he views as underpinning much evaluation. From this perspective, it is presumed that context can be held constant via randomisation and outcomes can be measured from those exposed or not exposed to the intervention (we have already noted Pawson's (2006) view of the limitations for such a methodology). Where these outcomes, in a statistically systematic fashion, are achieved, the intervention can be imputed to be causally related to its outcomes (Pawson and Tilley 2004). However, realists reject this essentially correlational perspective and adopt a 'generative approach' to causation and attribution. This asserts that outcomes are caused – i.e. generated – by underlying mechanisms rather than directly by the programmes themselves.

Dalkin et al. (2015: 1) argue that one of the key tenets of realism is:

> that observational evidence alone cannot establish causal uniformities between variables. Rather, it is necessary to explain why the relationships come about; it is necessary to establish what goes on in the system that connects its various inputs and outputs.

The basic idea is that things that we experience or can observe are caused by 'deeper', usually non-observable, processes. 'Realist evaluations try to identify the mechanisms that cause programme outcomes, not just an association between "the programme" and "the outcome"' (The Ramesis II Project no date a: 2).

Mechanisms

From this perspective, 'social regularities are constituted by the action of underlying generative mechanisms' (Pawson 2000: 284). Mechanisms are not variables or attributes and thus not always directly measurable or observable. Westhorp (2014: 5) outlines this perspective as follows:

> For example: we can open our hand and observe the tennis ball we held fall to the ground, but we cannot 'see' the gravity that causes the ball to fall. Similarly, we can experience a training programme and observe that participants use different language at the end of it than they did at the beginning, but we cannot 'see' the new content being stored in memory or the new connections being forged in the brain that enables them to do so. That is, the causal processes happen at a different level of the system than the observable outcomes. In realist philosophy, the underlying causal process is known as a 'mechanism'.

For Pawson (2006: 23), 'mechanisms are the engines of explanation in realist analysis'. Further, similar to Weiss (1998), the key mechanisms are cognitive. Pawson (2013: 133) argues that 'programmes do not 'work' in an off themselves; rather it is their subjects' choice that makes for success (or failure). . . . Programme mechanisms describe how the resources available in a programme influence the participants' reasoning and subsequent behaviour'.

Therefore, a programme theory seeks to identify the critical success factors of an intervention, *the mechanisms via which it works* (i.e. 'reasoning and resources'). It identifies the key components, mechanisms, relationships and sequences of causes and effects which are presumed to lead to particular short-, medium- and long-term outcomes and subsequent desired behavioural impacts.

The value of such an analysis is also that mechanisms provide the basis for generalisation. Reflecting Weiss's (1987) argument, Astbury and Leeuw (2010: 374) state that 'mechanisms are often 'portable' in the sense that they are building blocks for middle-range program theories, which may be transferable to different contexts and policy domains'. Consequently,

> getting more involved in (explanatory) theories about mechanisms adds value to the evaluation enterprise because it helps avoid the problem of one-off, discrete evaluations that do little to develop generalizable knowledge about social programming . . . with policy makers realising that many supposedly "novel" interventions share common underlying mechanisms of change (Astbury and Leeuw 2010: 376).

Context

However, for realists, mechanisms always operate in a particular context. This is in opposition to the randomised controlled experimental approach which seeks to control (i.e. reduce the influence of) context to enable it to conclude that the programme alone produces certain outcomes. Research or evaluation designs that strip away or 'control for' context with a view to exposing the 'pure' effect of the intervention 'limit our ability to understand how, when and for whom the intervention will be effective' (Wong et al. 2012: 13). For Pawson and Tilley (2004: 7):

> context describes those features of the conditions in which programmes are introduced that are relevant to the operation the programme mechanisms. Realism utilises contextual thinking to address the issues of 'for whom' and 'in what circumstances' a programme will work.

Context is clearly a potentially open-ended category, although Pawson (2010b: 16) argues that 'what counts as context will depend on the substantive problem under scrutiny' (the importance of context is asserted in Chapter 5). He lists some aspects of contexts which need to be considered (Pawson 2013: 37):

- Individual. The characteristics and capacities of the various stakeholders in the programme. [This will include the psychological and cultural orientation of participants].
- Interpersonal relations. The stakeholder relations that carry the programme [e.g. the social climate of the programme].
- Institutional settings. The rules, norms and customs local to the programme [both within the organisation and in the local community].
- Infrastructure. The wider social, economic and cultural setting of the programme.
    - (note: this is emphasised in Chapter 5).

Tilley (2000) suggests that context can be understood as the conditions needed for an intervention to trigger mechanisms to produce particular outcome patterns. Westhorp (2014: 6) states that 'the implication for evaluation is that what matters about context is what influences *whether* mechanisms operate, and *which* mechanisms operate'. Consequently, 'context is inextricably enmeshed with the mechanisms through which a programme works' (The Ramesis II Project no date c: 2). In certain circumstances, context can be defined relatively precisely. For example, Jolly and Jolly (2014: 33) refer to the 'program context' stating that 'learning environments are the context in which students decide what they will do with the learning opportunities on offer' and that 'course design has the power to explain learning outcomes when considered as a context in which a range of mechanisms are triggered'.

The evolution of evaluation 119

Variations within the target population can influence which mechanisms operate (gender, class, caste, culture, age, experience and so on), which is the basis of the 'for whom' question in realist evaluation. Access to resources and opportunities to implement decisions can also influence reasoning itself, as well as whether desired choices can be put into action. For example, community attitudes to gender may facilitate or constrain female participation in the labour market, which will strongly influence the effectiveness of an employability programme.

This approach relates to the role of theory within the realist perspective.

Theory

Realists' use of theory is different from the theory of change perspective, where theory is simply a means to understanding why a programme does or does not work. However, Pawson and Tilley (2004: 9) argue that 'realist evaluation is about theory testing and refinement'. Consequently, 'realist evaluation starts with theory and ends with theory' (Better Evaluation no date: 2). Therefore 'the purpose of a realist evaluation is as much to test and refine the programme theory as it is to determine whether and how the programme worked in a particular setting' (Better Evaluation no date: 2). This reflects the realist position that 'programme theories are immediately portable, whereas programmes are not'. (Pawson 2013: 88). Consequently, 'programme theories often have much in common, and it is the parallels between such ideas that are the prime focus of learning in evaluation' (Pawson and Tilley 2004: 18). Therefore, Pawson (2013: 8) argues that 'the place to start evaluation is with the *well-travelled* [emphasis added] programme theory that underpins it' and 'primary research is examined for its contribution to the developing theory'.

In terms of Lipsey and Pollards' (1989) typology, Pawson and Tilley (1996) argue that evaluation needs to be driven by quite specific propositions which guide the search for possible causal mechanisms and that some of these will derive from practitioners, some from social science theory and some from the results of previous evaluation studies.

Nevertheless, realists place emphasis on a 'social science' approach. Although realists will explore the programme theory underpinning programmes with stakeholders, the initial programme theory will also be based on previous research, knowledge and experience (Lipsey and Pollard's first source):

> *theory testing* is undertaken by synthesising existing research into elements of the programme theory, including evaluations of programmes or interventions that share the same programme theory. . . . The purpose is to synthesise findings from these studies and other relevant data to test and refine theories which explain in what circumstances and through what underlying causal processes interventions produce intended and unintended outcomes.
> (The Ramesis II Project no date a:2)

Blamey and Mackenzie (2007: 447) argue that the realist approach:

> shows less concern for prospectively articulated, well specified and consensual action plans and capacity building, and more interest in identifying promising hypothesized causal triggers. [the researcher] then goes on to suggest the most promising theories at more of a distance from the programme than in Theories of Change. This decision is based on the existing evidence base and evaluator knowledge and experience rather than on the relative importance placed on the theories by implementers per se. In this sense the theories generated, whilst partly emerging from discussions with stakeholders, are specified and owned more by the evaluators rather than approved and 'signed up to' by the stakeholders.

More generally, the difference between realist and other kinds of programme TBE approaches is that a realist programme theory specifies what mechanisms will generate the outcomes and what features of the context will affect whether those mechanisms operate. Ideally, these elements (context, mechanisms and outcomes) are made explicit at the evaluation design stage, as it enables data collection to focus on testing the different elements of programme theory (Better Evaluation no date).

Middle-range theory and the basis of generalisation

Middle-range theory is not a type of theory like implementation or programme theory but refers to a level of abstraction and ability to support generalisation. Pawson and Tilley (2004: 18) argue that 'realism supposes that evaluation can learn lessons from diverse programmes by operating at the middle range'. This is based on Merton's (1968: 39) definition of middle-range theories:

> Theories that lie between the minor but necessary working hypotheses that evolve in abundance during day-to-day research and the all-inclusive systematic efforts to develop a unified theory that will explain all the observed uniformities of social behaviour, social organization and social change.

Consequently, middle range theory needs to be 'specific enough to clearly explain the phenomenon and general enough to apply across cases of the same type' (Ramesis II Project no date b: 3).

Therefore, the aim of middle-range theorising is, via abstraction, 'to understand an event as an instance of a more general class of happenings' (Pawson 2013: 89). The basic premise is that although there is an empirical diversity of programmes, policymakers and practitioners 'they are, in truth, able to offer relatively few ways of inducing change. . . . The same processes are experienced in other walks of life and it is precisely the job of middle-range theory to provide the conceptual framework to establish a linkage' (Pawson and Tilley 2004: 18).

Consequently, realism supposes that 'evaluation can learn lessons from diverse programmes by operating at the middle range where there is a much greater opportunity for realising and transferring the findings of evaluations' (Pawson and Tilley 2004: 18). The result is that the same programme theories repeat themselves from initiative to initiative and jump from domain to domain. To illustrate this, they quote Bemelmans-Videc et al.'s (1997) contention that most social policies are reducible to one of three types of mechanism – 'carrots', 'sticks' and 'sermons'. Pawson and Tilley (1997: 123–124) state that

> the basic idea of middle-range theory is that these propositions do not have to be developed de novo on the basis of local wisdom in each investigation. Rather they are likely to have a common thread running through them traceable to more abstract analytic frameworks.

Astbury and Leeuw (2010: 376) continue

> by sharing and using the accumulated evidence on the level of the mechanisms at work (instead of the specific intervention as such), policy makers and evaluators may come to realize that many supposedly 'novel' interventions share common underlying mechanisms of change. Knowledge of these mechanisms could then be used to better inform the design and evaluation of social policies and programs.

The classic example of middle-range theory frequently quoted by realists is Merton's reference group theory which states that individuals compare themselves with reference groups of people who occupy a social role or status to which the individual aspires. Reference groups act as a frame of reference to which people refer to evaluate their achievements, their role performance, aspirations and ambition. Merton used this to explain the aspirations and behaviour of American soldiers and it has been used to explain educational inequality, social class attitudes, dealing with Parkinson's disease, behaviour in traffic queues and youth mentoring. Other middle-range theories which operate in a wide variety of contexts include Bandura's social learning theory, Durkheim's concept of anomie (i.e. normlessness and the lack of ethical and social standards), role conflict, cognitive dissonance theory and social differentiation theory (Pawson 2010a). Consequently, the function of middle-range theory is to combine diverse substantive areas by abstracting away from the concrete instances to a generic conceptual framework useful in explaining them all.

Conclusions: sport for development and the need for theory-based approaches

Weiss (1997: 520) argues that 'the clearest call for TBE [theory-based evaluation] comes when prior evaluations show inconsistent results' – a situation which neatly sums up most sports-related research (Coalter 2007). In this regard, a major defining characteristic of recent comprehensive reviews of research in SfD is the conclusion that there is an absence of TBEs. For example, Lyras and Peachey (2011: 311–312) argue that 'there is little research on the sufficient conditions and processes needed for achieving positive outcomes in specific settings'.

Similarly, Adams and Harris (2013: 142–143) refer to

> the lack of attention afforded to processes underpinning SFD programmes. . . . Clearly, design or theoretical fallibilities may ensure that 'ill-defined outcomes' elicit evangelical performance indicators which, based on the presumed intrinsic values of sport, become the indicator or mechanism of change. The consequence of which, is to identify evaluation questions that are limited in both scope and value, giving rise to questions such as 'did the sport intervention have an impact?' rather than asking 'why and how did sport have an impact'?

This has two consequences. The first is articulated in Cronin's (2011: 12) review of SfD research:

> organisations were often lacking a theory of change, such that it was difficult to establish what elements of a programme might deliver the intended impact. This makes it harder to conduct relevant and informative research in the first place. It also means that where no effect is detected (e.g. no increase in leadership skills), this may be because the intervention was not actually focused on delivering this in the first place.

Such concerns are reinforced by Jones et al. (2017: 140), who point to the limitations of much descriptive outcome-based research and the lack of analysis of process, because 'without this information it is unclear if the evaluative criteria used by the researchers matched the programme model, or if the constructs being measured were an intended or unintended consequence of participation'. More generally Whitley et al. (2018: 9), on the basis of their systematic review of 70 research studies, argue for the need for 'intervention theories (i.e., programme theories), rather than focusing predominantly on intervention outcomes and benchmarks'.

The second consequence is Schulenkorf et al.'s (2016: 36) comment that much existing research is limited in terms of 'transferability' or the ability to generalise 'results to wider populations and contexts'. This issue of generalisability has produced two responses.

Firstly, Darnell (2012) questions whether in such a diverse field as SfD, it is possible to develop transferable or generalisable evidence-based practice. Secondly, Schulenkorf et al. (2016: 36) propose that research adopts a rather positivistic approach by moving 'towards designing standardised SfD questionnaires, surveys and models. . .'. The problem with the latter response has already been outlined by both Cronin (2011) and Jones et al. (2017) in that any measured outcomes (no matter how often) without an understanding of the underlying programme theory can tell us nothing about the nature of the programmes and the meaning and relevance of the measured outcomes.

With regard to Darnell's concerns that diversity precludes generalisability the solution to this is provided by Pawson's (2013) realist argument that although programmes are not portable, middle-range programme theories are. This is also related to Weiss's (1997: 510) argument that 'knowing the mechanism that works is even more important for other sites that want to adopt the successful program'. Consequently, given the empirical diversity of SfD programmes, the realist emphasis on middle-range theory means that evaluation does not have to start afresh for each programme, as 'many supposedly 'novel' interventions share common underlying mechanisms of change' (Astbury and Leeuw 2010: 376).

References

Adams, A. and Harris, K. (2013) 'Making sense of the lack of evidence discourse, power and knowledge in the field of sport for development', *International Journal of Public Sector Management*, 27(2), 140–151.
Astbury, B. and Leeuw, F.L. (2010) 'Unpacking black boxes: Mechanisms and theory building in evaluation', *American Journal of Evaluation*, 31(3), 363–381.
Bemelmans-Videc M-L, Rist, R., and Vedung, E. (1997) *Carrots, Sticks, and Sermons: Policy Instruments and their Evaluation* Brunswick, NJ: Transaction.
Better Evaluation (no date) *Realist evaluation*. Available HTTP: www.betterevaluation.org/en/approach/realist_evaluation
Blamey, A. and Mackenzie, M. (2007) 'Theories of change and realistic evaluation: Peas in a pod or apples and oranges?', *Evaluation*, 13(4), 439–455.
Center for Theory of Change (no date) *What is theory of change?* Available HTTP: www.theoryofchange.org/what-is-theory-of-change/
Chen, H.T. (1990) *Theory-driven evaluations*, Newbury Park, CA: Sage.
Chen, H.T. and Rossi, P.H. (1980) 'The multi-goal, theory-driven approach to evaluation: A model linking basis and applied social sciences', *Social Forces*, 59, 106–122.
Chen, H.T. and Rossi, P.H. (1983) 'Evaluating with sense; the theory-driven approach', *Evaluation Review*, 7, 283–302.
Chen, H.T. and Rossi, P.H. (1987) 'The theory-driven approach to validity', *Evaluation and Program Planning*, 10, 95–103.
Chen, H.T. and Rossi, P.H. (1989) 'Issues in the theory-driven perspective', *Evaluation and Program Planning*, 12, 299–306.
Clark, H. and Anderson, A.A. (2004) *Theories of change and logic models: Telling them apart*, Presentation at American Evaluation Association Atlanta, GA, November. Available HTTP: www.theoryofchange.org/wp-content/uploads/toco_library/pdf/TOCs_and_Logic_Models_forAEA.pdf
Coakley, J. (2011) 'Youth sports: What counts as "positive development"?', *Journal of Sport and Social Issues*, 35(3), 306–324.
Coalter, F. (2007) *A wider social role for sport: Who's keeping the score?*, London: Routledge.
Connell, J.P. and Kubisch, A.C. (1998) *Applying a theory of change approach to the evaluation of comprehensive community initiatives: Progress, prospects, and problems.*

Available HTTP: www.dmeforpeace.org/sites/default/files/080713%20Applying+Theory+of+Change+Approach.pdf
Cronin, O. (2011) *Mapping the research on the impact of sport and development interventions*, London: Comic Relief.
Dalkin, S., Greenhalgh, J., Jones, D., Cunningham, B. and Lhussier, M. (2015) 'What's in a mechanism? Development of a key concept in realist evaluation', *Implementation Science*, 10, 49. DOI: 10.1186/s13012-015-0237-x
Darnell, S. (2012) *Sport for development and peace: A critical sociology*, London: Bloomsbury.
Emler, N. (2001) *Commonly-held beliefs about self-esteem are myths, warns new research review*. Available HTTP: www.jrf.org.uk/pressroom/releases/281101.asp
Gasper, D. (2000) 'Evaluating the "logical framework approach" towards learning-oriented development evaluation', *Public Administration and Development*, 20, 17–28.
Gugiu, O.C. and Rodriguez-Campos, L. (2007) 'Semi-structured interview protocol for constructing logic models', *Evaluation and Program Planning*, 30(4), 339–350.
Harris, K. and Adams, A. (2015) 'Power and discourse in the politics of evidence in sport and development', *Sport Management Review*, 19(2), 97–106.
Hermens, N., Super, S., Verkooijen, K.T. and Koelen, M. (2017) 'A systematic review of life skill development through sports programs serving socially vulnerable youth', *Research Quarterly for Exercise and Sport*, 88(4), 408–424.
Jassey, K. (2004) 'The bureaucrat', in: L. Groves and R. Hinton (eds) *Inclusive aid: Changing power and relationships in international development*, London: Earthscan, pp. 128–134.
Jolly, H. and Jolly, L. (2014) 'Telling context from mechanism in realist evaluation: The role for theory', *Learning Communities: International Journal of Learning in Social Contexts* [*Special Issue; Evaluation*], 14, 28–45.
Jones, G.J., Edwards, M.B., Bocarro, J.N., Bunds, K.S. and Smith, J.W. (2017) 'An integrative review of sport based youth development literature', *Sport in Society*, 20(1), 161–179.
Kay, T. (2011) *Sport as a catalyst for achieving the millennium development goals – implementation*, 2nd International Forum on Sport for Peace and Development, Geneva, 10–11 May.
Kay, T. (2012) 'Accounting for legacy: Monitoring and evaluation in sport in development relationships', *Sport in Society*, 15(6), 888–904.
Kruse, S.E. (2006) *Review of kicking AIDS out: Is sport an effective tool in the fight against HIV/AIDS?*, draft report to NORAD, unpublished.
Lee, P.L. (2011) *What's wrong with logic models?*, Occasional Paper No. 1, Local Government Services Association. Available HTTP: www.lcsansw.org.au/documents/item/210
Levermore, R. (2011) 'Evaluating sport-for-development approaches and critical issues', *Progress in Development Studies*, 11(4), 393–353.
Lipsey, M.W. and Pollard, J.A. (1989) 'Driven toward theory in program evaluation: More models to choose from', *Evaluation and Program Planning*, 12(3), 317–328.
Lubans, D.R., Plotnikoff, R.C. and Lubans, N.J. (2012) 'Review: A systematic review of the impact of physical activity programmes on social and emotional well-being in at-risk youth', *Child and Adolescent Mental Health*, 17(1), 2–13.
Lyras, A. and Peachey, J.W. (2011) 'Integrating sport-for-development theory and praxis', *Sport Management Review*, 14, 311–326.
Merton, R. (1968) *Social theory and social structure*, 3rd edn, New York: Free Press.

Pawson, R. (2000) 'Middle range realism', *Archives Européennes de Sociologie*, 41(2), 283–325.

Pawson, R. (2004) *Evaluating Ill-defined interventions with hard-to-follow outcomes*, Paper Presented to ESRC Seminar Understanding and Evaluating the Impact of Sport and Culture on Society, Leeds Metropolitan University, Leeds, January.

Pawson, R. (2006) *Evidence-based policy; a realist perspective*, London: Sage.

Pawson, R. (2010a) 'Middle range theory and programme theory evaluation: From provenance to practice', in: J. Vaessen and F. Leeuw (eds) *Mind the gap: Perspectives on policy evaluation and the social sciences*, Transaction Press, pp. 171–202.

Pawson, R. (2010b) *Causality for beginners*. Available HTTP: http://eprints.ncrm.ac.uk/245/

Pawson, R. (2013) *The science of evaluation*, London: Sage.

Pawson, R. and Tilley, N. (1996) 'What's crucial in evaluation research: A reply to Bennett', *The British Journal of Criminology*, 36(4), 574–778.

Pawson, R. and Tilley, N. (1997) *Realistic evaluation*, London: Sage.

Pawson, R. and Tilley, N. (2004) *Realist evaluation*. Available HTTP: www.communitymatters.com.au/RE_chapter.pdf

Power, M. (1997) 'The audit explosion', in: G. Mulgan (ed) *Life after politics*, London: Fontana, pp. 286–293.

Public Health England (no date) *Introduction to logic models*. Available HTTP: www.gov.uk/government/publications/evaluation-in-health-and-well-being-overview/introduction-to-logic-models#limitations-of-logic-models

The Ramesis II Project (no date a) *Realist evaluation, realist synthesis, realist research – what's in a name?* Available HTTP: www.ramesesproject.org/

The Ramesis II Project (no date b) *"Theory" in realist evaluation*. Available HTTP: www.ramesesproject.org/

The Ramesis II Project (no date c) *What realists mean by context; or why nothing works everywhere for everyone*. Available HTTP: www.ramesesproject.org/

Robb, C. (2004) 'Changing power relations in the history of aid', in: L. Groves and R. Hinton (eds) *Inclusive aid: Changing power and relationships in international development*, London: Earthscan, pp. 21–41.

Rossi, P.H., Lipsey, M.W. and Freeman, H.E. (2004) *Evaluation: A systematic approach*, 7th edn, Thousand Oaks: Sage.

Rossi, P.H. and Wright, J.D. (1984) 'Evaluation research; an assessment', *Annual Review of Sociology*, 10, 331–352.

Schulenkorf, N., Sherry, E. and Rowe, K. (2016) 'Sport for development: An integrated literature review', *Journal of Sport Management*, 30(1), 22–39.

Scriven, M. (1994) 'The fine line between evaluation and explanation', *Evaluation Practice*, 15(1), 75–77.

Spaaij, R. and Schaillee, H. (2020) 'Inside the black box: A micro-sociological analysis of sport for development', *International Review for the Sociology of Sport*, 56(2), 151–169.

Stame, N. (2004) 'Theory-based evaluation and types of complexity', *Evaluation*, 10(1), 58–76.

Tilley, N. (2000) *Realist evaluation: An overview*, Paper Presented at the Founding Conference of the Danish Evaluation Society. Available HTTP: www.researchgate.net/publication/252160435_Realistic_Evaluation_An_Overview

UNICEF (2006) *Monitoring and Evaluation for Sport-Based Programming for Development: Sport Recreation and Play*, Workshop Report, New York: UNICEF van Kampen, H. (ed) (2003) *A report on the expert meeting 'the next step' on sport and development*, Amsterdam: NCDO. Available HTTP: www.toolkitsportdevelopment.org/html/resources/0E/0E00BE53-2C02-46EA-8AC5-A139AC4363DC/Report%20of%20Next%20Step%20Amsterdam.pdf

Weiss, C.H. (1972) *Evaluation research: Methods of assessing program effectiveness*, Englewood Cliffs, NJ: Prentice-Hall.

Weiss, C.H. (1987) 'Evaluating social programs; what have we learned?', *Society*, 25, 140–145.

Weiss, C.H. (1993) 'Where politics and evaluation meet', *Evaluation Practice*, 14(1), 93–106.

Weiss, C.H. (1995) 'Nothing as practical as good theory: Exploring theory-based evaluation for comprehensive community initiatives for children and families', in: J. Connell, A. Kubisch, L. Schorr and C.H. Weiss (eds) *New approaches to evaluating community initiatives: Concepts, methods, and contexts*, New York: The Aspen Institute, pp. 65–92.

Weiss, C.H. (1997) 'How can theory-based evaluation make greater headway?', *Evaluation Review*, 21(4), 501–524.

Weiss, C.H. (1998) *Evaluation*, 2nd edn, London: Prentice Hall.

Wells, S. and Arthur-Banning, S.G. (2008) 'The logic of youth development: Constructing a logic model of youth development through sport', *Journal of Park and Recreation Administration*, 26(2), 189–202.

Westhorp, G. (2014) *Realist impact evaluation: An introduction*, London: Methods Lab Overseas Development Institute.

Whitley, M.A., Massey, W.V., Camiré, M, Blom, L.C., Chawansky, M., Forde, S., Boutet, M., Borbee, A. and Darnell, S.C. (2018) 'A systematic review of sport for development interventions across six global cities', *Sport Management Review*, 181–193.

Win, E. (2004) '"If it doesn't fit on the blue square it's out!" An open letter to my donor friend', in: L. Groves and R. Hinton (eds) *Inclusive aid: Changing power and relationships in international development*, London: Earthscan, pp. 123–127.

W.K. Kellogg Foundation (2004) *Logic model development guide*, Battle Creek, MI: W.K. Kellogg Foundation.

Wong, G., Westhorp, G., Pawson, R. and Greenhalgh, T. (2012) *Realist synthesis RAMESES training materials*. Available HTTP: www.ramesesproject.org/media/Realist_reviews_training_materials.pdf

7 Realist inquiry and action research

Guy Kegels and Bruno Marchal

Introduction

As discussed in Chapter 1, the second phase of the *community sport for AT-risk youth: Innovative strategies for promoting personal development, health and social CoHesion* (CATCH) project consisted of 'action-oriented research' in three community sport contexts, with the aim of developing and testing interventions to further the goals of personal development, healthy attitudes and social cohesion. Our purpose in this chapter is to explore if and how a *realist inquiry* frame-of-mind can contribute to substantiate, structure and deepen action research (AR), thus increasing its practical and theoretical relevance. We refer here to realist evaluation (RE) as proposed in Pawson and Tilley's *Realistic Evaluation* (Pawson and Tilley 1997) (i.e. searching for interacting contexts and mechanisms to explain outcomes). In order to do this, we will first clarify what we understand AR to be and what we think it could (or should) be. We will then describe what we consider to be the essential elements of the realist inquiry approach. To end, we will bring AR and realist inquiry together and articulate what could be the realist's contribution to better AR practice.

Action research: theory and practice

When scanning the classic academic (peer-reviewed) literature, it is striking to see how much easier it is to find publications on concepts, justification (or not) and relevance (or lack thereof) of AR than on actual AR carried out. Considering ourselves to be members of the AR tribe, we do not find this very surprising. Part of the explanation lies in the fact that participants in AR projects most often are more interested in the outcome of the action rather than in sharing the learning with an audience outside the project universe. Another part of the explanation may be that the practice of AR is felt to be its own reward and that it does not need to be exploited for scholarly prestige. Maybe the main reason is that the methods, processes and results of AR are just very difficult to correctly formulate in a scientifically explicit way; it is certainly a challenge to wangle such results into the academically accepted format of most journals. A final obstacle, in many cases, is that AR is often understood to be 'one-context-specific' and as a consequence 'of-no-use-for-other-contexts', which seriously reduces the inclination to share the results and possible learning with the academic community. We will return to this further on.

That having been said, let us take a look at writings *about* AR.

The first use of the term 'action research' (although identifying a 'first' is always a hazardous undertaking) is traditionally attributed to Kurt Lewin, in 1946, who described it as 'a comparative research on the conditions and effects of various forms of social action and research leading to social action' (Lewin 1946) – a somewhat bland and not (yet) very enlightening formulation, in our view. When groping for a more formal definition, the most often cited texts are Rapoport (1970), Susman and Evered (1978) and Meyer (2000). Key paragraphs include: 'Action research aims to contribute both to the practical concerns of people in an immediate problematic situation and to the goals of social science by joint collaboration within a mutually acceptable ethical framework' (Rapoport 1970), to which Susman and Evered (1978) add 'and to develop the self-help competencies of people facing problems'.

Meyer (2000) cites Reason and Rowan (1981), 'research in which the researchers work explicitly with and for people rather than undertake research on them' (our emphasis), and underscores the participatory character, democratic impulse (participants as equals, with a view to empowerment) and the simultaneous contribution to social science and social change. A more recent publication by Auriacombe (2015) provides a highly readable overview of the (published) views on AR and ends up providing a list of ever-mentioned characteristics, including: 'problem-focused, context-specific, democratic, participative, practical, evaluative action and change oriented, dynamic, cyclic, critical and reflexive'.

The overall tendency of this narrative seems reasonably clear: committed researchers collaborating on an equal footing with system actors at the operational level, in the service of a good cause, throwing the traditional (positivist) scientist's insistence on detachment (or neutrality) to the winds – and probably proud to do so. In Byrne and Callaghan's (2014: 208) formulation, it is 'research undertaken as part of the processes of transformative change themselves. A key term is praxis . . .'[1]. In epistemological terms, they link AR with Paolo Freire's notion of *dialogical research*, which asserts that both the scientist and the people in the field of investigation bring frames of understanding, from the synthesis of which useful knowledge emerges: equality of participants, democratic attitude, empowerment-oriented, critical, etc.

The challenge seems to be: how to ensure this is a respectable (and actually respected) form of scientific practice? If the narrative may seem to point to an over-weighting of the 'action' part in AR, there also exist alternative narratives that shift the balance towards (due) emphasis on knowledge production and sharing – although the element of researcher involvement and commitment in the action always remains an essential characteristic.

The image Kurt Lewin introduced more than 70 years ago was one of a *spiral*, standing for an iterative process of ever more accurate understanding and predictability, in an ever-closer approximation of the ideal solution to the problem at hand. Although very suggestive as a visual image and intellectually seductive, this description remains quite generic. Actual AR practice attracted criticisms of lacking methodological rigour, of being indistinguishable from consulting and of tending to result in either 'action with little research' or 'research with little action' (Foster 1972 cited in Dickens and Watkins 1999).

One attempt to remedy the 'paucity of methodological guidance' is Davison, Martinsons and Kock's *Principles of canonical action research* (Davison et al. 2004), in which they elicit a set of five principles aiming to assure both relevance and rigour. These principles (researcher–client agreement; cyclical process model; theory; change through action and learning through reflection) are accompanied by associated criteria to be met in a detailed sort of quality assurance checklist. The spirit in which their contribution is made is one of trying to resolve the tension (academic) action researchers always face: they are supposed to 'serve at least two demanding masters – the client and the academic community' (Kock et al. 1999: 582). Although for some (Hammersley 2004), this conundrum cannot be solved (either 'inquiry would be subordinated to action' or the AR would 'resolve itself into specialised research'), we think there are reasons to be more optimistic about the possibility to satisfy both masters.

We can – broadly but accurately, we think – define *research* as a purposeful approach to create valid new knowledge and/or improve insight in and understanding of the world. In the case of AR – involving both a 'researcher–client' and a 'researcher–academic peers' relationship – the client may be more interested in demonstrable immediate *relevance* (or usefulness *in situ*), whereas the academic peers are traditionally more critical about *validity* (or truth-content) and generalisability. If we acknowledge that there may be a real tension between these interests, this does not have to mean that they are necessarily antagonistic or incompatible. The point of formal AR as we see it is to be a *theatre of valid learning* in the course of a problem-solving project; the validity of the learning that hopefully ensues depends on the design of the action and its implementation and evaluation. The link with the increase of pre-existing knowledge lies in the *inferences* drawn from the evaluation: it is there that the academic AR practitioner needs to exercise the utmost rigour in order to avoid the multiple potential pitfalls the human mind is prone not to be aware of – and convince her peers. This must be, at least theoretically, possible.

A systematic practice of AR

Having thus sketched our position epistemology-wise, for the purposes of this chapter we will take inspiration from the model developed by Grodos and Mercenier (2000, in turn based on Nitayarumphong and Mercenier 1992), which we will tweak somewhat in light of our own experience and progressing insights.

The procedural (pragmatic) narrative we favour begins, classically enough, with an assessment of the existing situation, which, in a context of AR, is *a priori* considered a problematic or suboptimal situation. In order to achieve such an

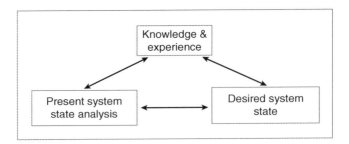

Figure 7.1 Contributing elements in constant interaction

assessment/analysis, two contributing elements are necessarily in constant interaction, as is illustrated in Figure 7.1: (1) a clear idea of what would be the *desired* situation and (2) the available stock of knowledge and experience that needs to be mobilised to make sense of the existing (problematic) situation and of the desired situation and – if possible – to formulate ways to pass from the former to the latter.

Several comments are already in order. To begin with, the three elements are in constant and necessary interaction as parts of one intellectual dynamic. The relevance of the analysis of the (problematic) present is necessarily dependent on what the desired situation is supposed to be, in turn depending on the intellectual frames and theories applied to both – and to the possible transition between them. Furthermore, in order to be able to contribute to solving the problem(s) of the present, their analysis involves not only intelligent description but also (retrospective) *explanation* in terms of causation: *why* things are as they are (and *how* have they come to be what they are: 'how did we come to this?').

Clearly, as Charles Lindblom famously stated already in 1979 in his essay *Still muddling, not yet through*, in the case of complex social problems such an analysis can never be *complete* or comprehensive (Lindblom 1979). He offers a defence of the 'incrementalistic' alternative (in his vocabulary this means *limited*, not trying to be exhaustive) in the form of what he calls 'strategic analysis': applying a 'thoughtfully chosen set of stratagems to simplify complex problems' – or in his idiom, 'muddling with some skill'. Lindblom does not offer much guidance on how this is to be done, which seems to imply that it involves expertise based on (long) reflective experience. Finding out what are *crucial* elements or mechanisms to explain a given situation is a skill not easily mastered by any single individual. Groups can have a better chance to achieve this than isolated individuals – if the group processes are well managed. The key criterion of relevance (or 'cruciality') is, ultimately, the strength of the case that can be made for it, its persuasiveness among intelligent people and so on.

Harnessing the knowledge and experience that is available within the group is a great and often satisfying exercise, resulting in an answer to the question 'what do we know and understand now'? Most often, though, it is useful or necessary to push this question further to 'what else is known – or can be known?' (more than what we, among us, now know we know). Working on this question is a time-consuming exercise for which the academic participant(s) – from outside the group of mostly very busy insiders in the organisation where the AR project is carried out – are the most obvious resource: this is the kind of thing they do. How far this search should go – how deep, how broad – is to be decided on the basis of reasonableness or good sense (cf. Lindblom's previous statements).

In the diagram, we have introduced the term *system state*, substituting for the generic term *situation* (present or desired). This is because we claim that looking at (social) reality in terms of systems (and complex systems, at that) can yield vastly superior results. Systems thinking means being aware that the whole is made up of components, modular or not, *in interaction*, and if we are dealing with living, complex systems, this includes positive and negative feedback mechanisms and agents interacting within the constraints or opportunities of a structuring environment that they may want to reproduce or modify. Trying to make sense of such a complex thing inevitably involves accepting (some might say 'embracing') *uncertainty* and learning how to live with that – in research and evaluation not the meanest of challenges.

The next step is clarifying the *desired* system state – what it *ought* to be.

This is a normative exercise. At the start, this may not be a very explicit or clearly formulated statement, but some hunch of what it should be (and what it should not be) is a necessary prerequisite for describing the present system state as problematic or suboptimal. A progressively more precise formulation of the desired state of affairs is of course necessary to decide on the product of the whole exercise so far: the AR project's *theory for change*, or how to move from the present system state to the desired one, formulated as a *change hypothesis* that will be tested.

Again, and obviously, formulating the desired situation is constrained by the other elements in the diagram: the present (suboptimal) system state constrains the possibilities for change as do the limitations of our knowledge and insights – this threesome remains shackled throughout the exercise. Finally, the precisely formulated desired state of affairs needs to be agreed upon by as many participants as possible if the AR project is to be carried forward through its further stages. Reaching this agreement is crucial but may take a lot of patience, negotiation and diplomacy.

From the previous comments, it should be very clear that this initiating phase of formal AR is challenging but crucial, typically involving multiple actors in a participatory approach 'having to engage in persistent reflexive thought about their own and others' practices' (Adelman 1993). To move the process forward, the next step is to formulate the *change hypothesis*, already alluded to previously.

The use of this term is not just to make a fit with a respectable 'research' paradigm of the hypothetico-deductive mould. It is first and foremost an expression of the fact that predicting what will be the effect of a chosen action in any complex social system is necessarily hypothetical in nature. The uncertainty inherent in the behaviour of live social systems is, however, not total. Certain regularities do exist, although they may not always work out as expected, depending on circumstances – hence the term 'demi-regularities'. Understanding how these circumstances ('context') exert their enabling or constraining influence on the demi-regularity constitutes an important space for learning.

Put simply, AR is a somewhat special case of learning from experience. Its main specificity lies in the *kind* of experience: it is the experience of trying to change something in the world (typically and originally in one of its organisations) based on some 'theory' or hypothesis that takes the following form:

> *Given* the present (problematic or suboptimal) state of affairs;
> *IF* we do 'this' (action introducing sets of constraints, enablers, sticks, carrots, sermons . . .);
> *THEN* we expect a new state of affairs will develop that is less problematic than the initial one.

Implicit is the hope that the elimination of the initial problem will not be accompanied by the creation of other problems, different but of equivalent weight in fact or in perception.

The question is then: how to test this hypothesis? Most AR practitioners will proceed by making a detailed list of what to do and how to do it; defining (desired) outcome variables and their indicators; putting into place an information system to monitor the implementation processes and planning/programming mid-term and end-term evaluations (summative and formative), which will add to the pre-existing stock of knowledge and insight, as shown in Figure 7.2. One of the

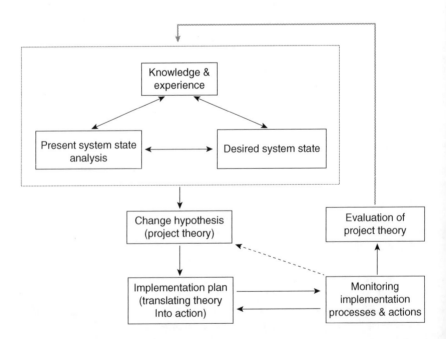

Figure 7.2 The action research cycle

advantages of such a diagram is that it offers a structure along which the necessary documentation and information system can be organised according to the elements shown.

What kind of learning will take place in this process depends in essence on the questions the *evaluation of the observed outcomes* ('evaluation of project theory' in the diagram) is supposed to answer.[2]

The first – and simplest – kind of question is, of course, 'did it work?' Suppose the evaluation shows that desired outcomes have been achieved, many will then be tempted to conclude that 'it worked' (in other words, there is a 'causal' link between the 'this' of the hypothesis – the 'action' part of the AR project – and the desired outcome). This is what most of us do most of the time in everyday life conditions – and how we build up most of our lifetime 'experience' – but of course the observed link is only of the correlation type, and its true interpretation can range from 'decidedly causal' to 'totally spurious': the old *cum hoc ergo propter hoc* fallacy.

From here on, the question of how to deal with this depends on the ontological/epistemological position one takes. The 'sceptical empiricist' Humean position is usually interpreted as implying that it is rationally impossible to establish (true) cause because *cause* as such cannot be observed; establishing *constant conjunction* is the farthest one can go. Therefore, establishing the constancy of the conjunction, in comparable circumstances – the *ceteris paribus* condition – through repetition would be the way forward. Roughly speaking, this is the path followed by much of present empirical research, as it can be said to be the basic axiom in epidemiologic research and the controlled trial study designs.

The 'realist inquiry' position[3], in contrast, starts from the reasonable premise that 'cause' does exist (as does reality, independently from the observer – hence the term *realist* inquiry), that it is a relevant category to investigate and that it is possible although difficult to establish, especially in social systems, as 'causal mechanisms' tend to operate at other strata of reality than the empirical one where outcomes are observed. The basic metaphor of this realism is that entities, in the broadest sense (material or immaterial), have causal powers that are activated when/if conditions are appropriate. Plant seeds have the 'power' to develop into mature plants but will only do so if environmental conditions of climate and soil are 'right'. The mechanisms through which this happens are not immediately visible/observable by looking at the outcome (i.e. the mature plant). Starting from the outcome, the causes have to be unearthed retrospectively in the form of *mechanisms*: a combination of descriptive 'hows' and explanatory 'whys'. A key commitment of such realist inquiry is that there are deeper levels waiting to be uncovered, beyond positive or negative correlation.

In practice, this translates into expanding the question 'does it work?' to 'what works, for whom, why, how and under which conditions?' And the *change hypothesis* on which the planned action is based (*given* A, *if* B, *then* C) is ideally extended to: '*given* A, *if* B, *then* C, *because* X'.

AR seeks to 'understand and improve the world by changing it' (Baum et al. 2006). It aims to optimise the *desired results of action* (in terms of relevance, effectiveness and efficiency) through a process of rigorous *pre-flection* – thinking through, *ex ante*, what is the most likely best way of doing things – and to optimise *learning* (in terms of the validity of its conclusions) through a process of rigorous *re-flection*: thinking through, *ex post*, how and why things have come to pass the way they have. Thus, ideally, *action* (for achieving desired change) and *research* (for generating new knowledge) can be brought into balance.

In a systems view of social reality, AR is dealing with systems (like organisations) that are said to be 'open': the system boundaries are permeable (i.e. open systems interact with their environment). However, AR projects must be seen as *experiments* if the validity of explanations is to be optimised. This implies *partial closure* of the open system. To a large extent, this can be accomplished by a *formal project status*, creating a protective bubble, so to speak, within which external influences can be partially controlled – apart from the one exerted by the external researchers. This may be especially important for AR projects within highly hierarchical metasystems like state bureaucracies, which are typically very change-averse on account of processes of strong procedural standardisation with direct supervision (Blaise and Kegels 2004).

It will come as no particular surprise that, epistemologically speaking, the (essential) evaluation component of AR is far from straightforward. To begin with, the explicit goal of AR is to arrive at a *more desirable* situation or system state, which inevitably implies a moral, political or aesthetic judgement, open to interpretation and contestation even inside the project or organisation universe. In that case, the outcome in terms of success or failure is likely to be perceived as mixed. For example, it may be considered desirable for community sports organisations to enhance social inclusion of youths in socially vulnerable situations, but this is a choice; not everyone is necessarily going to be equally enthusiastic about such a goal and there will likely be people who consider themselves losers or winners within this perspective. Working towards a more desirable situation within an organisation requires wide-enough shared *agreement* to begin with, both regarding the objectives and the course of action to be taken. In AR, absence of such an acceptable level of agreement equals what in log frame language is called a 'killer assumption' – meaning: forget it.

The (epistemological) search for knowledge or improved insight, in AR, is located in the formulation of the *change hypothesis*, which actually takes the following extended form:

> GIVEN starting situation A (and our understanding of how it has come about)
> IF we do X (action)
> THEN Y will happen, leading to desired situation B
> BECAUSE theory T, on which action X is based, is valid
> Under CONDITIONS postulated or to be discovered.

AR is thus conceived as an experiment, (1) mostly without simultaneous 'controls' (and for this reason, evaluation of its outcome will be most often of the *before-after* comparison type); (2) ranging on the complexity scale from simple 'mechanistic' interventions (like introducing new tools or routines) to complex behavioural or cultural changes loaded with uncertainty, requiring lots of time, patience and a continuous reflective attitude.

This implies that, for the action to have a chance of success, the change hypothesis needs to be rooted in robust substantive theory – not just any conjecture produced by the imagination.

Secondly, AR plays out in the social world, which is not static or constant. Changes are happening all the time: in the economic environment, the political priorities landscape, personnel composition, participants' flows and so on. In AR, the evaluation focuses on how the intervention produces results within a given context (rather than on which more or less static 'factors' explain some phenomenon of interest), and this context is likely to change significantly because of AR's actions (intended or not), external factors and other internal dynamics independent from the intended intervention package. Indeed, in AR the 'action' is almost always a set of interventions, not a single move. In evaluation terms, this of course poses the problem of attribution (how to attribute which result to which input). The way out of this conundrum is, theoretically, twofold. On the one hand, the design of the intervention package needs to be coherent, meaning that all elements need to fit the underlying robust substantive theory. On the other, the analysis of the link between results and project inputs requires 'system thinking', meaning the capacity to discern not only constituting elements but also their relationships and how to make sense of them. Here again, Charles Lindblom offers the useful words: in complex systems, we cannot be comprehensive (complete) in our analysis, but we can apply intelligent strategies to separate what is *crucial* from what is incidental. However, this may not be a skill easily acquired; it requires experience grounded in reflective practice and well-managed teamwork.

Thirdly, in AR, implementation of the intervention package is not necessarily carried out according to the initial plan, however carefully conceived. In a theoretical 'mechanical' world, we can make a clear semantic distinction between 'monitoring' (checking if *implementation* is going according to plan) and 'evaluation' (investigating whether the *change hypothesis* is valid). In practice, such monitoring may already reveal weaknesses in the initial implementation plan (in terms of feasibility and sometimes relevance) – and even in the validity of the change hypothesis itself – requiring rethinking and adjustment. Of course, this does not simplify the evaluation task and it underscores the necessity of systematic, accurate and detailed documentation of the AR process in order to support fallible human memory.

Fourthly, in AR, quantitative and statistical analyses are helpful but mostly insufficient, in the sense that they may establish *that* something significant is happening, but not *how*. Establishing quantitative patterns and their statistical significance just calls for further explanation, unless otherwise specified in the protocol: obviously, this depends on the action researchers' level of ambition, contrasting the evaluation question 'did it work' with 'how and why, for whom, under which conditions did it work?'

So far, we have used the space allotted to us to describe the potential – and some of the challenges – of AR in terms of optimising action-for-change as well as knowledge generation. We will now turn to realistic inquiry and try to find out what it is about this form of investigation that could contribute to better AR.

Essentials of realist inquiry

Scientific realism – in the twentieth century most famously pioneered by Roy Bhaskar (1978) but already introduced earlier by Harré (1972) – is not a methodology but rather a set of principles and metaphors concerning the nature of reality and our capacity to understand it. It is a paradigm that competes with (too) strong versions of positivism and constructivism, rejecting both as incomplete. It posits that it is possible to find a pragmatic way to go beyond these stances in a productive manner.

The *ontological* premise of realism can be captured, for our purposes, in two statements. Firstly, *reality exists independently of the observer* – it is not just a construction of the mind. Secondly, *this reality is 'stratified'* in three 'layers'. According to this stratification metaphor, there is the *empirical* stratum that is open to our experience and observation. However, what you see is not all there is: the empirical stratum is embedded in the *actual* stratum of what is really 'happening' (but only part of which is experienced/observed). In its turn, this is embedded in the stratum of the *real*, which includes the causal powers (the how and the why) leading to what is happening. These causal powers take the form of *mechanisms*, processes that express the inherent 'powers and liabilities' of objects to produce effects. This is illustrated in Figure 7.3:

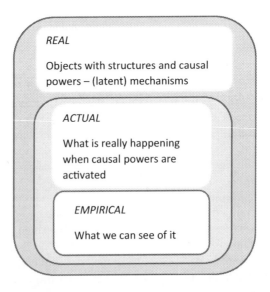

Figure 7.3 Layers of reality

Note that from this extremely brief summary, it follows that, in the realist narrative, the *actual* and especially the *real* are not open to direct observation or experience; only the *effects* can be observed as experience in the *empirical* layer of reality. Causal mechanisms are hidden 'underneath', so to speak, but that does not have to mean they cannot be uncovered.

The *epistemological* premise of realism is that knowledge of reality is relative to the agent; therefore, it depends on perspective, is partial and fallible, but it can be improved and corrected. We can rephrase this position as *weak epistemological relativism*, but without *judgemental relativism*: 'truth' remains a meaningful category, it *can* be known. Although knowledge is relative to the agent, it can be checked empirically: the *real* is inherently capable of 'regulating' knowledge (Sayer 1992) because it exists in an absolute way.

Astbury and Leeuw may have reduced the characteristics of 'mechanisms' to their purest essence by stating that they are (1) hidden, (2) context sensitive (i.e. they may only be 'fired' in specific contexts) and (3) 'generative of outcomes' (i.e. mechanisms are what generates effects) (Astbury and Leeuw 2010). As they are hidden (or at least not easily discerned) as well as potentially effective, they have often been likened to the content of the 'black box' that is so often present in projects: the often mysterious ways in which actions (or the preceding decisions) are linked with effects. The challenge of realist inquiry is to unpack this black box: find out what *explains* observed effects. Such theoretical explanation (in a retrospective mode) is said to proceeded by DREI (Isaksen 2016):

*D*escription of significant features of the observed regularity or pattern;
*R*etroduction to possible causal mechanisms;
*E*limination of alternatives through empirical analyses;
*I*dentification of the generative mechanism.

The term *retroduction* – initially called *abduction* by Charles S. Peirce, one of the fathers of the American 'pragmatist' school of philosophy – actually means formulating possible explanatory hypotheses. This may require some creative thinking[4] – see also Jagosh (2020).

The DREI procedure as described here may look unnecessarily pompous, but it is totally natural, for instance, for medically trained people. Replace the *description* part with *clinical examination and history taking*, the *retroduction* with *differential diagnosis* (the list of possible candidates for diagnosis), the *elimination of alternatives* with *clinical work-up* (additional tests and examinations) and you get a quite accurate description of the classical diagnostic process[5]. Readers of Arthur Conan Doyle will have noticed that the procedure also applies to, or coincides with, Sherlock Holmes' method (which in the novels is – mistakenly – described as 'deduction').

The aforementioned principles of realist inquiry have been incorporated and applied – with some twists – to programme evaluation in Pawson and Tilley's book *Realistic Evaluation* (Pawson and Tilley 1997). Program evaluators are among the best placed people to know that what works in one place does not necessarily work in another. For the inquisitive mind, the simple evaluation question 'did it work?' is hopelessly superficial. In their 1997 publication, Pawson and Tilley propose to replace it with 'did it work, for whom, how and under which conditions?' – a formulation that can be extended *ad libitum* with 'to what extent, over what duration, in what respects and why'. Here, realist inquiry's quest for explanation in the form of *mechanisms* is quite clear. If programmes inject resources of some kind into a given social context (they need not always be material but can also be symbolic, or cognitive, or delicious carrots and/or punitive sticks and/or persuasive sermons and/or gentle nudges), Pawson and Tilley conceptualise *mechanisms* as the reactive *reasoning people develop* when confronted with these changes: how do they react to these as *agents* (even if sometimes that reaction can be to ignore them all)? It is to be expected that the reactions will not be uniform across the whole spectrum of agents. The composition of the programme population in recognisable subgroups (reacting or expected to be reacting differently) becomes, in this perspective, an important element of context (as well as an important analytic category).

The heuristic Pawson and Tilley offer to operationalise this approach is the so-called context-mechanism-outcome configuration (CMOC), which they initially captured by the (admittedly simplistic) formula {C+M=O}. In plain language: how does *context* interact with *mechanism(s)* to result in the observed *outcome*[6].

As usual, the simplicity of the wording hides a lot of challenges. What is context? What are *relevant* context elements in this setting? What are possible mechanisms? Where to find them? How? (Recall they are hidden.)

Context is a lot of things. It includes features of history, culture, shared beliefs, organisation, income levels and ways of getting them, stability of currency or lack thereof, inflation levels, labour market conditions, demographic structure, education levels, security, supply chains and their stability, family structure, social cohesion, market controls and regulations, legislation, religions and lots of other things.

Recall Lindblom: in complex social systems, a *comprehensive* analysis is impossible; we need to make a *strategic analysis* ('muddling with some skill'), which means applying intelligent strategies to simplify the complexity to workable levels. One way to do this, in the case of AR projects – or programmes in general – is to start from the *theory for change* (the action hypothesis) of the planned intervention. Having made explicit, clarified and thought through how (we think) it will work, we will find it easier to come up with contextual elements that might reasonably be assessed to interfere (enabling or constraining) with desired outcomes. Again, brainstorming on such a topic is more fruitfully done as a group than as an individual. What is rather crucial in such an exercise is a capacity to imagine what could go wrong (in the *ex-ante* phase) or to clearly pinpoint what went wrong (in the *ex-post* stage). In both stages, this can lead to identifying *necessary conditions* for project success that need attention. From the management literature, we know the example of the *pre-mortem* (Klein 2007), an exercise in 'prospective hindsight'[7] that has been shown to have great potential, notably through reduction of overconfidence bias (Veinott et al. 2010).

Especially in projects/programmes where change is fully intended and directed, it may also be helpful to make sense of the dynamics of context by expanding the simple 'C+M=O' formula with an additional focus on the programme's *intervention(s)* (I) and on *actors* or identifiable (sub)groups of actors (A), thus modifying the 'CMO' into an 'ICAMO' analytic format: intervention(s)-context-actors-mechanism(s)-outcomes (Van Belle 2014). The advantage of this ICAMO heuristic design is to draw the analyst's attention, from the start, to the diversity of actors reacting in potentially different ways to the introduction of interventions in a given context. Attributing an explicit category to these actors pulls them out of the context configuration and accords them due importance in the whole process (Marchal et al. 2018).

Identifying *mechanisms* is equally challenging, but we do not really have to invent them from scratch. There is a lot of substantive theories that can be used. Many of them start from demi-regularities that are, strictly speaking, not theories (yet), of the form '*If A, then, more often than not, B*'. Such regularities need explanation – and this explanation takes the form of a theory, and if it is a correct one, it could be called a mechanism. We do not need, however, always to get to the bottom explanation of things; many regularities are sufficiently universal to be useful. For instance, parents care more for their own children than for those of others (but there may be exceptions); 'those to whom evil is done do evil in return' (but there are exceptions); losses loom larger than gains (but. . .); when prices go down, demand will increase (but. . .), etc. It is important to understand that the observed 'exceptions' (the 'but. . .' part) are an important source of learning about the 'demi-regs' (as they are called in the realist jargon): they invite us to search for relevant context elements that were important enough to modify or break the regularity.

An illustration may be in order. Economic theory would predict that devaluing a country's currency will stimulate export (the regularity). The explanation (or the theory) is that by making the currency cheaper for companies in other countries (with non-devalued currencies), a price advantage is created that can be expected to boost sales from the country with devalued currency (the mechanism). However, historical observation shows that between 2012 and 2015, the Japanese Yen's 'real effective exchange rate' went down by roughly 35 per cent but export volume did not budge – a case of 'uncompetitive devaluation' (Economist 2016). So, apparently, the initial theory (the explanation of the regularity) needs to be amended. A good deal of the deviation's explanation is to be found in the fact that the world's economies are ever more tightly intertwined, resulting in the fact that Japan's final products, meant for export, needed a lot of *imported* intermediate inputs. Because Japanese companies had to buy those imports with a weaker currency, they became more expensive, thus reducing (or totally wiping out) the end-price advantage Japanese firms would have hoped for. The empirically observed *outcome* (stagnant export) is explained by a changed *context* (increased importance of imported intermediary inputs) resulting in a different interaction with the intended *mechanism* (devaluation induces a price advantage), which consequently will have to be modified. We see a different CMO configuration emerging.

The example is an illustration of realist evaluators' process of *specification*. Mechanisms, even the sturdier ones, are only activated (or can be set to work) *IF* . . . knowledge of these conditions enriches the pre-existing theory and contributes to its 'portability' to different contexts. This is a possibly hot issue in the AR community. For many practitioners of AR, the learning that takes place throughout an AR project is strictly restricted to the actual AR context. Realist inquiry begs to differ, stating that from the particular case something can be learnt that is applicable to other settings (portability), on condition that the learning is formulated at a higher level of abstraction than the actual case studied (in the form of a theory). This does not mean that such theory is now immediately universal in its possible application, but that we (may) have come closer to generalisability, precisely through this process of *specification*.

This is closely linked to the notion of *middle-range theory* (MRT) (Merton 1949). A middle-range theory is *not* a grand theory of everything (which is not testable empirically); in Raymond Boudon's re-interpretation, 'broad range theorising' would be like trying to 'determine the overarching independent variable that would operate in all social processes' (Boudon 1991), which is illusory. It is also *not* an ad hoc explanation of an isolated observation or event – which is not at all applicable ('portable') to other contexts. What it *is*, is a theory at a *reasonable* level of abstraction that can be applied and empirically tested over time and space, in different contexts. A typical example (not coincidentally one of Merton's best known theories) is *reference group theory*, which states, in simple words, that in a given situation social agents tend to adopt attitudes and beliefs, which they think would be the prevalent attitudes/beliefs in the group to which they like or aspire to belong (the 'reference group'). This has proven to be a useful theory, because it contributes significantly to explaining many and varied empirical regularities that have been observed in the social domain. Applied to AR, realists will strive to refine the AR project's *theory for action* (which is a hypothesis) into a (more valid) *MRT*, using the AR process as a testing opportunity.

What can realist inquiry contribute to the practice of AR

Westhorp et al. (2016) argue that 'realist action research' would add depth and value to AR design in several ways: (1) realist inquiry contributes a useful and pragmatic epistemological approach (*weak epistemological relativism* but without *judgemental relativism*: 'truth' remains a meaningful category – cf. supra); (2) realism formulates the evaluation question in a potentially more informative way as 'for whom does this work, in what contexts, in what respects, to what extent and how?', seeking a realist understanding of causation; (3) this formally acknowledges the all-important role of contextual elements in the workings of the mechanisms that lead to outcomes and (4) incorporating realist evaluative activity within the AR cycle structures the kinds of lessons likely to be learnt about the AR intervention (Westhorp et al. 2016). We fully agree with this formulation as a description of the *potential* of incorporating the realist mindset in the design and implementation of AR. As to the role of theory, we might add that, simply put, realists would seek to extend the common format of the action hypothesis from '*IF we do this, THEN that will follow*' to '*IF we do this, THEN that will follow, BECAUSE* . . .', thus clarifying or at least making explicit the hypothesised causal mechanism(s). Of course, this simple term 'because' can cover a quite complicated set of mechanisms triggered or dampened by contextual elements and project inputs.

A further question, however, might be: is this realist mindset always 'necessary' to do good AR and/or to what extent should it be pursued? We think the answer to this should be: it depends. To begin with, there are many perspectives on what constitutes AR, as should be clear from the first section of this essay. At one end of the spectrum, there are those who see it as formal social research of a specific kind (with the purpose of producing social change and to produce formal learning from this process), dealing with complicated or complex situations which thus require great rigour and depth. At the other end, there are those who see it more as reflective practice to improve very practical aspects of performance – akin to quality management or improvement projects (cf. the extensive literature taking this stance in, for example, journals in the domain of nursing). So, there is large variation in the nature of the problems addressed with AR (their level of complexity), in the nature of the proposed solution (which may be, sometimes, technically rather simple) and in the degree of relevance to create 'transportable' knowledge or the felt need to do so.

Apart from this variability inherent to AR, we might also entertain the thought that the practice of realist inquiry can be variable in intensity. There is no doubt that extending the question 'does it work' with 'for whom, why, in which circumstances, to what extent', etc. has the potential to elicit far more relevant answers and better insights, but there is also no doubt that it requires more resources – human, intellectual and data-wise. Inevitably, then, a cost-effectiveness perspective enters the discussion: how much effort/time/resources is the additional depth of learning worth? We submit that the essential contribution is the realist *mindset* and that this can be applied to different degrees of thoroughness or depth. One version of realist inquiry 'light' – but already quite useful, in our experience – consists in the critical examination of the hypothesis-for-action with the specific purpose of identifying a priori *necessary conditions* for this action to succeed. This can often be done without painstaking research into the specificities of context, on the basis of intrinsic characteristics of the planned action and insights accumulated by experienced participants in the AR project. This approach can be likened to the 'pre-mortem' exercise mentioned earlier (imagining how the project will fail) but with a positive twist: identifying *ex ante* what needs to be avoided but also what needs to be ensured, firmly based in the realist mindset (that contexts interact with mechanisms to produce outcomes, desired or less so).

One typical case in which the full realist inquiry mindset with all its trimmings for depth and rigour comes close to being mandatory is the *pilot project* used in policy formation and implementation. Not all pilot projects can be likened to AR projects, but obviously they have a lot in common. They can come in a variety of forms, but let's say there are two extremes: one is 'to show something works', when tried out on a limited scale; the other extreme is 'to find out what the problems could be with implementation'. In the first type, extra resources will typically be injected to ensure success and the ultimate purpose of such a pilot is, for many people, to be able to say: 'we have shown that it works, therefore it should be scaled up'.

It will not come as a surprise when we state that this is the wrong way to go about it (although we have seen this happening time and again in development projects in the health sector, e.g. in cost-recovery strategies, community health worker strategies, community participation strategies and privatisation). With pilot projects (which are by definition intended to inform policymakers on issues of generalisation), more than with any other kind of projects in a contextually diversified social realm, the conclusion 'it works' is utterly insufficient. This is *par excellence* the situation in which the realist evaluator's *specification* comes into its full relevance (and more importantly: necessity): pilot projects are experiments that should produce a maximum of relevant information on the combinations of context-mechanism-outcome that is necessary for full(er) scale successful implementation in a variety of contexts. This means they should be designed with this objective in view and evaluated accordingly. RE in this case should be able to prove its worth.

A final note on competences. An eighteenth-century anecdote tells the story of a baffled musician who asked J.S. Bach how it was possible that he managed to play his organ music compositions so faultlessly well. His answer is reported to have been: 'You just have to press the right keys and the right pedals at the right time and the music plays itself.'

Of course, this is the kind of witticism an accomplished expert can afford to produce when surrounded by admirers. But what he was actually saying is: 'I am an expert organ player; I know how to press the right keys and the right pedals at the right time'. And, talented though he may have been, we can be sure it must have taken him a lot of time and effort to reach that expert status. It was not something he had acquired by reading a book on organ playing. Similarly, doing 'realist action research' is a challenge. The realist inquiry mindset can be embraced for reasons of intellectual seductiveness (this happened to us) but is not automatically acquired-because-admired. It requires hard work and lots of practice (preferably under the guidance of someone who is further advanced on this challenging road), and this practice needs to be underpinned by a lot of scholarly background. This learning process is a never-ending story.

But then, that is true of any research activity worth pursuing.

Notes

1 'Praxis' has its origin in Aristotelian thought about human action as different from 'poiesis'. The latter is about making or producing things following the logic of 'techne' ('technology'); 'praxis' does not aim to produce an object but to realise some morally worthwhile good, following the logic of 'phronesis' (practical wisdom). In the twentieth century, Hannah Arendt was well-known for having revived this distinction as an important element of her philosophy.

2 This is not to say that learning cannot or does not take place elsewhere in the process; through the practice of reflective action, constant learning can take place throughout implementation and monitoring of the action.
3 This is a foretaste of what realist inquiry could contribute, which will be developed further in the text.
4 Charles Darwin and Alfred R. Wallace's theory of natural selection required a mighty act of creative 'out-of-the-box' thinking.
5 With this difference that ordinarily in medical practice the diagnostic entities (diseases) are – mostly – just *categories* (the image used for identifying the most plausible one is 'pigeonholing') and not (yet) explanatory *mechanisms*, although for progressively more disease categories the mechanisms are becoming clear.
6 The seemingly mathematical formulation as a simple sum is only misleading if taken literally.
7 A 'pre-mortem' starts with the statement, *before* implementation of the plan, that 'our project failed spectacularly'. Participants are then invited to come up with reasons for this imagined failure. In terms of group dynamics, it intends to avoid 'group think' (a malady in some decision-making groups where consensus is favoured over and above all rational critical thinking), blind optimism, 'overconfidence bias' and/or undesirable submission behaviour to hierarchy.

References

Adelman, C. (1993) 'Kurt Lewin and the origins of action research', *Educational Action Research*, 1(1), 7–24.

Astbury, B. and Leeuw, F. (2010) 'Unpacking black boxes: Mechanisms and theory building in evaluation', *American Journal of Evaluation*, 31(3), 363–381.

Auriacombe, C. (2015) 'Closing the gap between theory and practice with action research', *African Journal of Public Affairs*, 8(3), 1–16.

Baum, F., MacDougall, C. and Smith, D. (2006) 'Participatory action research', *Journal of Epidemiology and Community Health*, 60, 854–857.

Bhaskar, R. (1978) *A realist theory of science*, Hemel Hempstead: Harvester Press.

Blaise, P. and Kegels, G. (2004) 'A realistic approach to the evaluation of the quality management movement in health care systems: A comparison between European and African contexts based on Mintzberg's organizational models', *International Journal of Health Planning and Management*, 19(4), 337–364.

Boudon, R. (1991) 'Review: What middle-range theories are', *Contemporary Sociology*, 20(4), 519–522.

Byrne, D. and Callaghan, G. (2014) *Complexity theory and the social sciences: The state of the art*, London: Routledge.

Davison, R.M., Martinsons, M. and Kock, N. (2004) 'Principles of canonical action research', *Info Systems Journal*, 14, 65–86.

Dickens, L. and Watkins, K. (1999) 'Action research: Rethinking Lewin', *Management Learning*, 30(2), 127–140.

Economist, T. (2016) 'After the dips: Big currency devaluations are not boosting exports as much as they used to', *The Economist*, 9 January.

Foster, M. (1972) 'An introduction to the theory and practice of action research in work organisations', *Human Relations*, 25(6), 529–566.

Grodos, D. and Mercenier, P. (2000) *Health systems research: A clearer methodology for more effective action*, vol. Studies in Health Services Organisation & Policy #15, Antwerp: ITGPress.

Hammersley, M. (2004) 'Action research: A contradiction in terms?', *Oxford Review of Education*, 2, 165–181.

Harré, R. (1972) *The philosophies of science: An introductory survey*, London: Oxford University Press.

Isaksen, R. (2016) 'Reclaiming rational theory choice as Central: A critique of methodological applications of critical realism', *Journal of Critical Realism*, 15(3), 245–262.

Jagosh, J. (2020) 'Retroductive theorizing in Pawson and Tilley's applied scientific realism', *Journal of Critical Realism*, 19(2), 121–130. DOI: 10.1080/14767430.2020.1723301

Klein, G. (2007) 'Performing a project premortem', *Harvard Business Review*, September.

Kock, N., Avison, D., Baskerville, R., Myers, M. and Wood-Harper, T. (1999) 'Panel 8 – IS Action Research: Can We Serve Two Masters?' *Proceedings of the International Conference on Information Systems 1999*, 72.

Lewin, K. (1946) 'Action research and minority problems', *Journal of Social Issues*, 2, 34–46.

Lindblom, C.E. (1979) 'Still muddling, not yet through', *Public Administration Review*, 39(6), 517–526.

Marchal, B., Kegels, G. and Van Belle, S. (2018) 'Theory and realist methods', in: N. Emmel, J. Greenhalgh, A. Manzano, M. Monaghan and S. Dalkin (eds) *Doing realist research*, London: Sage, pp. 79–90.

Merton, R.K. (1949) 'On sociological theories of the middle range', in: R.K. Merton (ed) *Social theory and social structure*, New York: Simon & Schuster, The Free Press, pp. 39–53.

Meyer, J. (2000) 'Qualitative methods in health related action research', *British Medical Journal*, 320, 178–181.

Nitayarumphong, S. and Mercenier, P. (1992) 'Ayutthaya research project: Thailand experiences on health systems research', in: *Commission of the European communities; directorate-general XII: Science, research and development. Life sciences and technologies for developing countries. Area 'health'. Methodology and relevance of health systems research. Research reports. Contractholders meeting 8–10 April 1992*, Paris: Centre International de l'Enfance, pp. 55–78.

Pawson, R. and Tilley, N. (1997) *Realistic evaluation*, London: Sage.

Rapoport, R. (1970) 'Three dilemmas of action research', *Human Relations*, 23, 499–513.

Reason, P. and Rowan, J. (1981) *Human inquiry: A sourcebook of new paradigm research*, Chichester: Wiley.

Sayer, A. (1992) *Method in social science – a realist approach*, 2nd edn, London: Routledge.

Susman, G. and Evered, R.D. (1978) 'An assessment of the scientific merits of action research', *Administrative Science Quarterly*, 23, 582–603.

Van Belle, S. (2014) *Accountability in sexual and reproductive health: How relations between INGOs and state actors shape public accountability. A study of two local health systems in Ghana*, London: University of London.

Veinott, B., Klein, G. and Wiggins, S. (2010) *Evaluating the effectiveness of the premortem technique on plan confidence*, Proceedings of the 7th International ISCRAM Conference, Seattle, May.

Westhorp, G., Stevens, K. and Rogers, P. (2016) 'Using realist action research for service redesign', *Evaluation*, 361–379.

8 Problematising the concept of social inclusion through sport
Opportunities and challenges through the lens of aspirations and capabilities

Emran Riffi Acharki and Ramón Spaaij

Introduction

The previous chapters of this book have investigated the relationship between social inclusion and community sport, both conceptually and empirically, in the context of Flanders. The preceding chapters, and Chapter 2 in particular, further present programme theories and overarching strategies through which community sport practices may foster social outcomes in terms of personal development, health, and social cohesion among marginalised youths. The research question that guides these analyses is: "What are the working mechanisms and facilitating conditions in community sports initiatives that relate to the promotion of social inclusion for at-risk youth?" In this chapter, we aim to think and engage critically *with* the conceptual, methodological, and empirical insights offered in the preceding chapters. We seek to provide critical reflections on the concept of social inclusion and its application and operationalisation in social science research on community sport. More specifically, we draw on a capability approach and the first author's empirical research to foreground subjective aspects and experiences of social inclusion and their relationship to sport, through a focus on aspirations and capabilities.

The empirical research we draw upon in this chapter is closely aligned with the *community sport for AT-risk youth: Innovative strategies for promoting personal development, health and social CoHesion* (CATCH) study through its explicit focus on social inclusion through community sport, albeit with a specific focus on youth sport in the Netherlands. The empirical data, which is complementary to the data collated in the CATCH project, serves to provide concrete illustrations of how a capability approach can inform and shed an alternative light on evaluation by centring the voice of people and the question of what they have reason to value. In doing so, we seek to identify fruitful directions for future research and knowledge translation complement the central arguments and research findings presented in this book.

DOI: 10.4324/9780429340635-11

Social inclusion: conceptual agreements and disagreements

Social inclusion can be approached as a state of being (an outcome) and as a process (Hills et al. 2002; Spaaij et al. 2014). Reflecting both approaches, social inclusion can be typified as the inclusion of (marginalised) groups in society, by gaining access to rights, resources, and opportunities (Haudenhuyse and Theeboom 2015). Whatever approach or definition is used, social inclusion (like its often interchangeably used antonym, social exclusion) remains a complex and contested concept. Social inclusion and exclusion do not manifest as dichotomous states nor as simple linear functions or accumulations of dimensions but, rather, as ever-dynamic and multi-dimensional processes and states of being accepted and valued, in or shut out from, society, in a material and a symbolic sense (Silver 2007; Steinert and Pilgram 2007). The very understanding of social inclusion and exclusion is continuously subject to macro-level forces, such as underlying political and economic discourses. For this reason, Byrne (2005) argues that any adequate understanding of social inclusion requires a comprehensive, integrated approach.

The literature describes different typologies, including various and recurring general dimensions of social inclusion (Bhalla and Lapeyre 2004; Steiner and Pilgram 2007). For example, Taket et al. (2009) distinguish between the economic, political, and sociocultural domains of social inclusion and exclusion. All typologies imply "hard", tangible aspects, such as income, citizenship status and objective access, as well as "soft", subjective aspects, such as a sense of recognition, social appreciation, and belonging (Spaaij et al. 2014). Moreover, they acknowledge that social inclusion and exclusion can be experiences as entrenched and cumulative, or as more fleeting and fluid. McDonald et al. (2019) refer to the latter as "moments of social inclusion" at the level of micro-social interaction (see also Abrams et al. 2005).

Some scholars explicitly value the importance of subjective aspects and experiences of social inclusion and exclusion. Levitas et al. (2007: 46), for example, state that "greater emphasis is needed on indicators of the quality of young people's social relationships and transitions (for example, personal and familial relationships, social isolation and support, social participation, subjective well-being)". However, a vast amount of literature remains limited to social inclusion and exclusion in material and economic terms, focusing on objective, tangible, and material dimensions of the concept. Levitas et al. (2007) categorise social exclusion in three main domains: resources, participation, and quality of life, wherein the latter stays somewhat unexplained. The "softer" aspects of social exclusion are barely mentioned throughout the rest of the 246-page report, with the exception of brief bullet points such as "social support" (89), "civic efficacy" (p. 92), and "vulnerability to stigma" (93). This tendency to avoid the soft aspects of social inclusion and exclusion might have something to do with their elusiveness. In this chapter, we are specifically concerned with the subjective aspects of dynamics of social inclusion.

An important notion to consider in understanding social inclusion in public domains such as youth sport relates to agency. Schuyt (2000) describes social exclusion as a subtle slide of people to the margin of society, which manifests itself in an interplay of being unable, not allowed, and unwilling to participate in key societal domains. This distinction reveals the relevance of agency in dynamics of social inclusion. More specifically, it raises the question to what degree willingness to participate can be interpreted as a precursor to, or a consequence of, one's ability and/or one's perceived social support (i.e. "being allowed"). Hence, how much agency is involved in one's willingness to be included in society? In the victim blaming approach, the position of disadvantaged youths is often attributed to the youth themselves (Crozier 2009). Concerning social inclusion, this is explained in refrains such as that "they" choose to have lower aspirations regarding being valuable members themselves (Archer et al. 2014). Consider the following example:

> Adam went into juvenile detention at the age of 15, for battery. Afterwards, he dropped out of school and fell on hard times. Although he didn't have the interest or money to apply for sports club membership, by coincidence, he took a trial training session at Kops boxing gym. Hereafter, the coach asked him to join the next class. Adam expressed how "for the first time, I had something to want . . ., to show that I'm kind of good at this boxing stuff". Although he lost his first three amateur bouts, he gradually improved and almost won the regional Amateur Championship. He reflected on this experience as follows: "When you get something, it tastes like more you know. At first, I was happy to just be allowed to join training. Then I wanted the respect of the coaches and teammates. Now I have that, there's a lot of stuff to want to keep and also to want next. I just got a temporary job you know, who knows, if I keep this discipline up, I can convince them to hire me. . . . You saw that girl at the counter? Yeah, but she's not like me you know. She's educated, classy. But I told her, if I score that job, I will definitely ask her out. Man, if I'd pull that off".

The excerpt from an interview, which was conducted as a part of the first author's current PhD research on social inclusion through sport, shows how "wanting" (willingness) can be a self-enforcing process, stimulated by factors such as social success. This willingness, which in the literature is formulated as aspiration, in itself requires a certain ability, which is referred to as the capacity to aspire (Appadurai 2004). This represents one's ability to have aspirations, such as aspirations for social inclusion. Adam's example highlights the need to recognise that in practice, and especially amongst marginalised youths, the capacity to aspire is not the same for everyone. As one might expect, levels of aspiration are closely related to wealth, as people with privilege (e.g. material or white privilege) often have more capacity to aspire, leading to greater aspirations. Members of marginalised groups, such as ethnic minorities with low socio-economic status, on the other hand, tend to face greater difficulties regarding their aspirations, even though they may not be aware of it themselves (Jensen and Frørup 2017). This seems especially important in the current European context of growing objective and subjective inequality (Otto et al. 2017).

In conclusion, one can consider social inclusion in tangible and in more elusive, subjective terms. Within the latter realm, we would argue that aspiration is an important dimension, which can be stimulated through youth sport. The next section will further explore dynamics of social inclusion through sport from this vantage point.

Social inclusion through lens of aspirations and capabilities

In the context of this book, explaining that sport holds great potential for youth development may be the equivalent of explaining to a dentist that flossing *might be* a good idea. The development of diverse forms of capital is often viewed as one of the positive outcomes of sport (e.g. Haudenhuyse et al. 2012; Spaaij 2012). Capital can be described as material and immaterial assets that can be specified as economic, social, and cultural. For the development of "soft" social inclusion through sport, social and cultural capital are particularly relevant.

Social capital can be described as social assets, concerning social networks, connections and sociability, meaning, the skill and disposition to sustain these networks (Morrow 2001). Cultural capital can be defined as the familiarity with the dominant culture in a society (Sullivan 2001) and is related to previously formulated aspirations (willingness) regarding social inclusion, especially amongst marginalised youths (Dumais 2002). Capital should not only be considered as an inherently important asset but as a part of one's experienced life environment. Bourdieu facilitates this idea with the concepts of habitus and field. Field can be described as a social competitive space and its configuration of relations between individuals and/or institutions (Hart 2016, 2013). Habitus concerns as a normative way of perceiving the world and acting in it (Navarro 2006). This concept relates to cultural and familial heritage, internalised to meaningful practices and meaning-giving perceptions, guiding future acquisition of associated cultural capital (Reed-Danahay 2005). Habitus and field are important aspects to keep in mind when examining how social inclusion and related aspirations are formed and influenced in youth sport. For example, general consideration of habitus and field help to understand how a young person from a disadvantaged urban area who has been engaged in a certain team sport might have internalised a certain appreciation of the direct community and the broader society, guiding his perception, behaviour, and subsequent development of capital, aspirations, and capabilities regarding social inclusion.

These Bourdieusian concepts give rise to at least two important notions regarding sport: capital and social inclusion. Firstly, it is important to note that sport contexts differ in their capacity to provide positive learning experiences that stimulate capital such as positive networks and role models. In addition, participants differ in their ability to accrue capital from sport and convert it into relevant

Problematising the concept of social inclusion through sport 149

capabilities to pursue goals such as social inclusion. This is referred to as conversion ability. Due to differences in conversion ability, one can accrue a positive social network, self-defence and psychosocial abilities through participation in sport while another person can find sport participation a less beneficial or even negative experience. To illuminate this point, we provide the following opposing examples from Emran's fieldwork:

> Amin explains how, as a youth football player, the majority of his coaches did their best to guide him both in football as in life. However, he increasingly struggled with putting their advice into practice. Amin explains that although he was technically skilled and actually "loved the game to death", he had a tough time to really develop in the sport and outside of it, because he struggled with the pressure of his single mother to "make it" as a professional athlete. He says: "It's hard for a teenager to listen to the coaches' advice of training consciously instead of just hard *and* being committed at school *and* being humble and sociable, while on the other hand, bearing the pressure of being the golden boy, the savior".
>
> Isra reports that she had a great time in Karate and she feels that she really developed social skills, made friends for life and eventually laid the foundation for her career as a teacher. She expressed: "Of course, nothing is perfect and neither is the sport. But I just had great role models inside and outside the dojo and I think I was kind of a resilient person myself".

A second notion is that when an individual is able to successfully transfer and convert capital into relevant capabilities, it is still uncertain to what degree he or she experiences being allowed to develop his or her own ideals and aspirations regarding social inclusion. We argue that society determines the value of types of capital, most probably in favour of its powerful and dominant members. In our example, it might be that acquired capital and formed capabilities still do not lead to one's ideal of social inclusion because one's capital and capabilities are less valued in society. Moreover, there is the possibility that one's aspirations (of social inclusion) can be restricted because they do not fit with the dominant normative view of what is worthy or even allowed to be aspired. For example, being an openly gay athlete or being an openly orthodox Muslim in some sport contexts can be very problematic aspirations.

Hence, Bourdieu's concepts provide important principles and elements for generating insights into how youth sport can contribute to the development of social inclusion, but they also leave some conceptual lacunae. To understand how youth sport "works" or does not "work" in real life, we need a broader framework that enables a comprehensive understanding of the dynamics of social inclusion through youth sport.

The capability approach seems fit for this purpose. The capability approach is a conceptual framework that was conceived by Sen and Nussbaum in the 1980s to provide insight into well-being (e.g. Nussbaum 2011; Sen 1999). While many frameworks until that era focused on economic wealth as an end in itself, the capability approach draws attention to individuals' ability to pursuit their own idea of well-being. In other words, it focuses on the degree to which individuals are able to pursue things (generally expressed as "beings and doings") that they find valuable, such as (their personal concept of) being socially included (Robeyns 2005, 2016).

For further specification of the capability approach, we use youth sport context as an example. Basically, the capability approach suggests that youth sport can help youths develop capabilities that support their pursuit of social inclusion. Capabilities are opportunities and options that help people in their pursuit of beings and doings that they value. In this sense, sport participation can build capabilities such as the formation of social capital (Lawson 2010) and self-regulatory and empathic self-efficacy. However, as the previous examples illuminate, whether youth sport actually leads to capability development is not guaranteed but rather depends on the pedagogical context wherein it is provided. For example, positive development through sport has more chance of occurring in sport practices that focus on more than winning; rather, coaches care for psychosocial development of youth participants, so they may gradually and increasingly develop aspirations and wider capabilities for pursuing social inclusion (Schulenkorf et al. 2016). Like the examples suggest, the capability approach also shows that positive development through sport depends on participants' conversion factors on personal (e.g. personal skills, motivation), social (e.g. family support and norms), or environmental level (e.g. pedagogical climate and safety), which altogether form one's ability to converse lessons and inspiration from sport to personally valuable capabilities.

In conclusion, capability theory accounts for the complex dynamics of social inclusion, complementing Bourdieu, by accounting for the fact that sport engagement does not lead to the same outcomes for everyone, as it depends on one's contextual circumstances and conversion abilities in particular (Sen 1992). The framework presented provides a broader conceptual basis for exploring and generating a deeper understanding of how youth sport coaches and youth sport participants perceive sport to expand capabilities and aspirations for social inclusion and how (e.g. in what pedagogical conditions) these processes can be stimulated. It is to these questions that we now turn through a discussion of empirical fieldwork conducted by the authors.

Empirical applications in research

So far in this chapter, we have explained how sport can contribute to aspirations and capabilities such as social skills to achieve desired social inclusion. Whether these outcomes materialise depends on conditions such as that sport is provided in an adequate pedagogical sport climate (Coakley 2011; Coalter 2007; Collins and Haudenhuyse 2015; Hartmann and Kwauk 2011; Schaillée et al. 2017). But (how) does the capability theory apply in practice? Empirical data, gathered by the first author as part of his PhD research, provides

Problematising the concept of social inclusion through sport 151

insights that serve as input for further clarification and reflection of the theory. The narrative of football coach Ishaan at AVV Zeeburgia in Amsterdam is a case in point. Ishaan explained:

> I now also have a boy [Quincy] from Ghana, who has been in the Netherlands for four years now. He is here with his father. His mother and his two sisters still live in Ghana, so his father has two or three jobs to ensure that they can come this way as soon as possible. I know that this boy occasionally visits another teammate who lives near him because he is afraid [to be] alone. I cannot expect such a boy to be brought by his father or uncle, get it?

Around six months later, Ishaan reported how Quincy in the meantime had gradually built a social network of friends who supported him in important matters such as transport for away games, learning Dutch, and school homework. Ishaan pointed out how this network developed gradually, a process that began at the football club. It took Quincy a while to get used to the rules and obligations of AVV Zeeburgia, such as being on time and complying with team routines, before Ishaan found him ready to participate in matches. Concurrently, Quincy gained confidence, social skills and trust from his peers, which helped him to build a supportive social network. Ishaan explained how he supported this process by not rushing into expectations towards Quincy, encouraging him and his teammates to help each other out and not portraying Quincy as less capable. Putting Quincy's case in a model of capability approach, it can be illustrated in simplified form as follows.

In similar vein, youth participants explained how, through sport, they expanded their capabilities and aspirations, which contributed to a sense of social inclusion. In an elite youth sport context, an observation at football club Ajax's Under-12s youth team revealed the following:

> Participants perform an exercise whereby one player duels against a defender and a goal keeper. Jael starts dribbling towards the goal, but seems to hesitate when he approaches the opposing defender. He gets pushed into a corner and seems to be in trouble. From the sideline, coach Lars screeches: "What are you going to do Jael? You're out of breath, you're out of power, what are you gonna do?" Jael gasps for air, holding the defender of the ball. "You can't keep this up Jael. What are you going to do? You must do *something now!*" Jael spontaneously skips the ball to free space and almost scores with a volley. Although it is not a goal, teammates applaud. Lars gives Jael a high five. "Firemen! Firemen!"
>
> Later in the training session, Lars calls Jael and ties his shoelaces (Lars recurrently uses tying shoelaces as a reflective moment). "Are you okay?" Jael nods. . . . Lars: "It's okay to be afraid you know. We all are sometimes. It's about how you handle it. Fear is like fire you know, it's just there. But . . . it's okay. You can use it". Jael nods: "We are firemen". Lars holds his shoulders: "Exactly! We control the fire!" . . . .

In a brief reflection, Lars explains that Jael is a new member of the team and he coaches him in handling the pressure that comes with playing for Ajax. "The first step is that he recognises things such as pressure and learns to think of them in a positive way. That's where learning starts you know [points to his head]".

Although Lars did not specifically formulate it as such, he seems to point to a constructive mindset, wherein challenges are perceived as learning opportunities. This relates to the stimulation of abovementioned personal conversion ability.

These and other examples show us how the capability model provides a useful framework to study and understand dynamics of social inclusion through sport. However, it also reveals some interesting theoretical notions. The following subsections illuminate valuable aspects and application challenges for the capability theory in the context of social inclusion through sport.

Valuable aspects of the capability approach

The capability approach can provide an important framework for contextual understanding of youth sport dynamics and its contribution to youth development such as social inclusion. The approach broadens the informational basis of assessment and provides the possibility to generate deep insights on the process in its context (Robeyns 2005; Svensson and Levine 2017). This responds to the call for further theorisation of youth sport, beyond the present frameworks and beaten paths (Schulenkorf and Spaaij 2015). More specific, the capability approach can provide a framework to engage in dialogue with local stakeholders about how sport is perceived to expand individuals' capabilities and social inclusion and how (e.g. under what pedagogical conditions) these processes can be stimulated (Svensson and Levine 2017).

Furthermore, the capability approach accounts for diversity in the youth sport context, by implying that youth sport does not lead to the same outcomes for everyone. Instead, it shows how outcomes depend on factors such as one's conversion abilities. In the context of social inclusion, this emphasises the importance of an appropriate pedagogical sport climate that contributes to the capabilities and conversion abilities of target groups. Therefore, the capability approach is especially valuable for research that is concerned with inequality and disability issues, because this approach makes it possible to account for specific circumstances of marginalised youths.

Taken together, the capability approach provides a participant-centred approach to personal and community development. It enables us to obtain insight into the black box of inclusion through sport by providing a framework for identifying how sport is perceived to expand individuals' capabilities to social inclusion and under what (pedagogical) conditions these processes occur (Harris and Adams 2016; Svensson and Levine 2017). It helps us break up the process to concrete questions such as "what aspects or activities have impact on the expansion of the capabilities of the respondents?" or "what related barriers do respondents perceive restricting their capabilities and (how) do they overcome them?" The capability approach further enables the consideration of subjects, in our case youth sport participants, as active social agents in their communities with their own ideas, priorities, strategies and aspirations (Ballet et al. 2011).

Application challenges of the capability approach

There are some significant limitations and challenges associated with the capability approach. Firstly, it seems conceptually challenging to adequately assign elements from practice to the theoretical dimensions of the model presented. This has to do with the ambiguous distinction of dimensions such as capital, capability, and social inclusion as an ideal outcome. Figure 8.1, for example, raises the question to what extent the capabilities (enrolment, practicing, playing matches, etc.) are (dis)similar and distinguishable from other dimensions such as conversion ability and social inclusion. Furthermore, it seems that conversion ability, aspirations, and choice work as moderators throughout the process. We acknowledge that, generally, in the complex thick of life, theoretical dimensions tend to blur into one entwined whole. However, this model seems to allow this to happen quite easily.

Secondly, the capability theory posits that from capabilities, people develop agency to choose their goals for well-being, such as their ideal of social inclusion (Sen 1992). This seems plausible; as capabilities develop, new choices arise. Hypothetically, a young athlete may develop extraordinary football skills and get the opportunity (thus agency) to promote to a certain team or club level. But how does this work for social inclusion? In the first section, we explained how social inclusion also concerns a sense of willingness, which we described as the capacity to aspire and, alongside this, the degree to which one perceives oneself to be "allowed" to pursue their ideals, such as the ideal of social inclusion. However, this notion seems to be somewhat overlooked in the capability approach.

Our final observation concerns the self-reinforcing nature of social inclusion. It is plausible that social inclusion and exclusion occur as a self-reinforcing process. If one experiences a feeling of social rejection, this may materialise into "real" social rejection, for example, if this feeling comprises one's ability to engage in

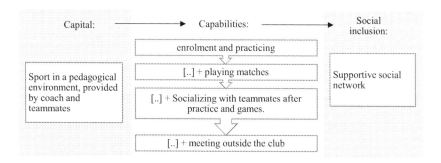

Figure 8.1 Development of social inclusion through sport, through the lens of capability theory

social activities such as sport. Social exclusion is not only a matter of perceptions of one's past trajectories and experiences but also of future expectations. The latter, as previously described, are closely related to aspirations and the capacity to aspire. The one-way directional arrows in Sen's (1992) model, however, do not seem to take these dynamics into account. In the final section, we draw together the main arguments and findings reported in this chapter.

Conclusion

In this chapter, we have sought to provide critical reflections on the concept of social inclusion by drawing on capability theory and the first author's empirical research to foreground subjective aspects and experiences of social inclusion and their relationship to sport. This focus on aspirations and capabilities is still in its infancy in research on sport for development, but it has been gaining increased attention over the past few years (Dao and Smith 2019; Darnell and Dao 2017). While the Bourdieusian concepts of capital, habitus, and field have been quite popular in community sports research (e.g. Skinner et al. 2008; Spaaij 2011; Adams et al. 2018), a conceptual approach to social inclusion that is grounded in capability theory provides an original contribution to this field of research. In particular, its focus on aspirations and capabilities can enrich mechanism-based approaches such as the realist evaluation approach advocated by Fred Coalter in this book (see Chapter 6). It can also inform the development of programme theories and theories of changes, including those presented in the preceding chapters within the context of the CATCH research, by accounting for young people's contextual circumstances and conversion abilities and for how these shape their capacity to aspire, their aspirations, and their capacity to fulfil their aspirations.

Considering the aforementioned application challenges of the capability approach, we advocate for a more dynamic and flexible reading of the capability approach, wherein the dimensions are not presorted as fixed stages in a predetermined linear process. Methodologically, this requires an in-depth, primarily qualitative, process-orientated approach to data collection and analysis. The use of life-history interviews, ethnography, and narrative analysis could be of particular value in order to identify how young people's capabilities and aspirations may evolve or shift over time as a consequence of, or in tandem with, their participation in community sport programmes.

References

Abrams, D., Hogg, M.A. and Marques, J.M. (eds) (2005) *The social psychology of inclusion and exclusion*, New York: Psychology Press.

Adams, A., Harris, K. and Lindsey, I. (2018) 'Examining the capacity of a sport for development programme to create social capital', *Sport in Society*, 21(3), 558–573.

Appadurai, A. (2004) 'The capacity to aspire: Culture and the terms of recognition', in: V. Rao and M. Walton (eds) *Culture and public action*, Stanford, CA: Stanford University Press, pp. 59–84.

Archer, L., DeWitt, J. and Wong, B. (2014) Spheres of influence: what shapes young people's aspirations at age 12/13 and what are the implications for education policy?, *Journal of Education Policy*, 29:1, 58–85, DOI: 10.1080/02680939.2013.790079

Ballet, J., Biggeri, M. and Comi, F. (2011) 'Children's agency and the capability approach: A conceptual framework', in: M. Biggeri, J. Ballet and F. Comim (eds) *Children and the capability approach*, Houndmills: Palgrave Macmillan, pp. 22–46.

Bhalla, A. and Lapeyre, F. (2004) *Poverty and exclusion in a global world*, 2nd edn, Houndmills: Palgrave Macmillan.

Byrne, D. (2005) *Social exclusion*, Maidenhead: Open University Press.

Coakley, J. (2011) 'Youth sports: What counts as "positive development?"', *Journal of Sport and Social Issues*, 35(3), 306–324.

Coalter, F. (2007) *A wider social role for sport: Who's keeping the score?*, London: Routledge.

Collins, M. and Haudenhuyse, R. (2015) 'Social exclusion and austerity policies in England: The role of sports in a new area of social polarisation and inequality?' *Social Inclusion*, 3(3), 5–18.

Crozier, G. (2009). South Asian parents' aspirations versus teachers' expectations in the United Kingdom. *Theory Into Practice*, 48(4), 290–296.

Dao, M. and Smith, T. (2019) 'The capability approach as a conceptual bridge for theory-practice in sport-for-development', *Journal of Global Sport Management*. DOI: 10.1080/24704067.2019.1703117

Darnell, S. and Dao, M. (2017) 'Considering sport for development and peace through the capabilities approach', *Third World Thematics*, 2(1), 23–36.

Dumais, S.A. (2002) 'Cultural capital, gender, and school success: The role of habitus', *Sociology of Education*, 75(1), 44–68.

Gano-Overway, L. and Guivernau, M. (2014) Caring in the gym: Reflections from middle school physical education teachers. *European Physical Education Review*, 20(2), 264–281.

Harris, K. and Adams, A. (2016) 'Power and discourse in the politics of evidence in sport for development', *Sport Management Review*, 19(2), 97–106.

Hart, C.S. (2013) *Aspirations, education and social justice: Applying Sen and Bourdieu*, London: A&C Black.

Hart, C.S. (2016) 'How do aspirations matter?' *Journal of Human Development and Capabilities*, 17(3), 324–341.

Hartmann, D. and Kwauk, C. (2011) 'Sport and development: An overview, critique, and reconstruction', *Journal of Sport and Social Issues*, 35(3), 284–305.

Haudenhuyse, R. and Theeboom, M. (2015) 'Introduction to the special issue "sport for social inclusion: Critical analyses and future challenges"', *Social Inclusion*, 3(3), 1–4.

Haudenhuyse, R., Theeboom, M. and Coalter, F. (2012) 'The potential of sports-based social interventions for vulnerable youth: Implications for sport coaches and youth workers', *Journal of Youth Studies*, 15(4), 437–454.

Hills, J., Le Grand, J. and Piachaud, D. (eds) (2002) *Understanding social exclusion*, Oxford: Oxford University Press.

Jensen, N.R. and Frørup, A.K. (2017) 'Aspirations of young people living in disadvantaged areas in Denmark', in: H.U. Otto, V. Egdell, J.-M. Bonvin and R. Atzmüller (eds) *Empowering young people in disempowering times*, Cheltenham: Edward Elgar, pp. 232–248.

Lawson, H. A. (2010) Empowering people, facilitating community development, and contributing to sustainable development: The social work of sport, exercise, and physical education. Programs, *Sport, Education and Society*, 10(1), 135–160.

Levitas, R., Pantazis, C., Fahmy, E., Gordon, D., Lloyd, E. and Patsios, D. (2007) *The multi- dimensional analysis of social exclusion*, Bristol: University of Bristol.

McDonald, B., Spaaij, R. and Dukic, D. (2019) 'Moments of social inclusion: Asylum seekers, football and solidarity', *Sport in Society*, 22(6), 935–949.

Morrow, V. (2001) 'Young people's explanations and experiences of social exclusion: Retrieving Bourdieu's concept of social capital', *International Journal of Sociology and Social Policy*, 21(4–6), 37–63.

Navarro, Z. (2006) 'In search of a cultural interpretation of power: The contribution of Pierre Bourdieu', *IDS Bulletin*, 37(6), 11–22.

Nussbaum, M.C. (2011) *Creating capabilities*, Cambridge, MA: Harvard University Press.

Otto, H.U., Egdell, V., Bonvin, J.M. and Atzmüller, R. (eds) (2017) *Empowering young people in disempowering times: Fighting inequality through capability oriented policy*, Cheltenham: Edward Elgar.

Reed-Danahay, D. (2005) *Locating Bourdieu*, Indianapolis, IN: Indiana University Press.

Robeyns, I. (2005) 'The capability approach: A theoretical survey', *Journal of Human Development*, 6(1), 93–117.

Robeyns, I. (2016) 'The capability approach in practice', *Journal of Political Philosophy*, 14(3), 351–376.

Schaillée, H., Theeboom, M. and Van Cauwenberg, J. (2017) 'Peer-and coach-created motivational climates in youth sport: Implications for positive youth development of disadvantaged girls', *Social Inclusion*, 5(2), 163–178.

Schulenkorf, N., Sherry, E. and Phillips, P. (2016) 'What is sport development', in: E. Sherry, N. Schulenkorf and P. Phillips (eds) *Managing sport development: An international approach*, London: Routledge, pp. 3–11.

Schulenkorf, N. and Spaaij, R. (2015) 'Commentary: Reflections on theory building in sport for development and peace', *International Journal of Sport Management and Marketing*, 16(1–2), 71–77.

Schuyt, C.J.M. (2000) *Sociale uitsluiting: Essay en interviews* [Social exclusion: Essays and interviews], Amsterdam: SWP.

Sen, A. (1992) *Inequality reexamined*, Oxford: Clarendon Press.

Sen, A. (1999) *Development as freedom*, Oxford: Oxford University Press.

Silver, H. (2007) 'Social exclusion', in: G. Ritzer (ed) *Blackwell encyclopedia of sociology*, Oxford: Blackwell Reference Online. Available HTTP: http://philosociology.com/UPLOADS/_PHILOSOCIOLOGY.ir_Blackwell%20Encyclopedia%20of%20Sociology_George%20Ritzer.pdf

Skinner, J., Zakus, D. and Cowell, J. (2008) 'Development through sport: Building social capital in disadvantaged communities', *Sport Management Review*, 11, 253–275.

Spaaij, R. (2011) *Sport and social mobility: Crossing boundaries*, New York: Routledge.

Spaaij, R. (2012) 'Beyond the playing field: Experiences of sport, social capital, and integration among Somalis in Australia', *Ethnic and Racial Studies*, 35(9), 1519–1538.

Spaaij, R., Magee, J. and Jeanes, R. (2014) *Sport and social exclusion in global society*, London: Routledge.

Steinert, H. and Pilgram, A. (eds) (2007) *Welfare policy from below: Struggles against social exclusion in Europe*, Aldershot: Ashgate.

Sullivan, A. (2001) 'Cultural capital and educational attainment', *Sociology*, 35(4), 893–912.

Svensson, P.G. and Levine, J. (2017) 'Rethinking sport for development and peace: The capability approach', *Sport in Society*, 20(7), 905–923.

Taket, A., Crisp, B.R., Nevill, A., Lamaro, G., Graham, M. and Barter-Godfrey, S. (eds) (2009) *Theorising social exclusion*, London: Routledge.

Part 4
General reflections

9 General reflections

*Marc Theeboom, Hebe Schaillée,
Sara Willems, Emelien Lauwerier,
Rudi Roose and Lieve Bradt*

Overview

Against the backdrop of a substantial number of young people in the EU living at risk of social exclusion, this book has explored different perspectives regarding the presumed potential of community sport for facilitating specific aspects of social inclusion of young people in socially vulnerable situations. It draws upon the findings from a comprehensive study conducted in Flanders (Belgium) entitled: *Community sport for AT-risk youth: Innovative strategies for promoting personal development, health and social CoHesion* (CATCH). The aim of the study – which was commissioned by the *Flanders Innovation and Entrepreneurship Agency* of the Flemish Government (VLAIO) – was (1) to obtain insights into processes of community sport provision in relation to three selected objectives (i.e. *personal development, health* and *social cohesion*) as indicators of aspects of social inclusion and (2) to exchange knowledge between researchers, practitioners and policymakers (i.e. *knowledge translation*). The CATCH project's central research question was: *What are the working mechanisms and facilitating conditions in community sport initiatives that relate to the promotion of social inclusion for young people in socially vulnerable situations?*

This book is not merely another report of the project. An overview of the project's scientific output is available elsewhere (www.isbvzw.be/671/papers/434). Instead, it provides insights in a number of specific aspects of the CATCH project and includes contributions each focusing on one particular topic with relevance to the central aim of the project. In the book's first section (*Introduction and general findings*: Chapters 1 and 2), Chapter 1 presents a description of the study's rationale, design and methodology, as well as of the specific context and objectives of community sport in Flanders. It also elaborates on how the concept of social inclusion was operationalised for the purpose of this project. Chapter 2 presents an evidence-based framework including the contextual assets and practices that shape the necessary and sufficient conditions through which community sport programmes may foster social inclusionary outcomes. The three chapters in the second section (*Thematic insights into community sport and social inclusion*: Chapters 3, 4 and 5) address the different foci of the CATCH project: personal

DOI: 10.4324/9780429340635-13

160 *Marc Theeboom et al.*

development, health and social cohesion. Chapter 3 outlines widely recognised theoretical models and how they can be used as conceptual frameworks for reflective practice in community sport in relation to personal development. Chapter 4 outlines the development and implementation and evaluation plan of an intervention aimed at promoting health in the context of community sport practice, based on insights into the inner workings and conditions through which this context may have an impact on health outcomes. Chapter 5 elaborates on the efforts of community sport practitioners to achieve a socio-pedagogical shift and develop a more structural understanding and approach to social cohesion. In the third section (*Broader perspectives on community sport and social inclusion*: Chapters 6, 7 and 8), a broader, international perspective is provided with regard to specific issues relevant for the central topic and/or approaches used in the CATCH project. Chapter 6 examines the evolution of different approaches to monitoring and evaluation (M&E) and its relevance for sport for development (SfD). It elaborates on the value and specifics of theory-based evaluation approaches (theory of change approach; implementation theory and programme theory; a realist generative approach based on a context, mechanism and outcome framework). Chapter 7 explores if and how a realist inquiry frame-of-mind can contribute to substantiate, structure and deepen action research (AR), thereby increasing its practical and theoretical relevance. For that purpose, it provides clarifications as to what can be understood as AR and what can be considered to be the essential elements of the realist inquiry approach. Chapter 8 provides critical reflections on the concept of social inclusion and its application and operationalisation in social science research on community sport. It draws on a capability approach and uses examples from other empirical research.

All chapters in the second and third section address specific aspects directly or indirectly related to the CATCH project and have formulated specific conclusions and recommendations for research and/or practice. Insights from each separate chapter contribute to a better understanding into *why*, *how* and *in what circumstances* community sport involvement can be effectively linked to indicators of social inclusion of young people in socially vulnerable situations. In this final section (*General reflections*: Chapter 9), we look back at what we have learned through our involvement in the CATCH project. One of the important outcomes of the project was knowledge translation, and the project aimed at reaching valorisation outcomes, some of which related to community building and stakeholder involvement, and others to the development of guidelines and tools that are useful in practice. A few examples are available that show the projects' (lasting) impact. Among others, an online tool (the *Community Sport Impact Wizard*: https://buurtsport.impactwizard.be) was developed in 2020 helping community sport organisations to design their own programme theory. Furthermore, a mobile web-based application to facilitate reflective practice for city coach trainees (see Chapter 3) is being developed in 2021 with implementation opportunities for a variety of other Flemish community sport practices. Throughout 2021, a number of online courses are being organised to further support organisations in using this tool. Also, a group-based programme promoting health-supportive behaviour among community sport coaches has been developed to be used as a module within in-service sports coaches training in Flanders. The focus on knowledge translation is as important as the realisation of the project's scientific objectives. It is easy to see why policymakers, funders, practitioners and other stakeholders may be keen to invest resources and time into projects that provide long-term viable solutions. A few key elements have been identified that are predictive of sustainability of interventions or new approaches in public health in general (Whelan et al. 2014), some of which may be informative for optimising research and practice within the domain of community sport practice. One element is the use of evidence to identify the core issue, the mechanisms at work, and the essential conditions leading to impact. Through the first phase of the CATCH project, our in-depth analysis of community sport practices has led to the gathering of appropriate information and targeted actions in phase 2 and the project as a whole. A second important element is the commitment and support from a diversity of stakeholder organisations which was crucial for adoption of the project but is also key for sustained change, even now the project has come to an end. A third element is evaluation, and we believe that a realist evaluation and visualisation of what brings about impact, how and under which circumstances has been of major importance to many stakeholders to take action. Whether the project is viable or sustainable on the long term is still to be awaited. For sure, some conditions may hamper its enduring effects, among which the extent to which the valorisation activities have not yet been fully embedded in policies, frameworks and organisations. Also, as project funding has come to an end, there is always the difficulty of maintaining initiatives in case there are no other funding sources or possibilities (Whelan et al. 2014).

Content-wise, this project is also unique as to the diversity of research approaches and inputs on understanding the context of community sport for social inclusion. This element pertains to the multidisciplinary nature of the research team involved. As described in Chapter 2, the project's general findings show that the potential of community sport programmes to contribute to participants' personal development, health and social cohesion largely depends on a number of necessary and sufficient conditions. These conditions refer to *building caring relationships with mentors and coaches, creating an experiential learning context* and *developing an enlarged and diversified social network*. In each of the chapters, more insights are provided into why and how these conditions could facilitate achieving the pursued objectives. The importance for identifying necessary and sufficient conditions has further been underlined in Chapter 6, where their relevance was emphasised for M&E of SfD programmes. The CATCH project was not designed to evaluate the actual effectiveness of the community sport programmes in contributing to the three selected social inclusion objectives. In order to do so, more appropriate methods are needed: one of which relates to identifying clear indicators and measurable outcomes, which is often a challenge in SfD programmes (Coalter 2007). In addition, measuring outcome without an understanding of its causes would not make sense. We therefore opted for an approach where researchers from different scientific disciplines focused on specific process-related aspects of community sport provision. These included, among others, the relevance of reflective practice for personal development, the use of a participatory approach to lead to better health and the implementation of strategies of structural work. To our knowledge, until now there have been no multidisciplinary studies on SfD programmes investigating these aspects. For this reason, it is interesting to first look at the extent to which this multidisciplinary character of the CATCH research team has affected the actual approach and outcomes of the project.

Challenging multidisciplinary approach

As indicated in Chapter 1, the team comprised of researchers from three university teams each from different academic disciplines: social sport science, health science and social work/social pedagogy. Alongside this team, there was a large number of non-academic partners (including 18 community sport programmes and 22 umbrella organisations representing stakeholders from, among others, youth work, organised sport, local health services and welfare organisations). We also collaborated with ISB, an expertise centre on community sport in Flanders, to ensure knowledge translation between researchers, practitioners and policymakers.

This particular collaboration provided a good opportunity, for the first time ever in Flanders, to investigate the asserted potential of community sport for realising social inclusion of young people in socially vulnerable situations. Bringing academics from different disciplines together with a common goal and working actively with and for practitioners also allowed us to experience the potential and complexities of a multidisciplinary approach. This potential was most apparent during the first phase of the study. Although each research group collected data in different local community sport settings and focused on only one of the three selected objectives, all researchers involved sought to identify the necessary and sufficient conditions in which community sport programmes may foster social inclusionary outcomes (see Chapter 2). During this phase, there were frequent interactions between the different research team members exchanging experiences and insights they got from the selected practices they were involved in. These interactions contributed to a shared understanding of the assumptions and critical factors underlying most community sport programmes.

The initial intention was to use an overarching *theory-based evaluation approach* for all local cases selected in phase 2 (intervention phase). Among others, this included testing the applicability of a generic programme theory. However, it was felt by the research team that the specificity of each setting and selected objective required a different approach. For the objective of 'personal development', the focus for the *Sport and Society* research group from the *Department of Movement and Sport Sciences*, an AR approach was used within an existing training course for 'city coaches' that were recruited from youths in socially vulnerable position. The emphasis of the research was on the development and refinement of reflective practice as an essential part of the developmental trajectory of the city coach trainees. In relation to the 'health' objective, addressed by the *Department of Public Health and Primary Care*, a health-promoting intervention was developed and evaluated. It made use of a participatory approach and behaviour change theories to bring depth of understanding of the underlying causal assumptions through which risk or protective factors may impact health outcomes among youths at risk. For the 'social cohesion' objective, the focus of the team from the *Department of Social Work and Social Pedagogy* was an in-depth explorative approach through a single-case study that was used to uncover strategies of structural work of community sport practitioners. In that sense, the latter approach was more a continuation of the first phase of the CATCH project as no specific intervention or AR was organised.

This variation of approaches during phase 2 of the project seems to be in line with the different perspectives on responsibilities within social inclusion policies. As indicated in Chapter 1, two different policy discourses on social exclusion have been described in the literature, each emphasising specific strategies at another level (e.g. Smyth 2017; Veit-Wilson 1998). While one policy discourse focuses on the individual (or personal) level, the other addresses the structural (institutional) level. Veit-Wilson (1998) labelled the former discourse as the 'weak' version and the latter as the 'stronger' form. According to Smyth (2017: 1), variation in social inclusion policy discourses is linked to where 'causation' of social exclusion resides:

> in individuals and their alleged deficiencies; or in the way societies are organised and structured that produce situations of inequality in the first place, where some people remain on the periphery. Where the former interpretation is adopted, the policy attempts that follow are reparative and designed to try and mend the bonds that bind people to society, and which are seen as having been disrupted. The attempt is to try and help those who are excluded to transgress the exclusionary boundaries holding them back. In the second interpretation, the focus is upon the way in which power is deployed in producing exclusionary social structures.

The choice of approach (i.e. at individual/micro or at structural level) that was used in CATCH's second phase seemed to be more in line with research traditions within each of the participating groups. The sport and health scientists focused primarily on facilitating developmental/behavioural changes within the individual, albeit the latter situated their approach at the micro-level as the target of the intervention were coaches and not at-risk youths themselves; the social work researchers emphasised the need for change at a more broad, structural level. Considering the complexity of the central topic of the CATCH project, using a variety of perspectives provides an opportunity to take multiple critical factors into consideration. Consequently, it illustrates the added value of a multidisciplinary approach. However, Choi and Pak (2006) argued that multidisciplinarity is only the basic level of involvement. On the basis of an extensive literature review on multiple disciplinary approaches in health sciences, they described the multidisciplinary approach as the (parallel or sequential) collaboration of different disciplines, but without challenging their disciplinary boundaries. Choi and his colleague (2006: 359) referred to interdisciplinarity and transdisciplinarity as more advanced types of scientific collaboration. They indicated that

> Interdisciplinary brings about the reciprocal interaction between (hence 'inter') disciplines, necessitating a blurring of disciplinary boundaries, in order to generate new common methodologies, perspectives, knowledge, or even new disciplines. Transdisciplinary involves scientists from different disciplines as well as nonscientists and other stakeholders and, through role release and role expansion, transcends (hence 'trans') the disciplinary boundaries to look at the dynamics of whole systems in a holistic way.

The authors illustrated the differences between these approaches by everyday food examples: multidisciplinarity as a mixed salad (with ingredients still intact and clearly distinguishable); interdisciplinarity as a stew (with ingredients only partially distinguishable) and transdisciplinarity as a cake (with ingredients no longer distinguishable). Choi and Pak also indicated that as these different terms are often ambiguously defined and used interchangeably, they suggested to use the general term 'multiple disciplinary' when the exact nature of the collaboration is not known. Looking back at the project, the collaboration within the CATCH consortium can best be described as a multidisciplinary approach. Stepping into the next levels remains challenging. Choi and his colleague reported that multiple disciplinary teamwork does not always work nor does it always deliver what it promises to deliver. Similarly, although there is a longstanding plea for interdisciplinary research in sports, to date, the number of studies that combine several disciplines remains limited (Spaaij 2014; Weiss 2008). Buekers et al. (2016: 4–5) emphasised that the fields of movement and sport would also have a lot to win when different scientific disciplines join forces, but they described a number of reasons why this is a challenge:

> For example, funding strategies and validation issues may have a strong negative impact on the commitment of researchers to be involved in interdisciplinary research. . . . the cooperation of different disciplines requires an extremely solid preparation and a very thorough discussion of the research goals, protocols, procedures, and designs. Even though this rigor is a normal prerequisite for all research, regardless of its nature, the differential approaches delineating and defining each of the disciplines certainly do not facilitate the integration process.

However, apart from these challenges, the CATCH project not only resulted in a better understanding of the conditions that could lead to effective community sport programmes in achieving social inclusion objectives, it also enabled us to have a better view on the actual status and functioning of these programmes. Through the unique configuration of the CATCH consortium, several academic and non-academic partners (or *social users*) were actively involved in the setup, implementation and valorisation of the project. This has provided an interesting basis for further thoughts on a number of aspects which we, as members of the research team, consider to be relevant for practitioners and policymakers. Our frequent observations and the intense collaborations we had with many practitioners and organisations in Flanders over the past years allow us to assess the extent in which the abovementioned described conditions can be provided by these organisations. In other words, are community sport organisations in Flanders at present times capable of enabling these necessary and sufficient conditions? Therefore, in the remainder of this chapter, we reflect on the potential of community sport practice in Flanders for realising specific aspects of social inclusion of young people in socially vulnerable situations.

Relevant issues for reflection

Although the CATCH project has focused on a selected number of community sport organisations, through our close collaboration with the *Flemish Institute of Sport Management and Recreation Policy* (ISB) and the frequent interactions with a broader group of practitioners and other relevant stakeholders within the *community sport labs* (CSLs), we are able to reflect on a number of relevant issues regarding Flemish community sport in general. On the basis of our current understanding of what is essential for community sport organisations when targeting the selected social inclusion objectives, we have identified a number of issues we consider as relevant for these organisations and policymakers. These issues primarily relate to the expectations and ambitions that have been formulated regarding the social inclusion potential of community sport by policymakers and funders, as well as by many organisations themselves. As this potential has often been described in very general (and therefore vague) terms, it leaves room for different interpretations of its actual meaning. For example, in Chapter 1 we have referred to the variation of perspectives regarding the concept of social inclusion and to the difficulties in having a clear definition for community sport in Flanders. While we have opted for a specific operationalisation of social inclusion in the CATCH project based on insights from a benchmark study (Van Poppel 2015), we saw that practitioners and policymakers in Flanders are less clear about their definition of community sport and how it can be used to target social inclusion objectives for young people in socially vulnerable situations. Among other things, this relates to the nature of sport's actual role in community sport. As community *sport* is used as the overall term for these type of practices – and not community or social *work* – we need to reflect on the asserted contribution of sport in these programmes. Taking into account the current status of Flemish community sport organisations, we also need to look at whether it is realistic to assume that they can go beyond sport-related objectives for youths in socially vulnerable situations. For that matter, we specifically focus on the level of expertise of community sport coaches, as well as on the expectations regarding the social inclusion of community sport in general. Although the CATCH project has only investigated programmes in Flanders, we feel that these issues also have relevance for community sport initiatives or SfD programmes elsewhere.

Community sport typology and the role of sport

Although the term *community sport* is commonly used in local sport policy literature, more precise definitions are rarely given. As already indicated in Chapter 1, Platts (2018) argued that defining community sport becomes problematic because of the various forms that exist. For example, in Flanders the most common formats of community sport provision are regular open access activities, one-day events, tournaments and initiation courses (Van Poppel 2015). While some organisers explicitly focus on broader social outcomes, others do not. This is in line with the most recent definition in Flanders (Van der Sypt 2019: 31), which states that community sport is:

> an umbrella term for low-threshold and community-oriented initiatives, based on a vision that seeks to guarantee optimum accessibility of sport for disadvantaged groups. Sport is used with or without an explicit focus on development at the individual and/or community level.

While this definition clearly emphasises accessibility for disadvantaged groups, it is less explicit regarding the targeted outcomes of community sport. In the CATCH project, we selected local practices that claimed to focus on social inclusion objectives for youth in socially vulnerable situations. But even though all these initiatives were labelled as community sport, it is important to look at how much 'sport' is actually involved in their work to achieve these objectives. Are these programmes not mere social projects that, to some extent, have a link with sport? In other words, what is the specific role and importance of sport within these practices? If we continue to refer to these programmes as community sport initiatives with social inclusion objectives, it would make sense to know at least the specific contribution of 'sport' and the extent to which these initiatives differ from social work initiatives in general. A mere focus on whether these programmes target social objectives is just not enough. In that sense it is relevant to look at how local SfD initiatives in Flanders have been described, where – similar to many other regions and countries – generic terms are often used to refer to a variety of organisational types and formats. For example, in his PhD study on local sport organisations in Flanders with an explicit social role that target 'hard-to-reach' groups, Smets (2019) used the term 'social sport practices' ('sociaal-sportieve praktijken' in Dutch) and identified the following four types: (1) *self-organisations* founded by ethnic minorities as an alternative to 'white sport clubs'; (2) *social sport initiatives from non-sport sectors* (e.g. youth welfare work, social work, integration, and education) that grew from a temporary offer into a permanent one; (3) *transformed classic sports clubs* driven by a compelling need to change (e.g. to survive because of demographic changes in their neighbourhood) and (4) *lifestyle (street) sport groups* united in apparent informal spaces. Smets (2019) used the term 'social sport practices' to refer to the assumption that these initiatives have broader objectives than mere sport-related ones. He indicated that it illustrates their 'intersectoral' ambitions as they develop

General reflections 167

sport programmes that connect to other areas of life such as education, housing, youth assistance, emancipatory work, etc. According to the author, the approach links their work to principles such as collective responsibility, equality and social justice. As most of these organisations come in contact (implicitly or explicitly) with youth work and community development initiatives, Smets argued that their ambitions and approaches resemble those of social work.

While in recent years, the term 'social sport practices' has increasingly been used in Flemish sport policy discourse when referring to local SfD organisations, its actual meaning remains vague. It is therefore questionable whether Smets' typology and characterisation helps us to better understand what local SfD organisations look like and, more importantly, what the actual role of sport is in their work towards attempting to achieve broader objectives.

Inspired by Coalter's (2007) classification on *sport*, *sport plus* and *plus sport*, which makes a distinction based on the specific role of sport in SfD initiatives, Buelens et al. (2018) have used the same typology to categorise community sport in Flanders (see Figure 9.1). Their typology has the following categories:

1 *Community sport*: While similar to sport-for-all as it also aims for increased sport participation, this category only targets hard-to-reach groups in a socially vulnerable situation. Sport provision is organised in specific locations to better reach out to specific populations (e.g. separate swim classes for female Muslims).

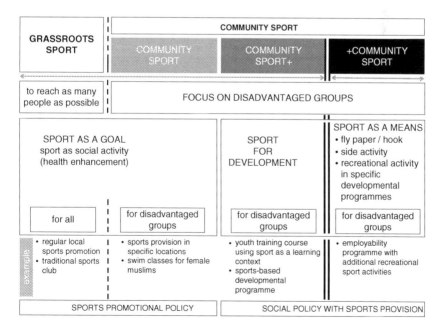

Figure 9.1 Positioning of community sport in Flanders (Buelens et al. 2018)

2 *Community sport plus*: Sports-based developmental programmes at community level for at-risk groups. Sport is the primary activity and is used explicitly as an experiential learning context aimed at producing individual developmental outcomes for participants (e.g. sport sessions intended to develop social skills, environmental awareness).

3 *Plus community sport*: Sport is used as a means to attract hard-to-reach groups in a socially vulnerable situation (as a 'fly paper' or 'hook'). It is primarily used as a recreational side activity within developmental (social inclusion) programmes. The sport activities can also help to facilitate positive contacts and social relationships between organisers and participants (e.g. emancipatory youth work practices using sport to connect and build relationships with youth).

Buelens et al.'s typology situates both 'community sport plus' and 'plus community sport' within a social policy perspective using sport as a vehicle for social inclusion for participants in a socially vulnerable situation. The main difference between these two types is the specific role of sport. From a community sport plus perspective, sport plays a central role as it is used as an explicit learning context. This means that sport activities are designed and delivered in such a way that participants are encouraged, for example, to (further) develop their social skills and to reflect on their own attitudes and behaviour, both in and out of sport. Within the context of plus community sport programmes, sport is not at the core of the intervention. Rather, it is a way to get into contact with often hard-to-reach people and is used to facilitate further communication and/or serves recreational purposes. In that sense, there is no deliberate use of sport as a learning context. If learning does occur during sport activities, it is rather a coincidental result of participants' involvement.

In the selected practices in phase 1 of the CATCH project, community sport activities primarily served the purpose of attracting and getting into contact with specific youth populations – i.e. plus community sport. It allowed community sport coaches to create a safe social climate in which they could connect with youth and build relationships of respect and trust. The community sport coaches indicated that the moments before and after the sport sessions provide further bonding opportunities where participants can talk informally about their feelings and daily life experiences. This is in line with the initial affective 'befriending' stage of Pawson's (2006) programme theory of mentoring at-risk youth in which affective bonds of trust/sharing of new experiences are created. As explained in Chapter 2, the building of caring relationships with mentors and coaches was identified as one of the necessary and sufficient conditions that were identified. However, except for a few cases where some (older) participants were encouraged to take up responsibilities during sport activities (e.g. as an occasional assistant coach), we did not encounter initiatives where sport activities were explicitly and regularly used as intentional experiential learning contexts targeting, for example, participants' personal development or active civic engagement. This seems to indicate that community sport programmes in Flanders do not provide the type of learning context through sport, which has been identified as an important condition in facilitating the achievement of social inclusion outcomes. In the selected community sport programmes we investigated, sport appeared to be primarily an attraction or context providing opportunities for other non-sport (follow up) activities or interactions. On the basis of Buelens et al.'s (and Coalter's) typology, the approach these organisations use therefore resembles more a plus community sport type: the extent to which they actually go beyond the initial stage of building relationships and respect and trust with participants through the use of sport remains unclear. Noteworthy here is also Pawson's (2006) identification of a number of youth mentoring stages beyond the initial affective befriending one. These include cognitive processes involved in a 'direction-setting' stage challenging personal identities, values and ambitions; and aptitudinal processes in a 'coaching stage' requiring youth to accept responsibility for their own development and contributing to developing maturity and advocacy (positional) processes in a 'sponsoring stage', in which mentors (or the organisation) advocate and network on behalf of youth and use their insider contacts and knowledge of, for example, education or employment opportunities to mediate participants' initial relationship with external agencies and services. However, whether these follow-up stages can be introduced depends among others on the type of (non-sport) partners of the community sport organisations and also on their own capabilities to provide additional support and to use sport as an experiential learning context to explicitly facilitate these processes. It is to this latter aspect that we now turn.

Towards realistic expectations

Understanding the role and contribution of sport in the programmes that were selected in the CATCH project is an important factor in determining the social inclusion potential of Flemish community sport. As mentioned earlier, we did not focus on the actual outcomes and impacts of the programmes that were investigated; instead, we have tried to understand the processes that are presumed to have an effect on one of the three selected outcomes. On the basis of the findings of the project, however, one can wonder whether Flemish community sport programmes are able to reach their full potential in terms of social inclusion. For example, in Chapter 5 it was reported that the objective of community sport programmes to work towards social cohesion in terms of developing structural approaches was described as 'a rather distant ambition' in practice. It was noted that this potential remained 'untapped' because of the organisation's inability to translate these ambitions into their actual work. Others have made similar remarks, such as Nols (2018: 117) in his study on the potential of Flemish SfD initiatives to work towards social change, as the author concluded that these initiatives:

> are often confined to work under precarious circumstances and have limited organisational capacity (e.g. resources, knowledge, skills) to combine their sport objectives with a wider social mission. . . . To expect even more from these initiatives, such as political education and social justice activities and actions, would be demanding too much.

This also touches upon a recurring challenge regarding SfD where policymakers and funders have high expectations regarding the social value of sport and, as a result, put pressure on (community) sport organisations to use a similar rhetoric and to promise more than they can deliver. In this regard, Weiss (1993: 96) referred, among other things, to inflated promises that are often made when bidding for social programmes. She argued that

> Because of the political processes of persuasion and negotiation that are required to get a program enacted, inflated promises are made in the guise of program goals. . . . Holders of diverse values and different interests have to be won over, and in the process a host of realistic and unrealistic goal commitments are made.

As a result, claims about the potential in terms of expected outcomes and impact often become far 'outstretched' and go beyond what is reasonable to expect from these organisations. We also encountered this problem in the CATCH project during our initial meetings with practitioners to ask for their involvement. Some organisations were concerned when we informed them about our intention to understand better how and what they do to work towards the selected objectives. There was a fear that our findings might reveal that they can achieve less than what is expected by funders or policymakers which would endanger their continued funding. This concern influenced our approach at the setup of the project by not only focusing on providing support to community sport organisations to optimise the effectiveness of their work and help them to explain better what they do (e.g. through programme theories), but also for us to organise regular meetings with policymakers in an attempt to manage their expectations. Whether we have been successful in this in the long run is yet to be seen.

Community sport plus: a bridge too far?

The finding that the selected community sport programmes in Flanders seemed to resemble more a 'plus community sport' approach than a 'community sport plus' one implies that their actual use of sport in working towards social inclusion objectives is limited. It is not clear why these organisations do not make more use of sport's potential as an experiential learning context. It might be possible that the conditions under which community sport organisations have to work are unfavourable to explore more opportunities to use sport in a broader sense (e.g. most programmes are open access and participation is voluntary). Or it is possible that most of them are only required by subsidising authorities or funders to focus on (quick) quantitative outputs (such as attracting as many participants as possible) instead of targeting long-term social outcomes and impacts, which are generally considered to be harder and more expensive to measure. Or perhaps these organisations regard sport's social outcomes as inevitable and self-evident and, as such, do not see the need to organise sport activities in a more deliberate and systematic way to target social objectives. The latter seems to be in line with how youth coaches in general organise sport activities focusing on social outcomes. For example, according to Petitpas et al. (2005), there are few programmes that teach life skills to youth through sport in a systematic and conscious manner. Similarly, Jacobs (2016: 20) who looked at how sport coaches and physical education teachers in the Netherlands work towards social skill development of youth, argued that:

> many coaches do not have an explicit pedagogical framework. They often base their practices on what they saw their own coaches and PE teachers do, on their feelings and intuition, and their own experiences as athletes and as coaches.

Jacobs (2016: 160) further noted that most coaches in his study merely focused on social skill development that will only benefit sport performance as they:

> rarely expressed a desire to teach the behaviours or life skills that policy makers often associate with sport participation. The coaches in general showed little concern for the players as individuals, but seemed to see them primarily as athletes. The social domain that these coaches wanted addressed primarily pertained to negative (anti-social) social behaviour of their players.

It has also been indicated that community sport coaches are often not trained to provide anything more than sports technical and tactical knowledge, which is reflected in the way they organise sport activities. Super et al. (2018: 174), who looked at the role of Dutch community sport coaches in facilitating life skill development for socially vulnerable youth, indicated that:

> although community sports coaches sometimes do receive formal coaching training, very often such training focuses on the technical aspects of sports coaching (e.g. exercises to develop specific sporting skills) and not on the pedagogical knowledge necessary for life skill development and transferability.

However, Turnnidge et al. (2014) indicated that coaches besides being able to facilitate skill development among their participants are also expected to ensure transferability of these acquired skills to other spheres of life, either by means of an explicit or an implicit approach. But research on the impact of SfD programmes showed that changes are often small scale and typically only occur at an individual or interpersonal level (Spaaij et al. 2016). Super and her colleagues (2018: 174) also argued that:

> Within community-based sports programmes, the sports coaches are often focused on developing skills without paying specific attention to the transferability of these skills to other societal domains.

172 *Marc Theeboom et al.*

The quote touches upon a fundamental question about the extent to which one can expect that those that are trained to deliver and guide sport activities for youth (such as sports coaches and physical education teachers) are well prepared and able to provide (community) sport plus activities and, in addition, ensure transfer of what was experienced and learned to other domains. For example, regarding the extent to which PE teachers know how to deal with issues beyond pure sports technical and tactical matter, Hardman and Marshall (2005: 51) concluded their study on the status of PE in Europe by stating that there is a 'broad-spread predisposition towards games and development of competitive sports skills'. Jacobs (2016) also commented that PE teachers are often not equipped with clear guidelines, curriculum, skills, teaching methods and evaluation criteria to integrate the social and moral development of their pupils systematically into their lesson plans and activities.

Expectations and conditions

Compared to the wide variety of statements and policy documents from official international agencies and NGOs repeatedly emphasising the distinct social value of sport, efforts to provide more concrete insights into how sport can actually be organised in a way that it facilitates social outcomes and impact are more limited. While over the years an increasing number of grassroots organisations have begun to develop their own strategies and methods about how to provide (community) sport plus activities to socially vulnerable youth, few comprehensive and practical guidelines are available. One that has often been referred to in this matter is Hellison's (2011) 'Teaching Personal and Social Responsibility model'. But to date, most of the literature that addressed the use of sport for youth in relation to social objectives refer to principles and guidelines for practitioners in general or are more theoretical in nature relating to specific concepts (e.g. positive youth development: Holt 2016; character development: Shields and Bredemeier 1995; moral development: Weiss et al. 2008; life skills: Danish and Nellen 1997; social and emotional skills: Kahn et al. 2019). In recent years – primarily within the context of the Erasmus+ sport funding framework – some efforts have been made to produce manuals or toolkits to help coaches and PE teachers in how to use sport activities in relation to specific objectives (e.g. intercultural education: Reynard et al. 2020; gender equality: GETZ 2020; life skills and employability: Schlenker and Braun 2020). But as described in Chapter 6, whether such programmes can be effective will largely depend on how they are implemented. This is in line with Patriksson (1995: 128) who argued that:

> When individuals have been socialized into sport or physical activity they are in a social environment that has the potential both to improve and inhibit their personal growth. The futility of arguing whether sport is good or bad has been observed by several authors. Sport, like most activities, is not a priori good or bad, but has the potential of producing both positive and negative

outcomes. . . . Questions like 'What conditions are necessary for sport to have beneficial outcomes?' must be asked more often.

Also, the very fact that most of this material has been produced recently indicates that, to date, many professionals in sports teaching and coaching have not been trained to work towards broader social outcomes when delivering sport activities to youth. Yet, there are high expectations regarding the required competences of sports coaches in relation to this issue. The recent 'Guidelines regarding the minimum requirements in skills and competences for coaches' formulated by the EU 'Expert Group on Skills and Human Resources Development in Sport' stated, among other things, that all coaches require much more than basic sports technical and tactical knowledge. According to the Expert Group (2020: 15), they 'also require so called "soft skills" to act as teachers and catalyst for personal development and social cohesion'. The guidelines further emphasise that a coach is generally regarded to be a role model and mentor and that he or she 'communicates positive values to society, teaches life transferrable skills and contributes to solving societal challenges, such as wellbeing, health and integration' (Expert Group 2020: 21). But other than the recommendation that 'specific and dedicated educational modules are needed' (Expert Group 2020: 18) in the coaches' training to work with disadvantaged groups in sport (thereby using the example of people with disabilities or senior citizens), there are no indications in these EU guidelines that additional training is needed for sports coaches to know how to work explicitly towards social objectives for youth in socially vulnerable situations. This is, however, in contrast to what has been repeatedly emphasised by scholars that specific conditions are required to facilitate personal and social development through sport (e.g. Coakley 1998; Coalter 2007; Green 2008). For example, Coakley (2011: 309) stated that 'by itself, the act of sport participation among young people leads to no regularly identifiable developmental outcomes. Instead, outcomes are related to and dependent on combinations of multiple factors'. Coakley referred to a multitude of research findings identifying these factors, among others, type, norms and culture associated with particular sports (experiences), social relationships formed in connection with sport participation, orientations and actions of peers, parents and coaches, significant characteristics of sport participants, material and cultural contexts under which participation occurs, etc. He also stated that, while research on the developmental influence of sport for youth in socially vulnerable situations supports these general findings, it also suggests that specific contextual factors are prerequisites for positive developmental outcomes for this group. Coakley (2011: 310) further argued that 'sport participation must occur in settings where young people are physically safe, personally valued, morally and economically supported, personally and politically empowered, and hopeful about the future'. Although Jones et al. (2017) indicated that after years of research and practice, it is now commonly understood that intentionally designed and managed sport practices are required to direct sport initiatives, among others, towards youth development, whether this is a common understanding among most policymakers remains uncertain.

Looking for inspiration

On the basis of our experiences in the CATCH project, we can speculate whether the extent to which sport is used in the selected case studies as a means to work towards specific aspects of social inclusion for young people in socially vulnerable situations reflects the expectations from policymakers and funders. For example, can we expect from community sport organisations to deliver programmes for their participants under the specific conditions that we identified and as described by Coakley (2011) (e.g. personally and politically empowered)? Jeanes and Spaaij (2015) noted that an important constraining factor to work towards social objectives relates to the personality, background and social status of coaches and the conditions under which coaches (sometimes volunteers) have to work. Among other things, it raises the issue regarding which coaching staff competences are required in community sport plus approaches. As indicated in Chapter 1, findings from the Flemish community sport benchmark study showed that a majority of the community sport organisations indicated to work towards the three selected objectives in their work with populations in socially vulnerable situations (Van Poppel 2015). It also showed that most of the programmes include professionals to organise sport activities. Unfortunately, it is not clear what type of professionals are active as no data regarding their educational background exist. However, as the benchmark showed that in 75 per cent of the cases sport delivery is coordinated by the municipal sports service, we can assume that most professionals have a background in sports coaching. The study also revealed that most community sport organisations in Flanders made use of volunteers, who are primarily used for assisting in activities (73.1 per cent) and/or delivering activities themselves (50.8 per cent). But here too, no specific information was available regarding the background of these volunteers. Noteworthy is that Super et al. (2018) indicated that in Dutch community sport programmes targeting socially vulnerable youth, sports lessons are very often provided by volunteer sport coaches without any formal training.

As community sport organisations targeting social objectives for youth in vulnerable situations have a lot in common with a youth/social work approach, it is also interesting to see how youth education professionals regard the potential of sport. In a publication aimed at youth workers on the use of sport as an educational tool for youth in socially vulnerable situations, Schroeder (2011) emphasised a need for more links between the worlds of youth work and sport. The author also pointed at the differences that exist between sport coaches and youth workers, indicating that both could complement each other. With regard to sports coaches, Schroeder (2011: 9) indicated that 'while they are well-placed to encourage physical development, sport coaches often lack the training and know-how to cope with the personal development needs of individuals from this target group'. Regarding youth workers, she stated that they 'are mostly trained to recognise the social needs of individuals and to propose methods which directly respond to those needs. But youth workers are usually not experts in sport'. The author argued that many youth workers do not know how to maximise the potential of sport as an educational tool in their regular work, as they are often limited by their own experience of sport. It is interesting to note that, according to Schroeder, sport coaches and trainers often use reflective practice to make athletes more aware of how they can improve future sport performances. The question, however, remains to what extent sport coaches are able to facilitate experiences in sport that can also be applied to broader non-sport-related issues. As we noted before, most sports coaches when working towards social objectives also rely on their own experiences and appear not to be trained systematically in this domain. Consequently, only relying on sport coaches' expertise in sport delivery might not be sufficient.

Community sport organisations with professionals covering both types of expertise (i.e. sports coaching and youth work education) will have better options for organising a community sport plus approach. This can either be through a mix of different staff profiles or via staff members who can combine both sets of competences. In case of the latter, apart from bottom-up initiatives where sport coaches have developed their own system based on their experiences, a more systematic and structured formation does not seem to currently exist. As mentioned earlier, a number of modules and toolkits have been developed that seek to help coaches to work towards specific social objectives (including the ones we identified in the context of CATCH). However, to our knowledge, a generic curriculum to train professionals to become a '(community) sport plus coach/worker' or 'social sport coach' has yet to be developed. We can assume that the absence of such a resource is a consequence of the belief among many that sport's social outcomes are inherent, inevitable and self-evident and/or that most coaches are supposed to already have these competences (see, e.g. the EU guidelines regarding coaches' skills and competences). Another explanation could be that there is a lack of mutual understanding and dialogue between the worlds of sport and youth work. In this regard, Schroeder (2011: 6) argued that 'Organisations working with youth usually tend to define themselves as belonging to one camp or the other'. It is also noteworthy that using sport for broader social objectives when working with youth in socially vulnerable situations is not a new phenomenon. For example, Quensel (1982) described principles and challenges for introducing an alternative social-pedagogical approach when using sport for youth in socially vulnerable situations. Also, with regard to the Flemish situation, almost three decades ago, De Knop and Walgrave (1992) expressed the need for a collaboration between the sport and youth work sector on various levels when using sport as a means of social inclusion for youth in socially vulnerable situations. They argued that too often both sectors work alongside one another instead of setting up collaborative initiatives.

Some final thoughts

Claiming that nothing has changed in Flanders over the past decades would be unfair and many organisations – both in and outside community sport – have started to become involved in working with sport for youth in socially vulnerable situations targeting broader social objectives. However, considering our reflections regarding the current status of Flemish community sport practice in relation to its social inclusion potential, the question is if these ambitions are not too high. As indicated in Chapter 1, from the early 1990s onwards, community sport activities were organised in Flemish deprived inner-city areas specifically targeting these hard-to-reach groups and were focused on social inclusion for target groups in socially vulnerable situations. Could we not have expected more progress being made by now? This also raises the issue within which policy area community sport plus or plus community sport should be situated. In the case of Flanders, community sport falls primarily within the responsibilities of the sports policy domain, both at Flemish and local level (see Chapter 1). However, considering its emphasis on social inclusion, belonging to only one policy domain, might not be an ideal situation. A recent resolution of the Council of the European Union on the 'EU Work Plan for Sport 2021–2024' (2020: 1) emphasised that the promotion of sport should be supported through cross-sectoral cooperation as it covers many policy areas. More specifically, the resolution was formulated as follows

> Recognising that sport could contribute to achieve the overall political priorities of the EU, and in particular the goals of various other policy areas such as education, health, youth, social affairs, inclusion, equality, gender equality, urban and rural development, transportation, environment, tourism, employment, innovation, sustainability, digitalisation and economy; and that those policy areas could support the promotion of sport based on cross-sectoral cooperation.

Similarly, in his study on SfD organisations in Belgium, Nols (2018) recommended that local authorities need to set up a support policy for these organisations where different policy areas join forces. But Smets (2019) indicated that the sector of 'social sport practices' in Flanders is situated between various policy areas and is therefore often 'invisible' and in need of more recognition. We then arrive at a fundamental question regarding the social inclusion potential of community sport (or for that matter, SfD in general). Despite the high expectations among many, why is there not more recognition for this potential (e.g. in relation to collaborative efforts between different policy domains or regarding specific training opportunities for coaches)? We can only assume that more recognition depends on a cumulative evidence base for community sport's personal and societal impact. At present, this is still minimal, specifically in relation to the selected objectives. As pointed out in Chapter 6, Pawson's (2004) comment that many social policy interventions can be characterised as 'ill-defined interventions with hard to follow outcomes', has been used over the years by a growing number of researchers to criticise the policy rhetoric regarding sport's wider social role. Consequently, there is a need for a more theoretically informed and systematic approach to the design and delivery of programmes to facilitate optimal effectiveness. Determining critical success factors (such as key programme components, underlying mechanisms, relationships and sequences of causes and effects) can lead to the design of theoretically coherent programmes that can then be properly implemented. While the CATCH project has resulted in the identification of a number of necessary and sufficient conditions, we will need more precise definitions of expected outcomes and impact, both at an individual and at a structural level and on interactions between these levels. This will allow more opportunities for measuring effectiveness and, as such, could lead not only to the formulation of realistic expectations but also to more recognition of community sport's social inclusion potential.

References

Buekers, M., Ibáñez-Gijón, J., Morice, A.H.P., Rao, G., Mascret, N., Laurin, J. and Montagne, G. (2016) 'Interdisciplinary research: A promising approach to investigate elite performance in sports', *Quest*, 69(1), 65–79.

Buelens, E., Theeboom, M. and Vertonghen, J. (2018) *Een vernieuwende kijk op buurtsport: Bouwstenen en positionering* [*A new look at community sport: Building blocks and positioning*], Brussel: Vrije Universiteit – Research group Sport & Society.

Choi, B.C.K. and Pak, A.W.P. (2006) 'Multidisciplinarity, interdisciplinarity and transdisciplinarity in health research, services, education and policy: 1. Definitions, objectives, and evidence of effectiveness', *Clinical and Investigative Medicine*, 29(6), 351–364.

Coakley, J. (1998) *Sport in society: Issues and controversies*, 6th edn, Boston, MA: McGraw Hill.

Coakley, J. (2011) 'Youth sports: What counts as "positive development?"', *Journal of Sport & Social Issues*, 35(3), 306–324.

Coalter, F. (2007) *A wider social role for sport: Who's keeping the score?*, London: Routledge.

Council of the European Union (2020) *EU work plan for sport 2021–2024*, Resolution of the Council and of the Representatives of the Governments of the Member States, meeting within the Council, on the European Union Work Plan for Sport (1 January 2021–30 June 2024) (2020/C 419/01), Official Journal of the European Union, C 419/1. Available HTTP: https://eur-lex.europa.eu/legalcontent/EN/TXT/HTML/?uri=CELEX:42020Y1204(01)&from=EN

Danish, S.J. and Nellen, V.C. (1997) 'New roles for sport psychologists: Teaching life skills through sport to at-risk youth', *Quest*, 49(1), 100–113.

De Knop, P. and Walgrave, L. (eds) (1992) *Sport als integratie: Kansen voor maatschappelijk kwetsbare jongeren* [*Sport as integration: Opportunities for socially deprived youth*], Brussels: Koning Boudewijnstichting.

Expert Group on Skills and Human Resources Development in Sport (2020) *Guidelines regarding the minimum requirements in skills and competences for coaches*, Luxembourg: Publications Office of the European Union. Available HTTP: https://op.europa.eu/en/publication-detail/-/publication/8f28e3a0-6f11-11ea-b735-01aa75ed71a1/language-en/format-PDF/source-122543310

GETZ (2020) *Gender equality toolkit for generation Z*, Worcester: University of Worcester. Available HTTP: https://getzproject.eu

Green, B.C. (2008) 'Sport as an agent for social and personal change', in: V. Girginov (ed) *Management of sports development*, Burlington, MA: Butterworth-Heinemann, pp. 129–145.

Hardman, K. and Marshall, J. (2005) 'Physical education in schools in European context: Charter principals, promises and implementation realities', in K. Green and K. Hardman (eds) *Physical education, essential issues*, London: Sage, pp. 39–65.

Hellison, D. (2011) *Teaching personal and social responsibility through physical activity*, 3rd edn, Champaign, IL: Human Kinetics.

Holt, N.L. (ed) (2016) *Positive youth development through sport*, New York: Routledge.

Jacobs, F. (2016) *Addressing and navigating the social domain in sport: Coaches and physical education teachers*, Doctoral dissertation, Utrecht University, Utrecht, The Netherlands.

Jeanes, R. and Spaaij, R. (2015) 'Examining the educator: Toward a critical pedagogy of sport for development and peace', in: L. Hayhurst, T. Kay and M. Chawansky (eds) *Beyond sport for development and peace: Transnational perspectives on theory, policy and practice*, London: Routledge, pp. 155–168.

Jones, G.J., Edwards, M.B., Bocarro, J.N., Bunds, K.S. and Smith, J.W. (2017) 'An integrative review of sport-based youth development literature', *Sport in Society*, 20(1), 161–179.

Kahn, J., Bailey, R. and Jones, S. (2019) *Coaching social & emotional skills in youth sports*, Washington, DC: Aspen Institute.

Nols, Z. (2018) Social change through sport for development initiatives: A critical pedagogical perspective, Doctoral dissertation, Vrije Universiteit Brussel, Brussel.

Patriksson, M. (1995) 'The significance of sport for society – health, socialisation, economy: A scientific review', in: I. Vuori et al. (eds) *The significance of sport for society: Health, socialization, economy*, Strasbourg: Council of Europe Press, pp. 111–134.

Pawson, R. (2004) *Evaluating ill-defined interventions with hard – to-follow outcomes*, Presentation to ESRC Seminar, Leeds Metropolitan University, Leeds.

Pawson, R. (2006) *Evidence-based policy: A realist perspective*, London: Sage.

Platts, C. (2018) 'Introducing community sport and physical activity', in: R. Wilson and C. Platts (eds) *Managing and developing community sport*, London: Routledge, pp. 3–14.

Petitpas, A.J., Cornelius, A.E., Van Raalte, J.L. and Jones, T. (2005) 'A framework for planning youth sport programs that foster psychosocial development', *The Sport Psychologist*, 19, 63–80.

Quensel, S. (1982) 'Eine alternative Pädagogik für sozial behinderte Jugendliche: Prinzipien und Hindernisse [An alternative pedagogy for socially deprived youth: Principles and obstacles]', in: W. Nickolai et al. (eds) *Sport in der sozialpädagogischen Arbeit mit Randgruppen*, Freiburg im Breisgau: Larnbertus-Verlag, pp. 13–39.

Reynard, S., Moustakas, L. and Petry, K. (eds) (2020) *EDU:PACT module handbook: Teaching and learning guidelines on intercultural education through physical activity, coaching and training*, Vienna: University of Vienna.

Schlenker, M. and Braun, P. (2020) *Scoring for the future: Developing life skills for employability through football*, Berlin: Streetfootballworld.

Schroeder, K. (2011) *Fit for life: Using sports as an educational tool for the inclusion of young people with fewer opportunities*, Brussels: SALTO-YOUTH Inclusion Resource Centre.

Shields, D.L.L. and Bredemeier, B.J.L. (1995) *Character development and physical activity*, Champaign, IL: Human Kinetics Publishers.

Smets, P. (2019) *Sociaal-sportieve praktijken: Beleidspraktijken van onderuit in het stedelijke sportlandschap* [*Social sport practices: Policy practices at the bottom in the urban sports landscape*], Brussels: VUBPress.

Smyth, J. (2017) 'Social inclusion', *Education and society*, July. DOI: 10.1093/acrefore/ 9780190264093.013.129

Spaaij, R. (2014) 'Sports crowd violence: An interdisciplinary synthesis', *Aggression and Violent Behavior*, 19, 146–155.

Spaaij, R., Oxford, S. and Jeanes, R. (2016) 'Transforming communities through sport? Critical pedagogy and sport for development', *Sport, Education and Society*, 21(4), 570–587.

Super, S., Verkooijen, K. and Koelen, M. (2018) 'The role of community sports coaches in creating optimal social conditions for life skill development and transferability – a salutogenic perspective', *Sport, Education and Society*, 23(2), 173–185.

Turnnidge, J., Côté, J. and Hancock, D.J. (2014) 'Positive youth development from sport to life: Explicit or implicit transfer?', *Quest*, 66(2), 203–217.

Van der Sypt, P. (2019) 'Buurtsport in Vlaanderen en Brussel anno 2018. De 2-meting buurtsport' [Community sport in Flanders and Brussels anno 2018], *Vlaams Tijdschrift voor Sportbeheer*, 271, 30–35.

Van Poppel, M. (2015) Benchmark Buurtsport: Buurtsport in Vlaanderen anno 2014 [Benchmark community sport: Community sport in Flanders in the year 2014], Belgium: Flemish Institute of Sport Management and Recreation Policy.

Veit-Wilson, J. (1998) Setting adequacy standards, Bristol: Policy Press.

Weiss, C. (1993) 'Where politics and evaluation research meet', *Evaluation Practice*, 14(1), 93–106.

Weiss, M.R. (2008) '"Riding the wave": Transforming sport and exercise psychology within an interdisciplinary vision', *Quest*, 60(1), 63–83.

Weiss, M.R., Smith, A.L. and Stuntz, C.P. (2008) 'Moral development in sport and physical activity', in: T.S. Horn (ed) *Advances in sport psychology*, Champaign, IL: Human Kinetics, pp. 187–210.

Whelan, J., Love, P., Pettman, T., Doyle, J., Booth, S., Smith, E. and Waters, E. (2014) 'Cochrane update: Predicting sustainability of intervention effects in public health evidence: Identifying key elements to provide guidance', *Journal of Public Health*, 36(2), 347–351.

Index

Note: Page numbers in *italics* indicate a figure and page numbers in **bold** indicate a table on the corresponding page. Page numbers followed by "n" indicate a note.

abduction 137
action research (AR) 60–62; reflective practices; theory of change; causal mechanisms 133; ceteris paribus condition 133; change hypothesis 131, 134; client and academic peers 129; constant conjunction 133; contributing elements in constant interaction *130*; described 128; desired results of action 133–134; desired system state 131; dialogical research and 128; experiment 134–135; implementation of intervention package 135; learning from experience 132–133; obstacle 127–128; quantitative and statistical analyses 135; research defined 129; social reality 134; social world 135; strategic analysis 130; systematic practice 129–136; system state 131; theory and practice 127–129; *see also* realist inquiry
Adams, A. 106, 122
Anderson, A.A. 108
anecdotal evidence 88
anomie 121
anti-smoking interventions 65
anti-social others 86
Arthur-Banning, S.G. 108
Astbury, B. 103, 109, 111, 117, 121, 137
atheoretical experimentation 105
Auriacombe, C. 128

Bandura, A. 121
befriending relationships 30
behavioural indicators 55
behaviour change: methods 70, 72–73, **73**; selecting the methods and applications for 70; *see also* HAPA model

Bemelmans-Videc 121
Bhaskar, R. 136
black box approach 103; control groups 104; limitation 104; politically imposed aspirations 105; on SfD 106–107; *see also* logic models
Blackshaw, T. 86
Blamey, A. 15, 120
bottom-up accountability strategy 95
Boudon, R. 140
Bourdieusian concepts 148–150, 154
box-ticking exercise 110, 111
Bruges' Public Centre for Social Welfare 69
Buekers, M. 164
Buelens, E. 168, 169
Byrne, D. 128

Callaghan, G. 128
capabilities 150
capability approach 154; described 149–150; development of social inclusion through sport *153*; limitations and challenges 153–154; valuable aspects of 152–153
capital 148
caring relationships: cultural capital of the coaching staff 32–33; person-oriented approach 30–31; practitioners 31–32; thousand chances philosophy 31–32; two-way exchange of knowledge 34–35
case selection: co-design 24; criteria used 25; diversity among selected community sport programmes **25–26**
CATCH project 4, 9, 23–24, 88–89, 159–162, 174–175, 177; aims 14–17; choice of approach 163–164;

Index 181

empirical data 145; healthy behaviour 13; knowledge translation 16–17; research aim 14–16; social inclusion 12; understanding process 14–16; *see also* action research (AR); empirical research
causative theory 113
Chapman, J. 46
Chen, H.T. 105, 112–114
children and young people (CYP) 64, 66
Choi, B.C.K. 163, 164
City Coach 61; changes planned and implemented in second, third and fourth course of 2018 **52**; described 47; experiential learning 59; guidance during reflective conversation groups 56–57; number of participants per reflective conversation group 53; Sportfolio 53–56; trainers 62
Clark, H. 108
coaches: CYP 66; health promotion 65–66; role 45; selected actions and related change goals **72**; voluntary community sport coach 46
Coakley, J. 107, 173, 174
Coalter, F. 7, 9, 12, 29, 167
co-design 24
COM-B model 61
community sport 3–4, 167; accountability strategies 95; caring relationships with mentors and defining 10; issues 165; typology and role of sport 166–169; *see also* community sport in Flanders; community sport programmes; social cohesion
community sport coaches 29–35, 45, 46, 58, 161, 165, 168, 171
Community sport for AT-risk youth: Innovative strategies for promoting personal development, health and social CoHesion (CATCH) project *see* CATCH project
community sport in Flanders 9–10; expertise centre 11; open access sport activities 10–11; policy changes 10–11; positioning *167*; social inclusion objectives 11–14
community sport labs (CSLs) 17, 165
community sport plus 168, 170–172
community sport programmes 28; assets and practices **29**; case selection 24–26; data analysis 28–29; data collection 26–28; diversity among **25–26**; participants 33; social network 37–38; *see also* caring relationships; experiential learning

concept of convenience 14
Connell, J.P. 115
container concept 11
context: programme theory 118; realist inquiry 138; theory-driven evaluation 118–119
Context, Mechanism and Outcome (CMO) configurations 15, 116, 138, 139
control groups 104
cost-benefit analysis 104
Crabbe, T. 33, 86
Cronin, O. 122
cultural capital 148
cultural intermediaries 34

Dahlgren, G. 64
Dalkin, S. 116
Darnell, S. 122, 123
data analysis 28–29
data collection: field visits 26–27; focus groups 28; interviewed participants 27–28; interviewees 27; social user group 28
Davies, L. 8
Davison, R.M. 129
De Corte, J. 96
De Knop, P. 11, 175
demi-regularities 131
Department of Movement and Sport Sciences 162
Department of Public Health and Primary Care 162
Department of Social Work and Social Pedagogy (Ghent University) 4, 163
descriptive logic models 109
DesÉquilibres 30, 35
dialogical research 128
Dixon, M. 60
Doyle, A.C. 137
DREI procedure 137
du Toit, A. 5

ecological approach 67
economic theory 139
empirical applications in research: application challenges of capability approach 153–154; data 150–151; valuable aspects of capability approach 152–153
empirical data 145
empirical research 106, 133; *see also* social inclusion
Eurobarometer on sport and physical activity 9
European Commission 6

EU Work Plan for Sport 2021–2024 176
EU Youth Strategy 2019–2027 6
evaluation 103; Golden Age 103, 104; grey box 103; plan 70, 74–76, **75**; SfD and theory-based approaches 121–123; white box 103; *see also* black box; theory-driven evaluation
Evered, R.D. 128
evidence-informed policy and practice 8–9
experiential learning 12–13, 45; caring relationships 35; City Coach 59; experiences 59; hands on learning experiences 36; opportunities for young people 35–37; reflective practices 36–37
Expert Group on Skills and Human Resources Development in Sport 173

Fahmy, E. 5
field 148
Flanders: social cohesion 84; vulnerability rates 83; *see also* CATCH project; community sport in Flanders
Flemish Community Sport Benchmark 14–16
Flemish Institute of Sport Management and Recreation Policy (ISB) 4, 17, 89, 162, 165
focus groups 28
Forde, C. 85
Freire, P. 128

Gasper, D. 108–110
generalization: learning and 115–116; middle-range theory 120–121
Gibbs, G. 59
Gilbertson, J. 8
Gordon, D. 5
Green, B.C. 8
grey box evaluations 103
Grodos, D. 129
Gugiu, O.C. 108

habitus 148
hands-on learning experiences 45
hands-on learning opportunities 36–37
HAPA model 70
Hardman, K. 172
hard-to-reach groups 10
Harré, R. 136
Harris, K. 106, 122
Harris, S. 10
Haudenhuyse, R. 29, 88
health 13

health assets 13
health promotion 76–77, 162–163; Bruges 69; community sport as a lever 65–66; health and prevention among at-risk young people 64–65; methods 68–70; process evaluation 68; results 71–76; theory 66–68; *see also* intervention mapping (IM)
Hellison, D. 172
Hermens, N. 106
Hickey, S. 5
Hodkinson, A. 5
Houlihan, B. 10

ICAMO 139
illness in childhood 65
implementation theory 113; defined 112; programme theory *vs.* 112
individual 118
infrastructure 118
institutional settings 118
instrumental approaches 85–87
interdisciplinary approach 164
interpersonal relations 118
intervention 51–57; challenges on which intervention could build 47–50; data collected 51–52; *see also* City Coach; intervention mapping (IM)
intervention mapping (IM) 66–67, 76; behaviour change (step 3) 70, 72–73, **73**; evaluation plan (step 6) 70, 74–76, **75**; identifying community needs (step 1) 69–70; implementation plan identification (step 5) 70, 74; multi-theory approach 67; programme plan (step 4) 70, 73–74; selecting the methods and applications for behaviour change (step 3) 72–73; selection of actions and change goals **72**; stating programme aims (step 2) 70, 72, **72**
interview: guide 27; semi-structured interviews with practitioners 89

Jacobs, F. 171, 172
Jagosh, J. 137
Jassey, K. 111
Jolly, H. 118
Jolly, L. 118
Jones, G.J. 106, 111, 122, 173
judgemental relativism 137

Kay, T. 111
Keegan, R. 50

Kemmis, S. 50
Klein-Dossing, R. 46
knowledge translation: consultation with practitioners 16; defined 16; levels 16; non-academic research outputs 17
Knowles, Z. 53
Kock, N. 129
Koss, J. 107
Kruse, S.E. 107
Kubisch, A.C. 115

learning 59; generalization and 115–116; through reflection 96; *see also* experiential learning
Lee, P.L. 109–111
Leeuw, F.L. 103, 109, 111, 117, 121, 137
Levermore, R. 110
Levitas, R. 5, 12, 146
Lewin, K. 128
Lindblom, C.E. 130
Lipsey, M.W. 113, 119
Lloyd, E. 5
log frames: described 111; limitations 109–110; use 110
logic models: characteristics 108; described 107–108; limitations of log frames 109–110; purpose of 108; SfD and 110–111; sub-optimal log frames 109
Lorenz, W. 96
Lubans, D.R. 106
Lynch, D. 85
Lyras, A. 122

Mackenzie, M. 15, 120
marketization of youth work 94
Marshall, J. 172
Martinsons, M. 129
MaxQDA 47
McDonald, B. 146
McTaggart, R. 50
Mercenier, P. 129
Merton, R. 120, 121
Meyer, J. 128
Mezirow, J. 46, 57, 59
Michie, S. 61
middle-range theory (MRT) 140; basic idea 121; definition 120; described 120; function of 121; reference group theory 121
monitoring and evaluation (M&E) 107, 108, 111, 114, 160, 161
Moreau, N. 30, 35
mountain exercise 54, *54*
movement animator 47–48

multidisciplinary approach. 164
multi-theory approach 67

neither in education, employment nor in training (NEETs) 3, 83
Noddings, N. 35
Nols, Z. 169, 176
non-academic partners 4; *see also* social users
normative/prescriptive theory 113
Nussbaum, M.C. 149
NVivo 11 28

Omtzigt, D.J. 5

Pak, A.W.P. 163
Pantazis, C. 5
participant-centred approach 152
participants: changes to number of participants per reflective conversation group 53; guiding during reflective conversations 56–57; indicators 61–62
participation perspective 67
participatory action research 50, *51*
Paterson, C. 46
Patriksson, M. 172
Patsios, D. 5
Pawson, R. 30, 57, 104, 105, 116–121, 123, 127, 137, 138, 168, 169, 176
Peachey, J.W. 122
Peirce, C.S. 137
personal behaviour factors 64
personal development 12–13, 162
person-oriented approach 30–31
Petitpas, A.J. 171
pilot projects 141
Platts, C. 10
plus community sport 168
poiesis 142n1
policymakers 17
Pollard, J.A. 119
positive youth development (PYD) 12
post-intervention 57–58
post-welfare states 84–85
post-welfarism 85
Power, M. 110
practitioners: semi-structured interviews 89; in training 69; *see also* structural approach to social cohesion
praxis 128, 142n1
pre-mortem exercise 138, 141, 143n7
prescriptive theory *see* normative/prescriptive theory

184   Index

Principles of canonical action research 129
process evaluation 68
program context 118
program evaluators 137–138
programme plan 70, 73–74
programme theory 119–120; construction 113–115; context 118; defined 112; implementation theory *vs.* 112; mechanisms 117; sources 113

Q-methodology 61
Quensel, S. 175

Rapoport, R. 128
realism 116; epistemological premise 137; ontological premise 136
realist evaluation (RE) 116–117, 120, 127, 142
Realistic Evaluation 127, 137
realist inquiry 133; AR practice 140–142; CMOC 138; DREI procedure 137; economic theory 139; essentials of 136–140; ICAMO 139; layers of reality *136*; mechanisms 138, 139; MRT 140; process of specification 140; program evaluators 137–138; reference group theory 140; retroduction 137; scientific realism 136; strategic analysis 138; *see also* realism
Reason, P. 128
reference group theory 121, 140
reflective conversations 46
reflective practices 46, 96; intervention 51–57; methods 46; participant perspectives 61–62; participatory action research 50, *51*; post-intervention 57–58; value 46; voluntary community sport coach training programme 47–50, 58–60
reflective rose *58*, 60
researcher–academic peers 129
researcher–client 129
retroduction 137
Robb, C. 111
Rodriguez-Campos, L. 108
Roose, R. 96
Rossi, P.H. 104, 105, 112, 114
Rowan, J. 128
Rowe, K. 106
rubrics 56

Sabbe, S. 86
Schaillée, H. 106
Schroeder, K. 174, 175

Schulenkorf, N. 107, 122
Schuyt, C.J.M. 147
scientific realism 136
Scriven, M. 103, 111
self-exclusion 86
self-reflective cycles 59
self-reinforcing process 153–154
Sen, A. 149, 154
SfD programmes 33
shared cultural capital 33
Sherlock Holmes' method 137
Sherry, E. 106
Smets, P. 166, 176
smoking 64–65
Smyth, J. 6, 163
snowball technique 27
social capital 148
social cohesion 13, 14, 84; complexity of 94; defined 84; discourse on 87; facilitating conditions 91–95; instrumental approaches 85–87; on-the-ground-dimension 88–90; in post-welfare states 84–85; research perspectives 88–89; *see also* structural approach to social cohesion
social exclusion 5–6, 154; causation of 163; described 5; policy discourses 6; *see also* social vulnerability
social inclusion: aspirations and capabilities 148–150; capital and 148–149; conceptual agreements and disagreements 146–148; described 5, 147; empirical applications in research 150–154; health 13; objectives of community sport in Flanders 11–14; personal development 12–13; public domains 147; self-reinforcing nature 153–154; social cohesion and 14; sport and 7; typologies 146
Social Inequality in Health Care (Ghent University) 4
social learning theory 121
social network: anti-stigma interventions 37–38; interorganizational partnerships 38
social policy interventions 176
social reality 134
social science approach 114, 119
social sport practices 166–167, 176
social user group 28
social users 4; *see also* non-academic partners

social vulnerability 83; addressing issue of 84; defined 3; as ground of intervention 83–84; young people in 83–84
socio-pedagogical shift 14, 87, 88, 96, 97
soft skills 173
Spaaij, R. 24, 34, 61, 106
sport: social impact of 8–9; social inclusion and 7; *see also* community sport; sport for development (SfD)
Sport and Society (Vrije Universiteit Brussel) 4
Sportfolio 53–56, 60–62
sport for development (SfD) 169–170; black box and 106–107; inflated promises 107; logic models and 110–111; power of sport 106–107; theory-based approaches 121–123
sport-plus: concept 12; philosophy 84
stakeholder 15–17, 38, 51–52, 67, 77–78, 108, 114, 115, 118–120, 160–162
stakeholder approach 114
statements 25
Stead, V. 88
Still muddling, not yet through 130
structural approach to social cohesion 87, 95–96; accountability strategies 95; bottom-up strategies 95; facilitating conditions 91–95; network level 92–93; organizational level 92; policy level 93–95; social cohesion 'on the ground' 90; strategies, inside-out and outside-in 90–91
Super, S. 13, 45, 60, 171, 174
Susman, G. 128
systems thinking 131

Tacon, R. 8
Taket, A. 146
Tassignon, F. 61
Tayleur, W. 8
Taylor, P. 8
Teaching Personal and Social Responsibility model 172
Theeboom, M. 11
theory: defined 113; realist approach 120; testing 119
theory-based approach 114–115
theory-based evaluation (TBE) 9, 15, 23–24, 115, 162
theory-driven evaluation: causative theory 113; context 118–119; implementation theory 112–113; learning and generalization 115–116; mechanisms 117; normative/prescriptive theory 113; realist evaluation 116–117; theory defined 113; *see also* programme theory
theory for change 131, 138
theory of change: attributes of 115; defined 112; reverse mapping 114
thousand chances philosophy 31–32
Tilley, N. 118–121, 127, 137, 138
trainers: City Coach 62; role of 57
trusted relationships 66
Turnnidge, J. 171

UK Department for International Development 110
umbrella organizations 28
uncompetitive devaluation 139
US Agency for International Development 110

Veit-Wilson, J. 6, 87, 163
Vettenburg, N. 3
visual sociology 46; mountain exercise 54, *54*, 60; reflective rose *58*, 60
Vlaeminck, H. 96
Voldby, C.R. 46
voluntary community sport coach 46
voluntary community sport coach training programme: challenges on which intervention build 47–50; documentation 47; participatory observations, informal conversations and field notes 47

Walgrave, L. 175
wanting 147
weak epistemological relativism 137
Weiss, C.H. 104–107, 112–117, 121, 123
Weiss, M.R. 170
Wells, P. 8
Wells, S. 108
Westhorp, G. 117, 140
white box evaluations 103
Whitehead, M. 64
Whitley, M.A. 45, 111, 122
willingness 147
Win, E. 111
Wright, J.D. 104
written journals 46

Yin, R.K. 24
young people: health and prevention among at-risk young people 64–65; socially vulnerable situations 5–6; social vulnerability 83–84; *see also* City Coach; voluntary community sport coach training programme

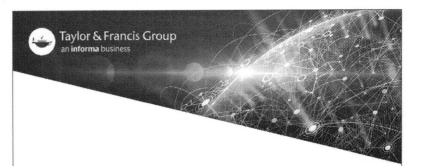

Printed in the United States
by Baker & Taylor Publisher Services